Asian American Literature

Edinburgh Critical Guides to Literature
Series Editors: Martin Halliwell, University of Leicester and
Andy Mousley, De Montfort University

Published Titles:
Gothic Literature, Andrew Smith
Canadian Literature, Faye Hammill
Women's Poetry, Jo Gill
Contemporary American Drama, Annette J. Saddik
Shakespeare, Gabriel Egan
Asian American Literature, Bella Adams
Children's Literature, M. O. Grenby

Forthcoming Titles in the Series:
Eighteenth-Century Literature, Hamish Mathison
Contemporary British Fiction, Nick Bentley
Contemporary American Fiction, David Brauner
Victorian Literature, David Amigoni
Crime Fiction, Stacy Gillis
Renaissance Literature, Siobhan Keenan
Modern American Literature, Catherine Morley
Scottish Literature, Gerard Carruthers
Romantic Literature, Richard Marggraf Turley
Modernist Literature, Rachel Potter
Medieval Literature, Pamela King
Women's Fiction, Sarah Sceats
African American Literature, Jennifer Terry

Asian American Literature

Bella Adams

Edinburgh University Press

© Bella Adams, 2008

Edinburgh University Press Ltd
22 George Square, Edinburgh

Typeset in 11.5/13 pt Ehrhardt
by Servis Filmsetting Ltd, Manchester, and
printed and bound in Great Britain by
Antony Rowe Ltd, Chippenham, Wilts

A CIP record for this book is available from the British Library

ISBN 978 0 7486 2271 9 (hardback)
ISBN 978 0 7486 2272 6 (paperback)

Contents

Series Preface   vii
Acknowledgements   viii
Chronology   ix

Introduction   1
  Some Thoughts on Ethnicity and Writing   1
  A History of Asian American Literature   7
  Asian American Canon Formation   17
  About this Book   20

Chapter 1 American Ways of Looking, 1880s–1920s   26
  Contexts and Intertexts   26
  Yan Phou Lee, *When I Was a Boy in China* (1887)   34
  Winnifred Eaton and Edith Eaton, Selected
    Short Stories (1900–15)   37
  Conclusion   44

Chapter 2 We are America, 1930s–50s   50
  Contexts and Intertexts   50
  Carlos Bulosan, *America Is in the Heart* (1946) and
    Toshio Mori, Selected Short Stories (1949)   55
  Monica Sone, *Nisei Daughter* (1953), John Okada,
    No–No Boy (1957) and Hisaye Yamamoto, Selected
    Short Stories (1949–51)   61
  Conclusion   67

Chapter 3 Noise, Trouble and Backtalk, 1960s–70s   72
  Contexts and Intertexts   72
  Jade Snow Wong, *Fifth Chinese Daughter* (1950)
    and Louis Chu, *Eat a Bowl of Tea* (1961)   76
  Frank Chin, *The Chickencoop Chinaman* (1972),
    The Year of the Dragon (1974) and *The Chinaman
    Pacific and Frisco R.R. Co.* (1988)   80
  Maxine Hong Kingston, *The Woman Warrior* (1976)
    and *China Men* (1980)   86
  Conclusion   101

Chapter 4 Between Worlds, the 1980s   107
  Contexts and Intertexts   107
  Joy Kogawa, *Obasan* (1981)   110
  Maxine Hong Kingston, *Tripmaster Monkey* (1989)
    and David Henry Hwang, *FOB* (1979) and
    M. Butterfly (1988)   116
  Amy Tan, *The Joy Luck Club* (1989)   121
  Bharati Mukherjee, *Jasmine* (1989) and Wendy
    Law-Yone, *The Coffin Tree* (1983)   128
  Conclusion   137

Chapter 5 Heterogeneity, Hybridity and Multiplicity,
    the 1990s   143
  Contexts and Intertexts   143
  Refugee Literatures   146
  Lan Cao, *Monkey Bridge* (1997)   149
  Sky Lee, *Disappearing Moon Café* (1990)   155
  Mei Ng, *Eating Chinese Food Naked* (1998)   161
  Chang-rae Lee, *Native Speaker* (1995)   167
  Conclusion   171

Conclusion   177

Student Resources   195
  Glossary   195
  Selected Electronic Resources   200
  Guide to Further Reading   204

Index   216

Series Preface

The study of English literature in the early twenty-first century is host to an exhilarating range of critical approaches, theories and historical perspectives. 'English' ranges from traditional modes of study such as Shakespeare and Romanticism to popular interest in national and area literatures such as the United States, Ireland and the Caribbean. The subject also spans a diverse array of genres from tragedy to cyberpunk, incorporates such hybrid fields of study as Asian American literature, Black British literature, creative writing and literary adaptations, and remains eclectic in its methodology.

Such diversity is cause for both celebration and consternation. English is varied enough to promise enrichment and enjoyment for all kinds of readers and to challenge preconceptions about what the study of literature might involve. But how are readers to navigate their way through such literary and cultural diversity? And how are students to make sense of the various literary categories and periodizations, such as modernism and the Renaissance, or the proliferating theories of literature, from feminism and Marxism to queer theory and eco-criticism? The Edinburgh Critical Guides to Literature series reflects the challenges and pluralities of English today, but at the same time it offers readers clear and accessible routes through the texts, contexts, genres, historical periods and debates within the subject.

Martin Halliwell and Andy Mousley

Acknowledgements

First of all I would like to thank Martin Halliwell and Andy Mousley for their careful editing and general support during the preparation of this book. I am also indebted to Jackie Jones, Máiréad McElligott and others at Edinburgh University Press, again for conscientious editing. Like Martin and Andy, my anonymous readers recognized the potential of such a project, for which I am very grateful. I would also like to thank John Thieme for encouraging me to pursue Asian American literature from this particular perspective, notwithstanding, as he and my readers acknowledged, the many other ways of reading Asian American literatures. I would also like to express my appreciation to my colleagues at Liverpool John Moores University, especially Colin Harrison, Ross Dawson, Morag Reid, Joanna Price, Ian Ralston and Elspeth Graham. Finally, my special thanks go to Paul and my family.

Chronology

The chronology of historical events is adapted from Sucheng Chan's chronology in *Asian Americans: An Interpretative History*. For other chronologies, as well as bibliographies, see Student Resources in this book

Date	Historical events	Literary events
1500s –1600s	Chinese and Filipinos arrive in New World on Manila galleon ships	
1700s	Filipinos settle in Louisiana; South Asians arrive in USA; Nationality Act (1790) only permits free whites to become citizens	
1830s	Chinese sugar masters work in Hawaii; Chinese peddlers and sailors arrive in New York	
1843	Japanese arrive in USA	

Date	Historical events	Literary events
1848	Gold discovered in California; Chinese labourers begin to arrive	
1852	Over 20,000 Chinese enter California	
1854	*People* v. *Hall* rules that Chinese cannot testify against whites in court	
1858	California passes law barring Chinese and 'Mongolians'	
1862	Six Chinese district associations in San Francisco form loose federation	
1865	Central Pacific Railroad Company recruits Chinese labourers	
1868	China and USA sign Burlingame Treaty affirming friendship and allowing free immigration; Fourteenth Amendment permits birthright citizenship to whites and blacks	
1869	Completion of first transcontinental railroad	

Date	Historical events	Literary events
1870	California passes law against importing Asian women for prostitution; The Naturalization Act excludes Chinese from naturalized citizenship	
1875	Page Law bars entry of Chinese, Japanese and 'Mongolian' prostitutes, felons and contract labourers	
1877	Anti-Chinese violence in Chico, California	
1878	*In re Ah Yup* rules Chinese ineligible for naturalization	
1880	USA and China sign treaty giving USA the right to limit but not prohibit Chinese immigration; California passes anti-miscegenation law	
1882	Chinese Exclusion Law suspends immigration of labourers for ten years; Chinese community leaders form Chinese Consolidated Benevolent Association (CCBA or Chinese Six Companies) in San Francisco	
1883	CCBA established in New York	

Date	Historical events	Literary events
1884	CCBA established in Vancouver; Chinese Exclusion Law of 1882 amended to require certificate for re-entry	
1885	San Francisco builds segregated 'Oriental School'; Anti-Chinese violence at Rock Springs, Wyoming	
1886	Chinese driven out of Tacoma, Seattle and other places in American West; Chinese immigration to Hawaii ends; *Yick Wo* v. *Hopkins* rules that law with unequal impact on different racial groups is discriminatory	
1887		Yan Phou Lee, *When I Was a Boy in China*
1888	Scott Act renders 20,000 Chinese re-entry certificates null and void	
1889	*Chae Chan Ping* v. *US* upholds constitutionality of Chinese exclusion laws	
1892	Geary Act renews exclusion of Chinese labourers for another	

Date	Historical events	Literary events
	ten years and requires Chinese to carry registration certificates; *Fong Yue Ting* v. *US* upholds constitutionality of Geary Act	
1896		Edith Eaton/Sui Sin Far, 'The Gamblers'
1898	*Wong Kim Ark* v. *US* rules that American-born Chinese cannot be stripped of citizenship; USA annexes Hawaii and Philippines	
1899		Winnifred Eaton/Onoto Watanna, *Miss Numè of Japan*
1902	Chinese exclusion extended for another ten years	
1903	Korean workers arrive in Hawaii; 1,500 Japanese and Mexican sugar beet workers strike in California	
1904	Chinese exclusion made indefinite and applicable to US insular possessions; Punjabi Sikhs enter British Columbia	

Date	Historical events	Literary events
1905	Chinese in USA and Hawaii support boycott of American products in China; Korean emigration ends; Asiatic Exclusion League formed in San Francisco; California forbids marriage between whites and 'Mongolians'	
1906	Anti-Asian riot in Vancouver; San Francisco earthquake destroys municipal records, allowing immigration of Chinese 'paper sons'	
1907	Japan and USA reach Gentlemen's Agreement preventing Japanese immigration to USA; South Asians driven out of Bellingham, WA	
1908	Japanese Association of America formed; Canada limits South Asian immigration by excluding immigrants who have not come by continuous journey from India (there is no direct shipping); South Asians driven out of Live Oak, CA	

Date	Historical events	Literary events
1909	Korean Nationalist Association formed	Yung Wing, *My Life in China and America*
1910	California restricts entry of South Asians; Angel Island Immigration Station opens to process and deport Asian immigrants	
1911		Anonymous, *Songs of Gold Mountain* (and 1915)
1913	Californian Alien Land Law prohibits Asian immigrants from buying land or leasing it for longer than three years; Sikhs in Washington and Oregon establish Hindustani Association; Korean farm workers driven out of Hemet, CA	
1914	South Asians charter ship to Canada by continuous journey but are denied landing in Vancouver	Tingfang Wu, *America through the Spectacles of an Oriental Diplomat*
1917	Arizona passes alien land law; Immigration Law defines a barred zone (including India) from which no 'Asiatics' can come	

Date	Historical events	Literary events
1920	10,000 Japanese and Filipino plantation workers go on strike; *Kwock Jan Fat* v. *White* rules that aliens seeking to immigrate have right to fair hearing	
1921	Japanese farm workers driven out of Turlock, CA; Washington and Louisiana pass alien land laws	
1922	*Takao Ozawa* v. *US* declares Japanese ineligible for naturalized citizenship; New Mexico passes alien land law; Cable Act removes citizenship from white women who marry aliens	
1923	*US* v. *Bhagat Singh Thind* rules Asian Indians ineligible for naturalization; Idaho, Montana and Oregon pass alien land laws; Canadian Chinese Exclusion Act	
1924	National Origins Act denies entry to all Asians, except Filipinos	
1925		Etsu Inagaki Sugimoto, A *Daughter of the Samurai*

Date	Historical events	Literary events
1928	Filipino farm workers driven out of Yakima Valley, WA	
1930	Anti-Filipino riot in Watsonville, CA; Japanese American Citizens League founded	
1931	Cable Act amended so that women can regain citizenship at a later date	Younghill Kang, *The Grass Roof*
1933		Jose Garcia Villa, *Footnote to Youth*
1934	Tydings–McDuffie Act grants eventual Philippine independence and limits Filipino immigration	
1937		H. T. Tsiang, *And China Has Hands*
1941	Japanese planes attack Pearl Harbor and USA enters Second World War	N. V. M. Gonzalez, *The Winds of April*
1942	Executive Order 9066 designates military areas from which people may be excluded, mainly targeting Japanese; Protests at Poston and Manzanar concentration camps	Carlos Bulosan, *Letter from America*; Hisaye Yamamoto, 'Death Rides the Rails to Poston'
1943	Tule Lake concentration camp becomes segregation	Pardee Lowe, *Father and Glorious Descendent*

Date	Historical events	Literary events
	centre; *Hirabayashi* v. *US* upholds constitutionality of detention order; Magnuson Act repeals Chinese exclusion laws, grants naturalization rights and immigration quota to Chinese	
1944	Draft reinstated for Nisei; Nisei 442nd Regimental Combat Team rescues another American battalion in Europe; Detention order revoked and some Japanese Americans permitted to return to West Coast	
1945	Second World War ends in Asia after USA drops atomics bombs on Japan	
1946	Luce–Celler Act grants naturalization rights and immigration quotas to South Asians and Filipinos; Last concentration camp closed; Philippines gains independence	Mine Okubo, *Citizen 13660*
1948	Displaced Persons Act grants immigrant status to Chinese stranded in USA because of Communist Revolution	Yutang Lin, *Chinatown Family*

Date	Historical events	Literary events
1949	USA breaks ties with newly formed People's Republic of China (PRC) and 5,000 highly educated Chinese in USA granted refugee status	Toshio Mori, *Yokohama, California*
1950	Korean War (1950–3)	Jade Snow Wong, *Fifth Chinese Daughter*
1952	McCarran–Walter Act grants naturalization rights and immigration quota to Japanese	
1953		Monica Sone, *Nisei Daughter*
1955	Cold War Confession Program (1955–late 1960s) tests loyalty of Chinese and those deemed pro-communist and subversive are deported	Bienvenido N. Santos, *You Lovely People*
1956	California repeals alien land laws	Diana Chang, *Frontiers of Love*
1957		C. Y. Lee, *Flower Drum Song*; John Okada, *No–No Boy*
1959	Hawaii becomes 50th state; Vietnam War (1959–75)	Milton Murayama, 'I'll Crack Your Head Kotsun' (part of *All I Asking for Is My Body*, 1975)

Date	Historical events	Literary events
1961		Louis Chu, *Eat a Bowl of Tea*
1962		Frank Chin, 'Food For All His Dead'
1963		Linda Ty-Casper, *The Transparent Sun and Other Stories*
1964	Civil Rights Act outlaws racial discrimination	Zulfikar Ghose, *The Loss of India*
1965	Immigration Law outlaws racial discrimination in immigration; Voting Rights Act outlaws racial discrimi-discrimination in electoral process	
1966		Wakako Yamauchi, 'And the Soul Shall Dance'
1968	Students strike at San Francisco State College to demand Ethnic Studies programmes	Joy Kogawa, *The Splintered Moon*
1970		Michael Ondaatje, *The Collected Works of Billy the Kid*; Nicotchka Rosca, *Bitter Country and Other Stories*
1971		Fusao Lawson Inada, *Before the War*

Date	Historical events	Literary events
1972		Momoko Iko, *Gold Watch*; Ved Mehta, *Daddyji*; Bharati Mukherjee, *The Tiger's Daughter*
1973		Jeanne Wakatsuki Houston and James Houston, *Farewell to Manzanar*; Ai (Ogawa), *Cruelty*
1974	*Lau* v. *Nichols* rules that schools with non-English speakers must provide bilingual education	
1975	More than 130,000 refugees enter USA from Vietnam, Cambodia and Laos	Jessica Hagedorn, *Dangerous Music*; Laurence Yep, *Dragonwings*
1976	Executive Order 9066 rescinded	Meena Alexander, *The Bird's Bright Ring*; Maxine Hong Kingston, *The Woman Warrior*; Mitsuye Yamada, *Camp Notes and Other Stories*
1977		Paul Stephen Lim, *Conpersonas*
1978	Boat people arrive from Vietnam	Janice Mirikitani, *Awake in the River*; Bapsi Sidhwa, *The Crow Eaters*
1979	Resumption of diplomatic relations between PRC and USA	David Henry Hwang, *FOB*; Philip Kan Gotanda, *The Avocado Kid*; Shawn Wong, *Homebase*

Date	Historical events	Literary events
1980	Orderly Departure Program enables legal immigration of Vietnamese	Darrell H. Y. Lum, *Sun*; Roberta Uno, *Asa Ga Kimashita*
1981	Commission on Wartime Relocation and Internment of Civilians concludes internment was a grave injustice and that Executive Order 9066 resulted from race prejudice, war hysteria and a failure of political leadership; Maya Lin designs Vietnam Veteran Memorial, Washington DC	Ruthanne Lum McCunn, *Thousand Pieces of Gold*
1982	Vincent Chin clubbed to death	Theresa Hak Kyung Cha, *Dictee*; Garrett Hongo, *Yellow Light*
1983	Some Japanese Americans file petitions to overturn convictions for violating wartime detention order	Tran Van Dinh, *Blue Dragon, White Tiger*; Cathy Song, *Picture Bride*; Wendy Law-Yone, *The Coffin Tree*
1986	Immigration Reform and Control Act creates programme to legalize undocumented immigrants resident in USA since 1982 or who had worked in agricultural for a minimum period	Ronyoung Kim, *Clay Walls*; Wendy Wilder Larsen and Tran Thi Nga, *Shallow Graves*; Li-Young Lee, *Rose*; Vikram Seth, *Golden Gate*; Merle Woo, *Yellow Woman Speaks*

Date	Historical events	Literary events
1987		Marilyn Chin, *Dwarf Bamboo*; David Mura, *A Male Grief*
1988	Senate supports redress and reparations for Japanese American wartime internment; Homecoming Act allows Vietnamese Amerasians to immigrate to USA; President Reagan signs the Civil Liberties Act for redress and reparations for Japanese American wartime internment	
1989	Entitlement programme pays surviving Japanese American internees $20,000 each; Vietnam allows political prisoners to immigrate to USA	Kimiko Hahn, *Airpocket*; Le Ly Hayslip, *When Heaven and Earth Changed Places*; Cynthia Kadohata, *The Floating World*; Evelyn Lau, *Runaway*; Shirley Lim, *Modern Secrets*; Rohinton Mistry, *Swimming Lessons and Other Stories*; Nguyen Thi Thu-Lam, *Fallen Leaves*; Sara Suleri, *Meatless Days*; Amy Tan, *The Joy Luck Club*; John Yau, *Radiant Silhouette*
1990	Immigration Act raises total quota and reorganizes system of preferences	Sky Lee, *Disappearing Moon Café*

Date	Historical events	Literary events
1991	First Gulf War begins	Gish Jen, *Typical American*; Gus Lee, *China Boy*; David Wong Louie, *Pangs of Love*
1992	Korean businesses damaged in Los Angeles uprising following Rodney King verdict	Timothy Liu, *Vox Angelica*; Sylvia Watanabe, *Talking to the Dead*
1993		Amitav Ghosh, *In an Antique Land*; Russell Leong, *The Country of Dreams and Dust*; Gita Mehta, *A River Sutra*; Fae Myenne Ng, *Bone*; Lois-Ann Yamanaka, *Saturday Night at the Pahala Theatre*
1994	California's Proposition 187 denies basic rights and government services to undocumented immigrants	Hiromi Gota, *Chorus of Mushrooms*; Ameena Meer, *Bombay Talkie*; Anchee Min, *Red Azalea*; Nguyen Qui Du'c, *Where the Ashes Are*; Shyam Selvadurai, *Funny Boy*; Abraham Verghese, *My Own Country*
1995		Denise Chong, *The Concubine's Children*; Wayson Choy, *The Jade Peony*; Chitra Divankaruni, *Arranged Marriage*; Chang-rae Lee, *Native Speaker*

Date	Historical events	Literary events
1996	Personal Responsibility and Work Opportunity Reconciliation Act and Illegal Immigration Reform and Immigrant Responsibility Act adversely affect Asian immigrants; Chinese Money Scandal about China's influence on US politics	Sophal Leng Stagg, *Hear Me Now*
1997		Lan Cao, *Monkey Bridge*; Nora Okja Keller, *Comfort Woman*; Catherine Lui, *Oriental Girls Desire Romance*
1998		Association of Asian American Studies revokes literary prize awarded to Lois-Ann Yamanaka's *Blu's Hanging* because of novel's alleged racism; Mei Ng, *Eating Chinese Food Naked*
1999		Jhumpa Lahiri, *The Interpreter of Maladies*
2000		Amitava Kumar, *Passport Photos*; Chanrithy Him, *When Broken Glass Floats*; Loung Ung, *First They Killed My Father*

Date	Historical events	Literary events
2001	9/11 terrorist attacks on New York and Washington; USA Patriot Act adversely affects civil liberties of immigrants from Middle East, South and Southeast Asia; Human Rights Watch documents increase in anti-Muslim and anti-Arab hate crimes following 9/11	
2003	Second Gulf War begins	
2007	Virginia Tech massacre by Cho Seung-Hui	

Introduction

SOME THOUGHTS ON ETHNICITY AND WRITING

> Didn't Baldwin say . . . that being a Negro was the gate he had to unlock before he could write about anything else? I think being an Asian American must be like that. Through that bodily gate the alphabets pour in. This is our life in letters.[1]

As a starting point for this book, this quotation from Meena Alexander's memoir, *Fault Lines* (1993), identifies several issues important to Asian American literature. In her first sentence, Alexander draws a comparison between African Americans and Asian Americans based on a shared preoccupation with identity, which is figuratively understood in terms of an unlockable gate. This spatial and temporal figure suggests that identity is not only a matter of responding to the question 'Who am I?' but also to a whole series of questions: 'Where am I? When am I?' (p. 176) and 'How did I become what I am? How shall I start to write myself, configure my "I" as Other, image this life I lead, here, now, in America?' (p. 3). On one level, the figure of the gate suggests a resolution to these questions in that it promises stability via the oppositions it sets up between here and there, before and after, becoming and being. On another level, however, the figure of the gate functions ambiguously: it marks the boundaries so necessary for being an Asian American, while at the same time acknowledging that these boundaries are permeable.

Alexander acknowledges this permeability via her reference to the African American writer James Baldwin and by extension inter-racial relationships. Her use of the antiquated term 'Negro', which is later replaced with 'African American', not only brings whites into these interracial relationships since Negro, from 'Negroid', has its basis in early European culture, but it also serves to highlight the impact of language on racially marked bodies and lives. This impact is most strongly felt when whites alone are accorded the privilege of naming. Their white alphabets pour in, although nonwhite letters gesture towards the possibility of self-naming. Names do essentialize, but, as Alexander proposes, there is a fault line that ensures they do not fit. 'No, not at all. There is very little I can be *tout court* in America except perhaps woman, mother. But even there, I wonder' (p. 193).

Such wondering informs the quotation, not least when Alexander, who is Asian American – if only since she immigrated to the USA in 1979 – thinks about what being an Asian American must be like. It also continues in the rest of the chapter, 'Real Places or How Sense Fragments: Thoughts on Ethnicity and the Writing of Poetry', and beyond. Alexander's wondering contrasts with alto-gether less tentative thoughts. Articulating the difference between minority memoir and American autobiography, she notes that 'this focus on the self is very peculiar to the culture of North America', as is the preoccupation with 'a perpetual present', apparently 'not touched by hierarchy and authority and the great weight of cen-turies' (pp. 198–9). She continues,

A constant attempt to vivify what one thinks of as identity by redefining oneself is a very American project ... I'm interested in how one's relationship to others defines where one is ... My story is only one among the many others that connect with it.[2]

Up to a point, Alexander does participate in this very American project of self-redefinition in imagined confrontations with racially unmarked American men. Near the beginning of 'Real Places', she defines herself as 'a poet writing in America. But American poet? What sort? Surely not of the Robert Frost or Wallace Stevens

variety? An Asian–American poet then? Clearly that sounds better.'
She does not stop here, however: 'A woman poet', 'a South Indian
woman poet', and 'a Third World woman poet, who takes as her
right the inner city of Manhattan . . . finding there, news of the
world' (pp. 193–4). The news she finds amid her prose is a poem,
'News of the World'. In this poem, Alexander's 'I' becomes a
Cambodian American who escaped the Pol Pot regime (1975–9).
Towards the end of this poem, 'A man approaches / muck on his
shirt / his head, a battering ram / he knows who I am' and, in the
last stanza, 'I stall' (p. 195).

This interracial confrontation, particularly as it comes after
Alexander's list of multiple identities, calls into question the possibility of her becoming whatever she wants in the USA. She continues: 'I can make myself up and this is the enticement, the
exhilaration, the compulsive energy of America. But only up to a
point. And the point, the sticking point, is my dark female body'
(p. 202), which, when viewed by those with battering rams for
heads, functions to reduce her identity. According to 'the white
man's naming patterns', she is a 'grotesque thing' and a 'black bitch'
(pp. 174, 168–9). Alexander counters this racism, as it also operates
more widely in the USA with respect to Japanese American internment camps and other anti-Asian practices, by asserting that 'we
have an ethnicity that breeds' and a poetry that plays. The fluidity
of both forms ensures that they 'will never be wholly spelt out'
(pp. 202–3).

Alexander's thoughts on ethnicity and the writing of poetry as
these two realms roughly coincide in their resistance to final conceptualization certainly present a number of challenges to this book
since it is compelled to spell out Asian American literature. This
book is thus implicated in the kind of power relationship described
in Alexander's poem 'News of the World' as it seeks to know and
therefore stall or essentialize Asian American literature and, with
it, the Asian American in Asian America. As different as these
phenomena are from each other and, moreover, from the term
'Asian American' invented in the late 1960s to politicize and racialize them, they are all 'about-to-be' because their meanings are 'continuously reinvented after the arrival of new groups of immigrants
and the enactment of legislative changes.'[3] Susan Koshy goes on to

propose in her essay 'The Fiction of Asian American Literature' (1996) that this about-to-be-ness makes the conceptualization and institutionalization of Asian Americanness through Asian American studies different from its racial minority equivalents.

This difference in part turns on the discrepancy between sign and literal referent. For Alexander, 'the literal is always discrepant, a sharp otherness to what the imagination conjures up' (p. 31). For Koshy, the fact that Asian Americanness exceeds ethnic, racial and national boundaries suggests that 'there is no literal referent for the rubric "Asian American," and, as such, the name is marked by the limits of its signifying power.' Yet, Koshy continues, ' "Asian American" offers us a rubric that we cannot not use. But our usage of the term should rehearse the catachrestic status of the forma-tion.'[4] In Alexander's terms, Asian American is 'a trope for the mind' (p. 202), enabling it to imagine Asian American in terms of *an* identity, *a* socio-political consciousness, *a* place and *a* literature for compelling theoretical, political and historical reasons to do with antiracist critique. Although the original self-definition of Asian American literature as Anglophonic US-centric prose, poetry and drama by Californian-based East Asian American writers is dis-puted, the reasons for it are less open to dispute since racist stereo-types continue to circulate in American culture. At the same time, tropes resist these imagined singularities as they emerge in the defi-nitions of Asian American from racists and antiracists alike for equally compelling reasons.

According to Koshy, and, presumably, the multiply-anchored Alexander as well, the articulation of a heterogeneous Asian Americanness is vital. Significantly, this articulation does not merely involve a competition between opposing sides, whereby one side emerges as the winner after eradicating or appropriating its other side(s). Instead, these sides remain contemporaneous in disruptive yet productive relationships. And, it is this side-by-side configur-ation that is arguably unique to Asian Americanness, whereby the latter can refer to an identity that is a middle-class Indian American émigré and a working-class Cambodian American refugee. It can also refer to an identity that is black, white, non-American and even non-Asian American, with, for example, South Asian Americans being classified as white, not Asian American in some US censuses.

To some Americans, Asian Americans are not Americans, consistent with the perpetual foreigner stereotype. Moreover, the writing resists traditional categorization since it comprises fiction, fact, poetry, prose, monologue, dialogue, polemic and theory.

In some respects, it is no coincidence that two South Asian American writers highlight this complicated configuration given that this regionalized constituency is commonly assumed heterogeneous to Asian America – narrowly defined as comprising East and Southeast Asian Americans who originate from Cambodia, China, Japan, the Koreas, Laos, the Philippines and Vietnam. In *A Part, Yet Apart* (1998), Rajiv Shankar also observes that South Asian Americans are 'easily marginalized within the house of Asian America'.[5] This marginalization may have been the case in the twentieth century, but, partly because of the US war on terror, this house has changed. As Rajini Srikanth proclaims in *The World Next Door* (2004), speaking specifically of South Asian American literature: it 'enjoys today . . . remarkable visibility' in the Western academy. She diversifies this house further by way of reference to the Americas (the USA, Canada, Latin America and the Caribbean), Asia (South, East, Southeast and West Asia or the Middle East) and the Asian diaspora.[6] Alexander is part of this diaspora since, prior to moving to the USA, she lived in Southern India, Northern Africa and the English Midlands. In this last location, 'Asian' is mainly associated with people from South Asia, typically, India, Pakistan and Bangladesh, rather than from, say, China, Tibet or Thailand.

Another critic who also values heterogeneity is an Indonesian-born and European-educated Chinese academic who resides in Australia. Indeed, Ien Ang complicates the labels 'Asian' and 'Chinese' with specific reference to Australia. Australia is categorized 'as part of "the West"', albeit as a 'far-flung outpost', and, more recently, as part of Asia.[7] Here, then, the West is in Asia and Asia is in the West. Of the apparently more specific label 'Chinese', as it applies to Chinese from the PRC, Taiwan, Hong Kong, Malaysia, Indonesia, Vietnam and East Timor, Ang observes:

In Sydney, the coming together of many different groups who have carried the label 'Chinese' to describe themselves has exposed its contested nature and its failure to operate as a term of diasporic integration. In this sense 'Chineseness' is put under erasure, 'not in the sense of being written out of existence but in the sense of being unpacked' . . . denaturalized and stripped of its self-evident cogency as a category of social and cultural classification.[8]

The first part of this Introduction has involved unpacking the category of Asian American, specifically through reference to contemporary writers who are responsive to the demographic and ideological heterogeneities within and beyond the category. It has highlighted the interracial and intraracial relationships that enable understanding of what being an Asian American must be like, at the same time briefly drawing attention to the critical part played by Asian American literature in the (de)construction of this identity and constituency. For Alexander, this preoccupation with identity also characterizes American culture, not least in the identity politics of Americans who protested against their racial, gender and sexual marginalization via civil rights and other minority movements. Not surprisingly, therefore, the literary forms privileged in the national canon and other so-called minor canons include the autobiography and the Bildungsroman, as they, too, are preoccupied with self-explanation and, ultimately, self-empowerment. Fundamental to Asian American literary critics are the relationships between these major and minor canons, and between Asian American literary forms and dominant American ideologies. Debate frequently focuses on whether or not Asian American literary self-explanation simply performs the work of these ideologies.

The remainder of this Introduction will now turn to Asian American literary texts as they form an Asian American literary canon, in order to consider its historical development. The section on literature from the 1880s to the 2000s and that on its institutionalization or canonization are interrelated: without the emergence in the late 1960s and 1970s of a canon consistent with a cultural nationalist agenda that included in its demands the development of Asian American studies, the longer history of Asian American literature and the even longer history of Asian Americans would not be as visible as they are today (see Chronology).

Although ideologically divided, Asian American critics attach such importance to visibility because their cultural history is marked by invisibility, which is, paradoxically, based on their visible differences in a racially bipolar cultural formation determined to categorize Asian American as perpetually foreign. The final section of this Introduction will outline the logic and some of the boundaries of this book.

A HISTORY OF ASIAN AMERICAN LITERATURE

It is common for Asian American critics to describe the historical development of Asian American literature in terms of 'periods' or, alternatively, 'modes' and 'patterns'.[9] These latter alternatives rightly problematize a developmental understanding of literature and cultural history, generally understood as moving from simplicity and naivety to complexity and sophistication in a manner ultimately consistent with both Enlightenment and national Bildungsroman narratives. Neither narrative is adequate since they misread both the past and the present. For example, early writer Edith Eaton or Sui Sin Far utilizes irony, a trope often associated with late twentieth-century postmodern literature, to highlight how Chinese Americans were excluded from national democratic ideals regarding individual freedom. Similar exclusions persist today, with, for example, Viet Thanh Nguyen and Angelo N. Ancheta noting in their respective books that many of the 'choices contemporary Asian Americans face bear an all too familiar resemblance to those that confronted the first pioneers of Asian American identity at the end of the [nineteenth] century.'[10]

Following and developing Michael Omi and Howard Winant's highly influential thesis in *Racial Formation in the United States* (1994), Ancheta and Nguyen also observe that the movement from racial dictatorship (1607–1865 and 1877–1964) towards racial democracy has been 'a slow, painful and contentious one; it remains far from complete' in so far as the dominant racial hierarchy now functions hegemonically. Like Omi and Winant, these critics assert that 'democracy has never been in abundant supply where race is concerned', unless that race is white or, at the very least, associated

with whiteness.[11] In the context of the USA's bipolar racial formation, 'people speak of "American" as if it means "white" and
"minority" as if it means "black"', thereby assuming a limited conceptualization of race that marginalizes not only biraciality but also
Asian Americans.[12] While neither black nor white, Asian Americans
have been identified as black and white, if not literally, as in the case
of South Asian Americans who were white in some US censuses,
then analogically via links between Chinese coolies and African
slaves.

Often in response to changing militaristic and economic relations
between the USA and Asian countries, the changing racial status of
Asian Americans typically underpins the organization of Asian
American literature into periods or, better, patterns. This book also
takes this cultural historical approach in so far as it comprises five
chapters, each of which foregrounds specific experiences of anti-
Asian violence and anti-Asian discrimination as they are negotiated
formally, thematically and politically in Asian American literature:
from early texts written during the exclusionary period, the 1880s–
1950s, when anti-Asian acts powerfully determined the preoccupations of Asian American writers (Chapters 1 and 2), to texts written
in the 1960s and 1970s, or the cultural nationalist period (Chapter
3), when racial discrimination was outlawed through new acts that
contributed to demographic and ideological diversity in contemporary Asian America (Chapters 4, 5 and Conclusion). Throughout
this history, nativist, racist and Orientalist ideologies have powerfully determined the way in which Asian Americans are viewed in
American culture, for the most part, as biologically and culturally
Other or, more precisely, the threatening 'yellow peril' and the controllable 'model minority'.

1880s–1920s

In the mid-to-late nineteenth century, after three centuries of Asian
immigration to the New World – first, through the Manila galleon
trade (1500s–1800s) and, later, through the Hawaiian sugar industry in the Sandalwood Mountains (*Tan Heung Shan*) and the
Californian gold mine, railroad and agricultural industries in the
Gold Mountain (*Gam Saan*) – Asian sojourners and settlers received

more attention from white Americans than at any time previously. Between the 1850s and the 1920s, immigrants from China, Japan, Korea, the Philippines and the Punjab formed a population of about one million, too many apparently for their European counterparts, of whom, historian Sucheng Chan estimates, there were 35 million. This so-called Mongolian horde constituted a yellow peril, particularly for white North American 'workers who felt threatened by the Asian competition and nativists from all classes who felt hostile toward them for racist reasons [and] agitated to stop their coming.'[13]

This agitation took various forms, with criminal acts of racial hatred through to legal acts of racial discrimination gaining representation, if not support, in mass media and literary forms. While American writers like Bret Harte, Joaquin Miller, Ambrose Bierce and Mark Twain were sympathetic towards Chinese immigrants, the vast majority of writers, including Atwell Whitney, Frank Norris, Wallace Irwin and Jack London, saw Chinese immigrants as heathen, if not plain evil in their apparently unwavering pursuit of vice – idolatry, gambling, opium smoking, tong violence and sexual deviancy. Such yellow-peril pursuits were also assumed to threaten the Western world, with the British writer Sax Rohmer offering in 1913 the most famous depiction of the yellow-peril stereotype in the form of a devil doctor. It was not until 1935 that Rohmer decided 'to reward his American supporters by transferring the activities of [Dr] Fu Manchu to the United States' at a time when East Asia, under Japanese imperialism, looked set to transfer its activities across the Pacific – eventually to Hawaii and the Philippines in the early 1940s.[14]

It is hardly surprising that early Asian American writers offered more realistic ways of looking at themselves and their experiences than those provided by the sensationalized depictions of Asianness that were otherwise circulating in American culture. This commitment to realism was evidenced formally and thematically, with many early writers publishing autobiographies or semi-autobiographies. For example, the first Asian American literary text published, by Yan Phou Lee (see Chapter 1), was autobiographical in form and aimed to correct 'false ideas in America concerning Chinese customs, manners, and institutions'.[15] Lee's *When I Was a*

Boy in China (1887) was the first in a series of volumes, of which New Il-Han's 1928 *When I Was a Boy in Korea* was one of the last. Similar to other early autobiographies such as Yung Wing's *My Life in China and America* (1909), Wu Tingfang's *America through the Spectacles of an Oriental Diplomat* (1914) and Etsu Sugimoto's *A Daughter of the Samurai* (1925), Lee's text was written from a position of class, educational and professional privilege, and, as such, marginalized the harsh conditions of working-class life both in Asia and the USA.[16]

Other less privileged writers similarly represent Asia in nostalgic, romantic or exotic terms, most obviously, Winnifred Eaton or Onoto Watanna (see Chapter 1), who achieved widespread recognition in the USA at the turn of the century with many best-selling sentimental and melodramatic interracial romances often set in an exoticized Japan. Edith Eaton did not achieve this level of success with her more realistic Chinatown-based short stories until they were recovered in the 1970s and later. The sisters' differences aside, both critically negotiate the yellow-peril stereotype and, particularly in Edith's writings, concomitant anti-Asian laws that make apparent the racial limits of American democratic ideals. Democracy could be withheld in immigration, property, education, employment and marriage because Asian immigrants, unlike, for example, foreign-born whites and foreign-born blacks who achieved citizenship in 1790 (Nationality Act) and 1870 (Naturalization Act) respectively, were categorized as aliens ineligible for citizenship until the mid-twentieth century.

Often figuratively represented in terms of the American dream-cum-nightmare, democratic ideals are also at issue in recovered early poetry in *Island: Poetry and History of Chinese Immigrants on Angel Island, 1910 to 1940* (1980) and *Songs of Gold Mountain: Cantonese Rhymes from San Francisco* (1987; see Chapter 1). Both texts contain poems about San Francisco's Angel Island Immigration Station, which opened in 1910 and was where, in the first place, predominantly Chinese working-class men were imprisoned, sometimes for months and even years, in atrocious conditions. Some of the poems were carved into the station's walls, whereas others circulated in newspapers, magazines and poetry clubs. The poems tend to adhere to popular forms of classical

Chinese poetry, as well as realistically describing harsh immigration experiences: 'America has power, but not justice. / In prison, we were victimized as if we were guilty. / Given no opportunity to explain, it was really brutal.'[17]

1930s–50s

Autobiography continues to be an important form in this period, and not only for the students, scholars, diplomats who comprise that privileged group of Chinese immigrant and Chinese American writers as it now also includes writers like Lin Yutang (particularly, *My Country and My People*, 1935) and his daughters, Adet, Anor and Meimei (*Our Family*, 1939 and *Dawn Over Chungking*, 1941), Helena Kuo (*I've Come Along Way*, 1942) and Mai-mai Sze (*Echo of a Cry*, 1945).[18] Although not of this class, Jade Snow Wong (*Fifth Chinese Daughter*, 1950; see Chapter 3) did tour Asian countries during the Cold War as part of diplomatic efforts to promote the USA as a world leader in democracy *vis-à-vis* communism. Other prose of Chinatown life include Pardee Lowe's *Father and Glorious Descendent* (1943) and Chin Yang Lee's *Flower Drum Song* (1957), which, like Wong's autobiography, were later criticized by andro-centric cultural nationalist critics for adhering to white racist stereotypes – for example, Dr Fu Manchu's contemporary and apparent antithesis, the compliant Chinese Hawaiian detective and incarnation of the model-minority stereotype, Charlie Chan.

Chinatown life is differently represented in H. T. Hsiang's 1937 novel, *And China Has Hands*, which in part envisages socialist pos-sibilities for the USA through interracial alliances between workers. Working-class Filipino Carlos Bulosan (see Chapter 2), although motivated to write by 'an aristocrat of sorts', Korean American Younghill Kang (*The Grass Roof*, 1931 and *East Goes West*, 1937), also envisages the possibility of an interracial brotherhood of workers in *America Is in the Heart: A Personal History* (1946).[19] This semi-autobiographical text describes the continuing discrep-ancy between democratic political rhetorical and dictatorial politi-cal reality in terms of the USA's colonial relationship with the Philippines, as well as highlighting colonization internal to the USA through segregationist working conditions in particular.

Bulosan's pioneering peers also began publishing at about this time: José García Villa in the 1930s, N. V. M. Gonzalez in the 1940s and Bienvenido Santos in the 1950s.

Segregationism, or 'No Orientals Allowed', saw its most fanatical expression in the forced internment of 120,000 Japanese immigrants and their American-born children in concentration camps after Japan bombed Pearl Harbor in December 1941. Before the Second World War Japanese American writers like Toshio Mori (see Chapter 2) and Toyo Suyemoto published in American journals. During their internment in Topaz camp, Utah, they published in the government-censored *Trek*. Mori's prewar short stories about everyday Japanese American life form the basis of *Yokohama, California* (1949), with two important exceptions: the war stories, 'Tomorrow is Coming, Children' and 'Slant-Eyed Americans'. In Poston camp, Arizona Hisaye Yamamoto published 'Death Rides the Rails to Poston' (1942), and after her release a number of other war stories including 'Wilshire Bus' and 'The Legend of Miss Sasagawara' (see Chapter 2). Two other important texts, Monica Sone's autobiography *Nisei Daughter* and John Okada's Bildungsroman *No–No Boy*, were published in 1953 and 1957 respectively, and both describe the detrimental impact of the internment experience on Japanese American families (see Chapter 2). Not without some irony, a number of characters in these Japanese American texts 'chase . . . that faint and elusive insinuation' of the American democratic 'promise' of equality and freedom.[20]

1960s–70s

With the racial formation of the USA undergoing transformation from dictatorship towards democracy via the passing of the Civil Rights Act (1964) and the Voting Rights Act (1965) Asian American writers were in a better position to demand the substantiation of the heretofore faint and elusive insinuation of the American democratic promise. Socio-political groups with a cultural nationalist agenda, including, for example, the Asian American Movement, Yellow Power and the Third World Liberation Front, mobilized a younger generation of Asian Americans in particular. In their literary and critical texts, this generation claimed America in forthright ways through a combination of American and Asian literary forms. Similar to Toshio Mori, Hisaye Yamamoto and John Okada, whose realistic prose narratives referenced Asian literary traditions such *shibai*, *haiku* and the Japanese children's story 'Momotaro' respectively, cultural nationalist writers combined popular American forms like cowboy and kung fu films with Asian ballads, operas, folk tales and children's stories.[21]

For example, Frank Chin's combative rhetoric was influenced by the god of war Kwan Kung from the Cantonese epic *The Romance of the Three Kingdoms* (AD 220). Not surprisingly, then, Chin is forthright in his critique and proclaims Chinatown 'a detention camp' and 'a game preserve for Chinese' historically endangered by anti-immigration and anti-miscegenation laws, to the point of genocide (see Chapter 3).[22] He accused certain Asian American writers of racism in their apparently uncritical support of white supremacy and, with it, racial self-hatred, specifically Christianized Chinese American autobiographers from Yung Wing and Jade Snow Wong to Maxine Hong Kingston (see Chapter 3).

Chin was also involved with the Combined Asian American Research Project, or CARP, which was instrumental in the republication of earlier texts by Bulosan, Okada, Sone, Santos and Louis Chu (see Chapter 3) throughout the 1970s. Chin and his co-editors, Jeffery Paul Chan, Lawson Fusao Inada and Shawn Hsu Wong, also republished excerpts from some of these earlier texts in *Aiiieeeee! An Anthology of Asian-American Writers* (1974). This influential anthology also included examples of literary writing from both their contemporaries and themselves. In their introductory chapters they made a powerful aesthetico-political statement – specifically a cultural nationalist statement – that was androcentric, as well as East-Asian-centric and US-centric:

> Our anthology is exclusively Asian-American. That means Filipino-, Chinese-, and Japanese-Americans, American born and raised, who got their China and Japan from the radio, off the silver screen, from television, out of comic books, from the pushers of white American culture that pictured the yellow man as something that when wounded, sad, or angry, or swearing, or wondering whined, shouted, or screamed 'aiiieeeee!'

Asian America, so long ignored and forcibly excluded from creative participation in American culture, is wounded, sad, angry, swearing, and wondering, and this is his AIIIEEEEE!!! It is more than a whine, shout, or scream. It is fifty years of our whole voice.[23]

The literary forms most suited to articulating this androcentric voice in respect of racial oppression and the heroic struggle against it on the frontier, in the bachelor societies and the internment camps include 'raging satires, polemic and slapstick comedies', not 'confession, autobiography, conversion. One form of betrayal leading to another, the self, the history, the moral integrity.'[24]

Polemic also marks women's writing in this period, as they, too, contended with racial and gender stereotypes. While Asian American men were desexualized in the figures of Fu Manchu and Charlie Chan, Asian American women were hypersexualized and exoticized in American culture as the Dragon Lady and the China Doll. Exclusionary legislation like the 1875 Page Law and the 1924 Immigration Act differently contributed to the sexual objectification of women as prostitutes and picture brides. There was also the war bride Madame Butterfly, who remains for Jessica Hagedorn the 'tragic victim/whore of wartorn [Asia, including, through the 1960s and 1970s, Vietnam], eternally longing for the white boy soldier who has abandoned her and her son.' Hagedorn continues: 'In our perceived American character – we are completely non-threatening. We don't complain. We endure humiliation. We are almost inhuman in our patience. *We never get angry.*'

The important question for Hagedorn and her 'co-conspirators' is: 'Could Asian Americans, in fact, be "militant"?' A quotation from Vietnamese American Trinh T. Minh-ha provides a response: '*Shake syntax, smash the myths*', which Hagedorn and other women writers like Janice Mirikitani (see Chapter 3), Kitty Tsui, Geraldine Kudaka, Nellie Wong, Genny Lim practised in their writings from the 1970s onwards.[25] In addition to protesting against sex, gender and racial hierarchies in and beyond the USA, Asian American writers embarked on an intraracial 'pen war', mainly divided along gender lines and mainly involving Chin and Kingston. In general, Asian American feminists pointed out that 'there were not many ways to be Asian American' since the *Aiiieeeee!* group's ideal was 'male, heterosexual, Chinese or Japanese American, and English-speaking'.[26] The representativeness of this ideal was also challenged by the demographic changes brought by the 1965 Immigration Act, particularly in terms of immigrants and refugees from South and Southeast Asia.

1980s–2000s

In the 1980s, Asian America shifted from a predominantly American-born to a predominantly foreign-born population, necessitating, as Lisa Lowe and others asserted, an acknowledgement of demographic and ideological heterogeneity. Such diversity effectively meant that Asian America was caught between worlds due to, in particular, different class allegiances. While some Asian Americans have made important advances economically and politically, including in the late 1980s financial redress for Japanese North American internment, others have not, typically refugees and 'illegals' or non-documented migrants. Intraracial and, as is often the case, intergenerational confrontation in the form of 'immigrant-bashing' occurs in literary texts by, for example, Maxine Hong Kingston, David Henry Hwang, Amy Tan, Wendy Law-Yone, Bharati Mukherjee and Chang-rae Lee (see Chapters 4 and 5).[27] Alongside immigrant narratives were refugee literatures by and about Southeast Asians. These literatures emphasized the importance of bearing witness to wartime traumas, as in, for instance, Chanrithy Him's and Le Ly Hayslip's autobiographies, Lan Cao's novel and Kimiko Hahn's poetry (see Chapter 5).

Such diversity generated a crisis in representation, with the apparently more stable definition of Asian American as formulated in the identity politics of the 1960s and 1970s struggling to operate as a term of both political and aesthetic cohesiveness. While antiracist critique may be 'the *only* safe description of any political consensus today', the ways in which this critique is pursued differs depending on institutional location (see Conclusion).[28] In terms of the US academy and, with it, the publishing industry, Rajini Srikanth summarizes this Asian America divided against itself in terms of ethnic studies versus postcolonial studies:

Postcolonial studies requires an understanding of the *global* forces of neocolonialism and global capitalism that affect any single nation's economic, political, and social realties. Ethnic studies, while acknowledging the importance of understanding the forces at play beyond U.S. borders, is based on the idea that what is ultimately important is the reality within the nation state: the condition of people of color, the resources denied them, the opportunities withheld.[29]

While some Asian Americans, most notably Sau-ling Cynthia Wong, identifies with ethnic studies, other Asian American critics, including Aijaz Ahmed, Arjun Appadurai, Homi Bhabha, Dipesh Chakrabarty, Partha Chatterjee and Gayatri Chakravorty Spivak and Sara Suleri are identified with postcolonial studies.[30] Moreover, some Asian Americans identify with both labels, with Meena Alexander, for example, using 'ethnic' in *Fault Lines* and 'postcolonial' in *The Shock of Arrival* (1996). Granted, Alexander highlights the limitations of labelling *per se*, but, at the same time, she risks an appropriation that could reinforce racial hegemony:

> Some practitioners of various ethnic studies feel somewhat displaced by the rise of postcolonial studies in North American English departments. If the rising institutional endorsement of the term *postcolonial* is, on the one hand a success story for the PCs (politically correct), is it not also a partial containment of the POCs (people of color)? . . . One has the impression that the postcolonial is privileged because it seems safely distant from 'the belly of the beast,' the United States.[31]

As heated as these intraracial debates can at times be, as when, for example, the Association of Asian American Studies 1998 literary award for Japanese Hawaiian Lois-Ann Yamanaka's *Blu's Hanging* (1997) was revoked on account of the novel's alleged anti-Filipino racism, they do, nevertheless, mark a general queering of contemporary Asian American literary studies. According to David L. Eng, Alice Y. Hom and other critics, this queering involves 'a political practice based on transgressions of the normal and normativity' as determined by white patriarchy.[32] Among the contemporary Asian American literary texts to represent sexuality as an important theme are David Henry Hwang's *M. Butterfly* (1988; see Chapter 4), Sky Lee's *Disappearing Moon Café* (1990; see Chapter 5), Shawn Wong's *American Knees* (1991), Shyam Selvadurai's *Funny Boy* (1994), David Mura's *Where the Body Meets Memory* (1996), Catherine Liu's *Oriental Girls Desire Romance* (1997) and Mei Ng's *Eating Chinese Food Naked* (1998; see Chapter 5). Norms are transgressed through an increased emphasis on multiculturalism within and beyond Asian America with respect to sexuality, biraciality and transnationality, as well as through an increased emphasis on deconstructive theorizing. The influence of deconstruction and poststructuralism contributed to a paradigm shift in Asian American literary criticism, which further enabled analysis of critical rigidity in the process of canon formation.

ASIAN AMERICAN CANON FORMATION

Fundamental to Asian American literary studies are the relationships between the national literary canon and the Asian American literary canon, and between Asian American literary forms and dominant American ideologies. Debate frequently focuses on whether or not Asian American literary texts simply perform the work of these ideologies. The national literary canon of American literature, featuring, among its most vivifying of texts, Walt Whitman's 'Song of Myself' (1855), and the Asian American literary canon do share some similarities, not least when Whitman's democratic vision is evoked for the purposes of antiracist critique. As it does for Meena Alexander and other Asian American writers, Whitman's poetry, specifically the line 'To be in any form, what is that?' (p. 196), continues to remain significant when markers of racial identity such as skin colour, nose and eyelid shape, hair texture, clothes, food and language limit the forms an American can take.

Just as national identity is limited, so, too, is the national canon, at least in terms of the genres taught in the Western academy. Poetic 'songs of myself' for the most part give way to similarly self-preoccupied prose narratives, most notably American auto-biographies and Bildungsroman. Traditionally, both forms focus on the personal development of a character, in autobiography a real character, and in the Bildungsroman a fictional character, as s/he struggles to understand self and world, albeit, as some critics argue, in keeping with dominant ideologies. The most widely taught Asian American prose also tends to be autobiographical. As Chan, Chin, Inada and Wong in their introduction to *The Big Aiiieeeee!* (1991) observe of the Asian American literature with the longest history of publication: 'Every Chinese American book ever published in . . . America by a major publisher has been a Christian autobiography or autobiographical novel', right up until Amy Tan's *The Joy Luck Club* (1989) and, presumably for Chin, her later family sagas as well.

But Tan is merely Kingston's 'literary spawn' for Chin and it is to the latter that much of Chin's criticism is directed, specifically at *the* example of this ideologically compromised form: *The Woman Warrior* (1976). Formal consistency suggests ideological consistency, with Chin et al. arguing that autobiographical texts are published because they uncritically sanction that very American project of self-redefinition according to dominant racial ideologies:

> Chinese American ventriloquizing the same old white Christian fantasy of little Chinese victims of 'the original sin of being born to a brutish, sadomasochistic culture of cruelty and victimization' fleeing to America in search of freedom from everything Chinese and seeking white acceptance, and of being victimized by stupid white racists and then being reborn in acculturation and honorary whiteness.

Such ventriloquism renders autobiographical texts and, with them, the Asian American literary canon fake. Chin constructs the real canon comprising those who, he insists, resist ventriloquism through writing that allows the facts about Asian American history to be told heroically, imaginatively and with intelligence, not with sentimentality of 'sob stories' and other 'melancholy slop'. To the *Aiiieeeee!* and *The Big Aiiieeeee!* editors it matters that the writers in their anthology, among them Edith Eaton, Toshio Mori, Hisaye Yamamoto, John Okada, Louis Chu and Joy Kogawa (*Obasan*, 1981;

see Chapter 4), 'make the difference between the real and the fake. It matters that the Asian American writers here are not . . . yellow engineers of the stereotype.'[33]

The binary opposition between the real and the fake, while it continues to inform Asian American literary studies, does so in ways responsive to the manner in which the texts exceed, and therefore complicate such a rigid distinction. Indeed, later texts often focus on ideological complicity as a theme (see Chapters 4 and 5), against the notion that dominant American ideologies are liable to simple transcendence via appeals to, for example, American democratic rights, universal human rights (see Chapters 1 and 2), Asian traditions (see Chapter 3) or interracial and intergenerational love (see Chapter 4).

In her discussion of the Asian American literary canon, Lisa Lowe notes how frequently even the most formulaic texts – autobiography, Bildungsroman, interracial and intergenerational romances and travel writing – 'reveal heterogeneity rather than reproducing regulating ideas of cultural identity or integration' of the kind so strongly criticized by Chin et al. Whether heterogeneity is understood demographically or ideologically, it functions in a critical way *vis-à-vis* 'a canonical function' determined to reconcile individuals inside and outside the texts to the social order, the inequality of their experiences apparently resolved in the process.[34] As oppositional as the critical and canonical functions seem to be, particularly for Asian American critics who tend to interpret texts as either resistant or accommodationist with respect to dominant American ideologies, there are nevertheless points of interdependence. Most obviously, interdependence is made apparent when the same text demonstrates both resistance and accommodation. This insight regarding interdependence underpins contemporary attempts to reread texts, often earlier texts proclaimed accommodationist because of their reliance on formulaic genres popular with white American readers, 'for signs of resistance' to American racism.[35]

By the same token, resistance can be accommodated or appropriated, if not by force then by consent, and, ultimately, in terms of a commodification, as would be expected in a late capitalist racial formation characterized by hegemony. As Viet Thanh Nguyen argues in *Race and Resistance* (2002):

> The emergence of a unique Asian American identity after [the late 1960s] was dependent upon . . . a post-civil rights understanding about the potential of racial identity, or panethnicity, as a mode of political resistance . . . but it also coincided with the maturation of a global capitalism that had the ability to turn even resistance into a commodity.[36]

The possibility that resistance is liable to commodification, that it can be marketed, purchased and consumed (see Chapter 5), problematizes the binary opposition between good resistant and bad accommodationist writers. For Nguyen and other critics, Asian American literary texts exceed the binary opposition in the sense that they occupy more ideologically ambivalent positions that function to 'demonstrate the *flexible strategies* often chosen by authors and characters to navigate their political and ethical situations.' Nguyen continues,

> At the same time, this plurality and flexibility does not exist absolutely; it must be read, received, interpreted, marketed, purchased, and, in general, 'used' ideologically by readers and critics who are members of not only a literary public but also a wider American [and Western(ized)] public permeated by racial attitudes and global capitalism.[37]

ABOUT THIS BOOK

This book is principally for undergraduate students and for lecturers planning courses in Asian American literary studies. It serves as an introduction to the field and provides close analyses of selected texts in the form of case studies. For the most, these texts are discussed separately, although, particularly in the earlier part of the book, a number of writers are discussed under the same subheading. Each chapter also highlights events important to its period, under the subheading 'Contexts and Intertexts'. This background material is derived from Asian American cultural history, as it is also negotiated in the literary texts selected for the case studies and others. Along with the Chronology, which cites 105 writers (out of several hundred), these references to other texts give more of a sense of the volume and diversity of Asian American literature beyond, as is often the case in the UK and to a lesser extent in Europe and elsewhere, the celebrity writers that students are introduced to at first: Maxine Hong Kingston, Bharati Mukherjee and Amy Tan. While the cultural historical material and the reference material provide a sound basis for researching these and other less familiar writers, postgraduate students should also find the analyses of recent critical and theoretical debates valuable to their current and future research.

The main body of the book spans over a hundred years of Asian American literary production. More attention is given to contemporary writing, from the late 1960s onwards, consistent with 'the presentist trend'.[38] Such a focus makes sense given that most scholarship, in the form of articles, monographs and anthologies, is typically done by students and lecturers in the context of Asian American literary studies (and sometimes in American studies and English studies), which gained university recognition as a field of research in area studies in the USA from the late 1960s onwards. Other institutions associated with the professionalization of Asian American literary studies, such as major publishing houses, major publishing retailers and award givers, also dictate the Asian American literary texts that are available for teaching and learning. But, this said, the services available through the Internet (booksellers and e-publications) and interlibrary loan do make it easier, especially for students, lecturers and other readers outside the USA, to access a more diverse range of Asian American literary texts.

For the most part, this book follows this presentist trend, along with reproducing other institutional biases. Indeed, most of the texts selected for case studies are considered standard or canonical for a variety of reasons ranging from novelty and originality to popularity and notoriety. Most are written in prose English or Englishes – standard, pidgin, 'Mainstreamese'[39] – and most are set in the USA, with a few being set or partially set on or over its borders with Canada and Hawaii. While it is possible to theorize Asian North Americanness, Asians in the USA, Canada and Hawaii resist simple conflation for important historical and ethico–political reasons. As Viet Thanh Nguyen observes of Asian American multiculturalism, although his argument could also apply to Asian American transnationalism: 'By claiming the local literature of Hawai'i as Asian American literature, Asian American studies reveals the geographical, political, and cultural investments Asian America has made in a continental America with an imperialist history that continues to shape the present.'[40]

Its institutional biases notwithstanding, this book does at least gesture towards less popular times, genres, writers and texts. For example, Chapters 1, 2 and part of Chapter 3 focus on early Asian American literature (1880s–1961), with two of these chapters also relying on poetry to provide important intertextual insights about the accompanying historical contexts. In Chapters 3 and 5, the case studies of Maxine Hong Kingston and refugee literatures also benefit from insights generated by Janice Mirikitani's and Kimiko Hahn's poetry. Chapters 3 and 4 discuss Frank Chin's and David Henry Hwang's plays, while, in Chapter 5, the case study of Lan Cao's novel *Monkey Bridge* is preceded by a discussion of other refugee literatures by or about Southeast Asian Americans. The first part of this Introduction, along with the book's Conclusion, gestures more pointedly at literatures considered marginal to the Asian American literary canon, not only South Asian American literature but also, following Tomo Hattori's argument, 'Asian literatures that bear traces of American culture' and 'American literature, not necessarily by or about Asians, but which felt the influence of Asian philosophy, religion, science, popular culture or consumer trends.'[41] Finally, the Student Resources section, alongside the Chronology, provides a comprehensive and up-to-date list of texts important to Asian American literary studies. It also contains a glossary of important terms, among them assimilationism, model minority, Orientalism, transnationalism and yellow peril, along with the key terms Asian American, Asian America and Asian American literature.

NOTES

1. Meena Alexander, *Fault Lines: A Memoir* (New York: The Feminist Press, 1993), p. 200. Hereafter references to this edition are given in the text.

2. Alexander, quoted in Rajini Srikanth, *The World Next Door: South Asian American Literature and the Idea of America* (Philadelphia: Temple University Press, 2004), p. 244.

3. Susan Koshy, 'The Fiction of Asian American Literature', *The Yale Journal of Criticism* 9:2 (1996), 315.

4. Ibid., 316, 342.

5. Rajiv Shankar, 'Foreword: South Asian Identity in Asian America', in *A Part, Yet Apart: South Asians in Asian America*, ed. Lavina Dhingra Shankar and Rajini Srikanth (Philadelphia: Temple University Press, 1998), pp. ix–x.

6. Srikanth, *World*, pp. 2–5.

7. Ien Ang, *On Not Speaking Chinese: Living Between Asia and the West* (London: Routledge, 2001), p. 189.

8. Rey Chow, quoted in Ang, *Not Speaking*, pp. 91–2.

9. Sau-ling Cynthia Wong, 'Denationalization Reconsidered: Asian American Cultural Criticism at a Theoretical Crossroads', *Amerasia Journal* 21:1 & 2 (1995), 17; Koshy, 'Fiction', 319.

10. Viet Thanh Nguyen, *Race and Resistance: Literature and Politics in Asian America* (Oxford: Oxford University Press, 2002), p. 31; Angelo N. Ancheta, *Race, Rights, and the Asian American Experience* (New Brunswick, NJ: Rutgers University Press, 1998), p. 39.

11. Michael Omi and Howard Winant, *Racial Formation in the United States, from the 1960s to the 1990s* (New York: Routledge, 1994), p. 66, p. 79. Their understanding of the racial formation in the USA informs the logic of this book, and their terms 'racial dictatorship' and 'racial hegemony' in particular are used throughout.

12. Frank H. Wu, *Yellow: Race in America Beyond Black and White* (New York: Basic Books, 2002), p. 20.

13. Sucheng Chan, *Asian Americans: An Interpretative History* (New York: Twayne Publishers, 1991), p. 3, p. 25.

14. William F. Wu, *The Yellow Peril: Chinese Americans in American Fiction, 1850–1940* (Hamden, CT: Archon Books, 1982), p. 13, pp. 164–5, p. 170.

15. Yan Phou Lee, *When I Was a Boy in China*, ed. and intro. Richard V. Lee (Philadelphia, PA: Xlibris, [1887] 2003), p. 52.

16. Elaine H. Kim, *Asian American Literature: An Introduction to the Writings and their Social Context* (Philadelphia: Temple University Press, 1982), pp. 24–32.

17. Karen L. Polster, 'Major Themes and Influences of the Poems at Angel Island', http://www.english.uiuc.edu/maps/poets/a_f/angel/polster.htm [Accessed March 2007].

18. Amy Ling, *Between Worlds: Women Writers of Chinese Ancestry* (New York: Pergamon Press, 1990), pp. 61–6.

19. Kim, *Asian American*, pp. 43–4, pp. 48–9.

20. John Okada, *No–No Boy* (Seattle: University of Washington Press, [1957] 1979), p. 251.

21. Toshio Mori, *Yokohama, California*, intro. Lawson Fusao Inada (Seattle: University of Washington Press, [1949] 1985), p. vi.

22. Frank Chin, 'Confessions of the Chinatown Cowboy', *Bulletin of Concerned Asian Scholars* 4: 3 (1972), 60.

23. Frank Chin, Jeffery Paul Chan, Lawson Fusao Inada and Shawn Hsu Wong (eds), 'Preface', in *Aiiieeeee! An Anthology of Asian-American Writers* (Washington, DC: Howard University Press, 1974), pp. vii–viii.

24. Frank Chin, 'This is Not an Autobiography', *Genre* 18 (Summer 1985), 123–5.

25. Jessica Hagedorn (ed. and intro.), *Charlie Chan is Dead: An Anthology of Contemporary Asian American Fiction* (New York: Penguin, 1993), pp. xxii–xxvi.

26. Elaine H. Kim, 'Beyond Railroads and Internment: Comments on the Past, Present, and Future of Asian American Studies', in *Privileging Positions: The Sites of Asian American Studies*, ed. Gary Y. Okihiro, Marilyn Alquizola, Dorothy Fujita Rony and K. Scott Wong (Pullman: Washington State University Press, 1995), pp. 12–13.

27. Sheng-mei Ma, *Immigrant Subjectivities in Asian American and Asian Diaspora Literatures* (New York: State University of New Press, 1998), p. 29.

28. Nguyen, *Race*, p. 3, p. 7.

29. Srikanth, *World*, p. 42.

30. Lavina Dhingra Shankar, 'The Limits of (South Asian) Names and Labels: Postcolonial or Asian American?' in Shankar and Srikanth (eds), *A Part*, p. 53.

31. Ella Shohat, 'Notes on the "Post-Colonial"', in *The Pre-Occupation of Postcolonial Studies*, ed. Fawzia Afzal-Khan and Kalpana Seshadri-Crooks (Durham, NC: Duke University Press, 2000), p. 135.
32. David L. Eng and Alice Y. Hom (eds), 'Introduction', *Q & A: Queer in Asian America* (Philadelphia: Temple University Press, 1998), p. 1.
33. Frank Chin, 'Come All Ye Asian American Writers of the Real and the Fake', *The Big Aiiieeeee! An Anthology of Chinese American and Japanese American Literature*, ed. Jeffery Paul Chan, Frank Chin, Lawson Fusao Inada and Shawn Wong (New York: Meridian, 1991), p. 50, pp. 90–2; Chan et al. (eds), 'Introduction' in *Big Aiiieeeee!*, pp. xi–xii.
34. Lisa Lowe, *Immigrant Acts: On Asian American Cultural Politics* (Durham, NC: Duke University Press, 1996), pp. 43–5.
35. Nguyen, *Race*, pp. 4–5, p. 7.
36. Ibid., p. 4.
37. Ibid., p. 4, pp. 23–4.
38. Keith Lawrence and Floyd Cheng, *Recovered Legacies: Authority and Identity in Early Asian American Literature* (Philadelphia: Temple University Press, 2005), pp. 2–3.
39. Gish Jen, *Who's Irish?* (New York: Vintage, 1999), p. 23.
40. Nguyen, *Race*, p. 157.
41. Tomo Hattori, 'China Man Autoeroticism and the Remains of Asian America', *Novel* 31: 2 (Spring 1998), 220.

CHAPTER 1

American Ways of Looking, 1880s–1920s

CONTEXTS AND INTERTEXTS

In her 1915 serialized novel, *Miss Spring Morning*, Winnifred Eaton, writing under the Japanese-sounding pseudonym of Onoto Watanna, depicts a conversation in Japan between two Irish Americans, Mrs Tyrrell and her son Jamy. Relying on hearsay for the most part about 'the massacres of Christians in heathen lands', the near-sighted Mrs Tyrrell informs Jamy of her wish to be at home: 'There's no telling what might happen to us here.' Although he tells his mother that she 'needn't worry about the Japs. They're on their good behaviour – trying to "make good," in the eyes of the civilized world', Mrs Tyrrell is far from reassured. To her, the Japanese are 'unreal – figures of some strange, fantastic world', who are, at best, 'a lot of foolish children' and, at worst, 'the yellow peril'. Not even her appreciation of the Americanized Japanese Captain Taganouchi is enough to overcome her prejudice towards a race whose history she considers more degraded than 'one whose history is that of slavery and degeneration'.[1]

When compared to the racist views of his mother, Jamy's opinions regarding the Japanese seem more liberal. His liberalism arguably coincides with his role of romantic artist concerning his beloved Japan – supposing, of course, that 'she does cease to barter and sell her women like cattle' and 'rid herself of her national immorality' (p. 669). One Japanese woman in particular infatuates

Jamy, and he is determined to save her from her working-class fate as a prostitute. Given that he 'has always been crazy about Oriental things and people', even collecting 'queer little fans and ivory figures and old tea-boxes and things' as a child, it is hardly surprising that he is proprietorial towards Miss Spring Morning (p. 688). Although she does not work as his model, Spring-morning does become Mrs Tyrrell's servant before marrying Jamy in a Christian ceremony. But she is already married to Yamada Omi who returns from the Russo-Japanese War of 1905 to claim his wife back from her American husband. While suspicious that Spring-morning has another lover, not least because he sees her marry Omi at the beginning of the story, Jamy's romantic vision overrides the reality of his wife's situation, until, that is, his ideals are quashed on confirmation of her deceit and death.

Through the Tyrrells, Winnifred offers two apparently opposite views of Japan, one, bad, the other, good or, at least, trying to make good. Significantly, both visions are not only mediated but also shortsighted. As the Tyrrells observe of each other: 'I'm not seeing Japan through glasses, but with admiring eyes wide open', Jamy says to his mother, although she is not convinced and insists that his 'glasses are quite rose-colored' (p. 681). From behind their glasses, and by extension through their racial lenses, the Tyrrells transform the Japanese into spectacle to be either feared or admired and, ultimately, controlled. References to the American view of Japan, as it is typically seen through rose-colored glasses, also appear in a number of Winnifred's other stories. Bespectacled white American characters effectively transform the Japanese characters, including those 'bent on becoming as American as possible', into acquisitions for amusement, study and profit, as if they were 'this or that bit of bronze or porcelain' or some other piece of 'oriental loot'.[2]

Winnifred's prose is consistent with the turn-of-the-century preoccupation with spectacle. Shows, fairs, exhibitions and tourist trips to Chinatowns and Little Tokyos, and, for the wealthier, Asia, contributed to the Orientalization of Asian immigrants and Asians. As spectacle for white American observers, in a power relationship that reinforced the dominant racial hierarchy, 'the Oriental' was accorded a racial essence that was biologically and culturally Other. According to Mrs Tyrrell, for example, this racial essence means that the Japanese, if not 'Oriental people' generally, are 'unlike us in every way', right down to 'the last drop of . . . blood' that not even a prolonged sojourn in the USA can change (p. 680).

The other Chinese American writers in this chapter are similarly preoccupied with 'the unwisdom of the American way of looking at things', specifically with respect to biological racism.[3] Unlike her literary peers, for example, Yan Phou Lee in *When I Was a Boy in China* (1887), Edith Eaton or 'Miss Sui' Sin Far in *Mrs Spring Fragrance* (1912; p. 218) and the anonymous poets in *Songs of Gold Mountain* (1910s), Winnifred blatantly fabricated her identity. Not a Canadian-born Chinese Eurasian, but a Nagasaki-born gentlewoman, so the story goes, she passed as Japanese. While critical of the act of passing, her British-born Chinese Eurasian sister understood the reasons for it, especially when the Chinese were proclaimed soulless, expressionless and 'beyond the pale of civilization' by even respectable Americans (p. 225). As Edith explains in her autobiographical essay, 'Leaves from the Mental Portfolio of an Eurasian' (1909),

> The Americans, having for many years manifested a much higher regard for the Japanese than the Chinese, several half Chinese . . . thinking to advance themselves, both in a social and business sense, pass as Japanese. . . . The unfortunate Chinese Eurasians! Are not those who compel them to thus cringe more to be blamed than they?
>
> (p. 228)

The Americans regarded the Japanese more highly partly because of Japan's efforts to make good through modernization. Modernization contributed towards domestic stability within Japan and so the economic factors so crucial to Chinese working-class men's immigration to the USA in the nineteenth century were largely absent. As Japanese immigration by both men and women increased in the 1900s, however, the USA and Japan signed a Gentleman's Agreement (1907), whereby Japanese immigration was limited, but not prohibited, in contrast to Chinese immigration. Exclusion of the Chinese, from 1882 onwards, shifted from this ethnic group to regionalized groups from the Asiatic Barred Zone in 1917 and eventually to the racial group in the 1920s and 1930s.

Although the Japanese were its primary target, the 1924 Immigration Act so successfully excluded virtually an entire racial group because of concomitant anti-Asian naturalization laws. This act, explains Angelo N. Ancheta, 'excluded any "alien ineligible to citizenship," which, because of the racial bar on naturalization, meant all Asians.' Barred from naturalizing until the mid-twentieth century, over a century and a half after white immigrants were permitted this right, Asian immigrants also saw their American-born children's birthright citizenship similarly deferred. In 1898, *United States* v. *Wong Kim Ark* recognized Asian American birthright citizenship, thirty years after the Fourteenth Amendment to the Constitution permitted other native-born Americans this right.[4]

Indicative of a racial dictatorship, these and other anti-Asian laws proved so tenacious because of nativist, racist and Orientalist ideologies. These ideologies systematically circulated in both official and popular culture and rendered 'the Oriental' perpetually foreign or un-American, if not anti-American. Even before the writers selected in this chapter arrived in the USA – Edith in New York in 1872, after which the family moved to Canada, Lee, a year later, in San Francisco, after which he moved to the East Coast and then back to China, and, finally, the Gold Mountain poets, presumably before the Chinese exclusion period (1882–1943) – diverse and at times contradictory opinions of the Chinese already circulated among Westerners on both sides of the Atlantic. Whether it was considered utopian or dystopian, China's military capacity meant that Westerners coming into contact with the country were often in less powerful positions than those to which they were accustomed in other colonial encounters. If not through violent colonization, then, Western hegemony would need to be achieved ideologically.

One particularly powerful ideology was, and still is, the yellow peril, enough to make it, in William F. Wu's opinion, 'a fundamental assumption of American culture'. In his book *The Yellow Peril* (1982), Wu describes how yellow-peril fears first emerged in the thirteenth century with the Mongol invasions of Europe. In the USA, however, these fears began to circulate around the time of the first Anglo-Chinese Opium War (1839–42) and other violent events in mid-nineteenth century China. These fears became more pronounced in the 1870s and 1880s.[5] As Marlon K. Hom notes in his

introduction to *Songs of Gold Mountain*, 'China boys' were first
regarded with 'benign tolerance' for their work in North America's
western states and territories, but after this work finished and reces-
sion ensued they were subjected to 'hysterical rejection'.[6] This hysteria was reinforced through journalistic and scientific discourses
that proclaimed the Chinese 'incapable of civilization', the so-called
proof of which came from their idolatry, gambling, opium smoking,
gang violence and sexual deviancy. Such activities apparently
rendered them 'a cancer' in 'the biological, social, religious and political systems'. Even more terrifying than cancer, however, were the
unnamed diseases to which Euro-American children, the 'infantile'
Asian and the 'foetal' African were most vulnerable.[7]

Chinese and Africans were not only linked by their presumed
immaturity but also by their associations with slavery, since it was
assumed that 'the Chinese was being imported to replace the Negro
slave who, now that he was emancipated, would simply die out like
the Indian.'[8] The coolie system of slave labour as it operated on
plantations in Southeast Asia and South America was mistakenly
applied to the credit fare system. Hom explains that in this latter
system 'a man would repay the loan that paid his passage by
working under contract for a specified period. He was then free to
pursue his own living' (p. 5). Although not slaves, Chinese immigrants were nevertheless rendered 'virtual slaves' by a racist system
of labour exchange in the mines, on the railroads and in other industries, assuming, that is, they made it past the officials at Angel Island
Immigration Station.[9] Between 1910 and 1940, this station
processed and deported Asian immigrants, some of whom were
detained for months and even years.

Whether in prison or in work, the forced detention of Chinese
working-class men undermined their masculinity and humanity.
Hence the importance given to these traits by a number of the Gold
Mountain poets: 'I am a man of heroic deeds; / I am a man with
pride and dignity' (p. 88). The poets also criticized a detention
system that reduced both Chinese and American men to animals:
'My countrymen are made into a herd of cattle!' 'Your officials are
wolves and tigers, / All ruthless, all wanting to bite me' (pp. 80, 85).
In her newspaper article, 'The Land of the Free' (1890), Edith
describes a similarly predatory Canadian immigration official who

'pounced' on a Chinese man and demanded 'in the name of the Queen of his marvellously free country, $50 or his immediate departure' (p. 179). Economic obstacles such as this, along with those brought about by old debts and poor job prospects, meant that it was 'hard to go anywhere without money'. The poets continue: 'With deep sorrow we Chinese sojourners must / face many calamities, / Wondering when we can expect to go home', an unlikely prospect for one 'Pitiful . . . twenty-year sojourner, / Unable to make it home' to his wife and family (pp. 109, 96). Wives and families were also prevented from joining the stranded sojourners because Chinese immigration was discouraged on both sides of the Pacific.

The Chinese restriction on female immigration served to reinforce the views of American feminists and missionaries in particular that 'all Chinese marriage is a form of slavery', and 'all women, whether prostitutes or wives, were "purchased"'.[10] Some Chinese women were bought and sold as sex slaves, although, according to American feminist, missionary and legal discourses, all Chinese women were prostitutes. For example, the 1875 Page Law and later anti-prostitution legislation effectively made prostitutes of all Chinese women. This legislation was so strictly applied that it discouraged female immigration. The resulting gender asymmetry in Chinatown, with women representing less than ten per cent of the population, effectively made bachelors of the men. The often sexually explicit poets go further, especially in 'Songs of the Hundred Men's Wife', which highlight how restrictions on immigration transformed the Chinese man into a 'john' and the Chinese woman into a 'whore' (p. 315).

In Edith's story, 'Lin John' (1912), the Chinese prostitute also seems to receive less sympathetic treatment than her male counterpart. After three years hard labour, the eponymous brother has earned enough money 'to release his only sister from a humiliating and secret bondage' in prostitution, only for her to steal the money and buy 'a sealskin sacque like the fine American ladies' (pp. 117, 119). The sister's desire for pretty clothes, and by extension Americanization, thus overrides the prospect of their freedom. Crucially, however, this freedom hardly constitutes a release from bondage: 'Now, what do I want to be free for?' asks the sister, 'To be poor? To . . . be gay no more?' (p. 119). These questions help to explain the sister's actions by providing an economic context for her desires and crimes. A number of the Gold Mountain songs also explain the apparent superficiality of the prostitute's consumerism: 'We in this business of pleasing men must keep / up with the trend'; 'The whore has changed her appearance: / Now she looks just like a cute young lass. / . . . Who dares to say she is just a prostitute by trade!' (pp. 312, 314).

The Gold Mountain songs about women serve several functions with respect to masculine identity. Hom argues that the songs provide the poets with 'a temporary form of solace', which is at times comparable to that provided by pornography, not least when Chinese women are described as 'the hibiscus tent' and 'scented / curtain' (pp. 254, 239, 258). Along with reinforcing their masculinity denied by anti-immigration, anti-prostitution and anti-miscegenation laws, the songs work against the stereotype of emasculated Chinese men. For example, 'Songs of the Young at Heart' typically proclaim 'I never tire of the lust for women; /At seventy . . . / Brothels and whorehouses are places of my / mad indulgence' (p. 285). Even in the more romantic songs, this androcentric stance is still discernible when the poets make wives lovesick and prostitutes love struck. One prostitute experiences love so overriding that 'She wants to sleep with him, so she even pays his / bills. / What a fantastic indulgence in passion!' (p. 315). Unlike the prostitute in Edith's 'Lin John', then, these women will incur poverty as one man's wife. Perhaps prostitution was curbed by love, although more probable explanations for its restriction were the American legal and missionary systems, along with proto-feminist campaigns on both sides of the Pacific.

Despite these various restrictions on already small bachelor societies, Chinese immigrants were still assumed to imperil the USA biologically, socially, religiously and politically via an essence peculiarly resistant, if not antithetical, to Americanness. If it was not through anti-Chinese acts, laws and taxes, then yellow peril gained expression in mass media and literary forms: from early 'xenophobic novels' of Chinese invasion, including Atwell Whitney's *Almond-Eyed: The Great Agitator; A Story of the Day* (1878), to short stories in the *Overland Monthly* (1868–75, 1883–1935) and the *Californian* (1880–2). Some of Frank Norris's stories were published in these magazines, with his white supremacist beliefs also underpinning representations of Chinatown by other nativist and racist writers like C. W. Doyle, Chester B. Fernald, Maud Howe, Lu Wheat, Wallace Irwin and Jack London. Bret Harte's popular poem, 'The Heathen Chinee' (1870), although sympathetic towards the eponymous character of Ah Sin, still adheres to anti-Chinese stereotypes.[11] The 'peculiar' Ah Sin, as 'his name might imply', ruins a card game by trickery, which his opponent understands in the wider anti-Chinese context: ' "We are ruined by Chinese cheap labor," – / And he went for that heathen Chinee.'[12]

Given the popularity of 'The Heathen Chinee', not just the poem but also the titular phrase, with its underlying binary opposition of Christian and heathen and arising from that the other conflicting associations of adult and child, normal and peculiar, freedom and slavery, it is hardly surprising that the Chinese American writers in this chapter struggle creatively and critically. Although yellow-peril fears circulated throughout American culture, and, for the most part, dictatorially so, Lee, the Eatons and the Gold Mountain poets still attempt antiracist critique in their prose and poetry. Their texts re-negotiate the dominant relationship between racial and national groups by asserting similarities and by reversing 'American Concepts of "Other-ness"' in nativist, racist and Orientalist discourses. Annette White-Parks clarifies the logic and the risks involved in such reversals with specific reference to Edith's fiction:

'a concept of fundamental differences' has been used to justify inhuman treatment of populations of the United States with skins darker than Anglo, from Indians and Blacks . . . to Asians and Mexicans . . . Such a concept implies that skin color (being 'white' or of 'European descent') has set the standard for humanness in North America since the European invasion, and supplies a reason why writers of non-European descent would choose 'mediation' – stressing the 'samenesses'.[13]

Although stressing the samenesses problematizes racism, thus conceived, it simultaneously risks reaffirming the dominant racial hierarchy through assimilationism. For Asian American critics there is

a question as to whether Lee and Winnifred negotiate as successfully as Edith these different ideological positions to claim a shared
humanness and Americanness for Chinese immigrants, while also
valuing Chinese culture enough to avoid assimilationism.

YAN PHOU LEE, *WHEN I WAS A BOY IN CHINA* (1887)

When I Was a Boy in China was the first Asian American literary text
published and was written in English. Yan Phou Lee (1861–1938?)
intended it for an American readership whom he addresses in a
direct and personal way: 'If you were living in China', the assumption being that they do not, and so must rely on Lee to take them to
various places inside and outside the upper-middle-class Chinese
home where he 'happened to be born'.[14] As a tour guide, Lee provides his readers with Chinese spectacle, albeit in the so-called
Western and Christian form of autobiography.[15] This combination
of the familiar and the unfamiliar, not quite the strange, but more
the exotic, as in, for example, Lee's chapters on 'Chinese Cookery',
'Games and Pastimes', 'Religions' and 'Chinese Holidays', appealed
to a culture preoccupied with spectacle. His prose made him something of 'a celebrity' (p. 16), if not, in Elaine H. Kim's words, an
'ambassador of goodwill to the West'.

Although not a member of the upper class, belonging to which
typically prohibited a young man's journey to the USA, Lee is nevertheless of this ambassadorial class because his autobiography
focuses on high culture and 'the charming superficialities of cere-
monies, and customs of food and dress', typically against the low
cultural pursuits of other Chinese and other Asians.[16] For the most
part, Lee's China is aestheticized, although, at points, his less than
charming prejudices do become apparent. For example: 'the edu-
cated classes despise both Taoists and Buddhists', presumably for
their 'gibberish' and 'criminal' tendencies respectively. Similarly
despised are other Asian religious practices: 'the idolatry of the
Chinese is superior to the brutal worship of India, and to the
brutish worship of the Egyptians' (pp. 68, 70–1).

While neither brutal nor brutish, Americans are criticized for
believing that the Chinese are incapable of education and culture.

As part of an educational experiment to Americanize and Christianize a group of Chinese boys, Lee hoped that his studies and, later, writing career in the USA would allow him to 'do a great deal of good in this country by simply correcting erroneous American ideas concerning Chinese affairs' (p. 15). American journalists and travel writers are openly criticized for their role in perpetuating such false ideas, although Lee's criticism of other Americans is more subtle and relates to inadequate kite making and fishing skills. Also criticized are American women, presumably as safe a topic to question as 'Games and Pastimes'. According to Lee, 'American girls are spoiled' by 'excess of liberty', especially when compared to properly raised Chinese women. But, this said, Lee does go on to assert that both groups of women of a certain class are too preoccupied with 'trifling things', from lesser literary genres to lives dominated by fashion and other pleasantries (pp. 56–7).

On the topic of Chinese women, Lee is at his most indignant: 'There is far less of truth told about the "fair section" of the Chinese people than of the sterner sex, because far less is known' (p. 52). He attempts to resolve this problem by highlighting stereotypically feminine virtues of 'skill, patience, quick wit and delicacy', along with insisting that famous Chinese women are worthy of oral representation (pp. 54–5). He also comments on the controversial topics of female infanticide and footbinding. As Lee explains it, footbinding involves a class-based choice: 'To be ranked as servants, working girls? Not they. The Chinese young lady chooses to be fashionable even though she undergo torture for several years and incur helplessness for life.' Still, her lot is altogether more pleasant than working-class women who have 'to "make way [*sic*]" with their babies rather than see them slowly starve to death' (pp. 56–7, 53).

In addition to correcting erroneous American ideas, Lee focuses on cross-cultural similarities. For instance, he discusses his English-style christening and Roman-style house, complete with ' "a skeleton in the closet," it is said here in America. It is no less true of Chinese families' (p. 46). Not only do these references to Anglo–European culture display his learning, together with his cosmopolitanism, but they also counter the Orientalist stereotype of uncivilized Chinese. Other Orientalist stereotypes are questioned and, at times, reversed, when Lee asserts that the Chinese are not 'naturally cruel', and 'Oriental tastes' are also marked by 'simplicity', against biological racism that renders the Chinese peculiar (pp. 37, 33–4). Moreover, Western tourists are exoticized and Orientalized when they are described as 'peculiar people' who constitute 'strange sights' in 1870s Shanghai and Hong Kong (pp. 91, 89).

For the most part, *When I Was a Boy in China* is concerned with correcting errors and emphasizing cross-cultural similarities, often by reversing dominant American ideologies. In so doing, Lee undermines biological racism by drawing attention to the way in which Americans are not exempt from the so-called natural traits that they attribute to the Chinese. Both groups share human traits – good and bad. On the odd occasion, however, Lee does emphasize Chinese difference by measuring it against a white American norm. With respect to sport and masculinity, for instance, he notes that there is 'a feeble apology for the manly sport of base-ball', although, for the most part 'there are hardly any sports, so called' in China. For this reason, Lee continues, Chinese youths are 'grave and staid as an American grandfather', hardly a challenge to the stereotype of emasculated Chinese men (pp. 47, 50).

However, Lee's radicalism does emerge elsewhere, in relation to politics, not sport. In 'First Experiences in America', Lee, clearly impressed by American modernity, remarks that 'San Francisco in 1873 was the paradise of the self-exiled Chinese' who came to study 'under the protection of the American eagle' (p. 96). Modernity and protection are soon questioned via old-fashioned violence when gun-wielding robbers hold up Lee's eastbound train. This questioning is reinforced by irony: how paradisiacal can this city and the state be given the extent of anti-Chinese discrimination and violence in the 1870s and 1880s? Lee protested about this sinophobia in articles for *North Atlantic Review*. Of particular concern to him was the Chinese Exclusion Law of 1882, which preceded the publication of *When I Was a Boy in China*, thus reinforcing further the irony of a Californian paradise. Not quite a goodwill ambassador, then, Lee, in his literary and critical writings, negotiates a position attuned to the fact the 'Nation, which Abraham Lincoln said was conceived in liberty, waxed great through oppression, and was really dedicated to the proposition that all men are created to prey on one another.'[17]

WINNIFRED EATON AND EDITH EATON, SELECTED SHORT STORIES (1900–15)

Like Lee, Winnifred Eaton (1875–1954) and Edith Eaton (1865–1914) are attuned to the discrepancy between democratic political rhetoric and dictatorial political reality. They also seek to negotiate a position between racism and assimilationism, albeit in ways considered very different. Winnifred achieved widespread recognition in the USA at the turn of the century with many best-selling sentimental and melodramatic interracial romances often set in an exoticized Japan, whereas Edith did not achieve this level of success with her more realistic Chinatown-based short stories until they were recovered in the 1970s. This is partly the reason why S. E. Solberg and other critics identify Edith as 'The First Chinese-American Fictionist' for her short story, 'The Gamblers' (1896), which was published before Winnifred's first novel, *Miss Numè of Japan* (1899).[18] Of the two sisters, Edith represents to cultural nationalist critics in particular the real originator of Asian American fiction, over and above her more prolific race-denying and Orientalist sister. More recently, however, Asian American critics have complicated this cultural nationalist binary opposition by arguing that the criterion of authenticity is impossibly idealistic. Its uncritical application bypasses the way in which both sisters negotiate a position between the real and the inauthentic, not least in their shared thematic concern with American ways of looking.

In her autobiographical essay, Edith describes how a number of English and Canadian people look at her 'very much in the same way that I have seen people gaze upon strange animals in a menagerie.' In these countries, her racial identity is determined by her physical difference: her 'English bred' Chinese mother's eyes and hair gives her 'a peculiar coloring', over and above her father's 'white blood' (pp. 218–20). In the USA, however, Edith passes for white, until, that is, she says: 'I am a Chinese' (p. 225). Race at this time was understood as a biological given, based on visible physical characteristics. In the words of one Gold Mountain poet: 'the exterior / . . . counts the most' in terms of cross-cultural interaction and racial political theory (p. 207). However, Edith's (and Winnifred's) experiences with respect to passing help to denaturalize race, shifting it from a biological to a cultural and linguistic category. Passing thus demonstrates the instability of racial categories, a theme the Eatons explore further in their fiction also with reference to other categories of identity such as class and gender. In one of Winnifred's stories, concepts of humanness – the human, inhuman and non-human – are at issue.

In her serialized novel, *The Old Jinrikisha* (1900), Winnifred makes a jinrikisha or rickshaw the narrator. This vehicle is given human qualities, not just a female narrative voice but also an aristocratic birth. With the fall of the samurai class, however, the jinrikisha works for the bourgeoisie, including wealthy American tourists, and is pulled by a runner who 'belonged to the very lowest type of ruffian'. This class hierarchy is reinforced by a racial hierarchy when the runner attacks a white American girl, despite his diminutive size: 'She was tall and well formed . . . with all the grace of a thoroughbred', while he is a 'miserable, skinny, little rat' who has to resort to 'a fiendish method' to overpower her (pp. 5–6). When read alongside the novel's other scenes involving foreign tourists, who also see Japan as 'some vague picture in a fairyland scene', *The Old Jinrikisha* extends its critique beyond the Orientalized working-class runner to Western Orientalists (p. 13). Their fairyland pictures, similar to the stereotype, 'freeze movement, variability, evolution, and growth' in the words of Stephen Foster. He continues, albeit about touristic discourse more generally, 'Selection of what is significant is given over to the observer, so that the resulting representations express mainly the observational style and social placement of the photographer, interlocutor, or outsider.'[19]

Following Foster's argument, *The Old Jinrikisha* and *Miss Spring Morning* say less about Japan and the Japanese than they do about the Western way of looking, which is not only unwise but also mistaken. To return briefly to the Tyrrells, who opened this chapter, and Jamy's wilful belief that Mrs Yamada Omi could be his Springmorning: more interested in her pose and his own role of romantic

artist-saviour-husband than the reality of his Japanese wife's situation, Jamy claims to see this situation clearly in a dramatic scene
involving the return of Spring-morning's husband from the Russo-
Japanese War of 1905. Winnifred's narrator questions the so-called
clarity of Jamy's vision. No longer in the 'far-away fairyland' of
Japan, Jamy undergoes an epiphany partly attributable to 'the
clean-cut, homely, preposterously conventional, inartistic landscape' of the USA. The pathetic fallacy aside, he still continues to
see his life before and after that 'sweet aberration' in Japan in
romanticized terms. Whether he has emerged from his 'Japan-
fever' a different, more insightful man, let alone a sane man, is thus
in question (pp. 719–20, 688).

Even when the glasses worn seem less than rose coloured, as in
'An Unexpected Grandchild' (1909), Winnifred emphasizes the
fact of mediation. This story centres on the 'tragic tale of a girl
victim and some brute countryman of our own', as the unexpected
grandmother, Mrs Howland remarks (p. 685). After reading
Madame Butterfly (1898), a novella written by Philadelphia resident
John Luther Long, Mrs Howland is so powerfully affected that she
misreads her American son's relationship with a Japanese woman.
On meeting this woman and her supposed child for the first time,
Mrs Howland is excited because 'here before her was one of the
very victims of which she had heard and read.' She proclaims,
'"My poor, poor child! . . . My heart bleeds for you. But" – and she
turned heroically toward the Japanese girl, whose face was hidden
in her sheltering sleeve – "but right is right."' Turning to her son's
American girlfriend, Mrs Howland announces: 'We as women, as
sisters to this poor, betrayed creature, owe her a duty and – repara-
tion! What my son refused to give her, I will – protection!' (pp. 687–
8). Significantly, the betrayed creatures are the Howlands, as well as
the real parents of the child abducted by the Japanese woman for
the purpose of financial exploitation through interracial relationships. 'I could not conceive of a Japanese adventuress. It seems
incredible even now', Mrs Howland admits to her son, the suggestion being that adventuring is unlikely to be conducted by the
Japanese, however rosily or tragically constructed (p. 700).

Edith also draws attention to the unwisdom of the American
way of looking with reference to 'Chinese-Amricans [*sic*]', who are

generally considered 'unworthy of a little notice' (p. 231). When they are noticed, as in, for example, the popular press, the emphasis is on so-called yellow-peril activities such as gambling, prostitution and gang violence. Such activities arguably attract the American journalist, Mark Carson, to Chinatown in Edith's story, 'Its Wavering Image' (1912). Described as 'a man who would sell his soul for a story', Carson is assigned to Chinatown to 'unveil' its inhabitants 'before the ridiculing and uncomprehending foreigner' in an underhand way through a romantic relationship with 'a half white, half Chinese girl' called Pan (pp. 62, 65, 61).

More precisely, Pan is Carson's pass into Chinatown. Not recognizing the violence of this objectification, she proudly assumes the role of tour guide, never once running into yellow-peril stereotypes such as the evil doctor, the violent gangster and the malicious dragon lady presumed to inhabit Chinatown. On these tours, the couple enjoy each other's company, perhaps not equally since Pan's biracial identity, which had initially puzzled Carson, becomes increasingly threatening to him. As Vanessa Holford Diana puts it, 'she disturbs the racial categorization on which the stability of his own identity relies; Pan represents to Carson "the spectre of racial ambiguity that must be conquered".'[20] Carson's newspaper exposé, 'Its Wavering Image', represents his attempt to conquer both Chinatown and Pan. He also tries to stabilize Pan by bringing to her consciousness traits apparently 'alien' to Chinese Americans, such as reading and romance (p. 63). After performing a platonic love song, to which she responds emotionally, he exclaims: 'Those tears prove that you are white' (p. 64). To the clever-eyed Carson, ironic, given his limited perception, Pan could pass for, if not be, white. 'You are a white woman – white', he fiercely insists, although she rejects this identity, as Edith also did: 'I am a Chinese woman' (pp. 61, 66).

Moving from journalistic discourse to missionary discourse, from selling souls to saving souls, Edith's short story, 'Pat and Pan' (1912), about an orphaned white boy and his Chinese sister, highlights the similarities between these apparently opposite discourses. Pat and Pan are discovered asleep in each other's arms in a Chinatown doorway by a white Missionary schoolteacher, Anna Harrison, who subsequently 'determined that Pat . . . should learn to speak his mother tongue. For a white boy to grow up as a Chinese was unthinkable' (p. 161). While Harrison's school is progressive in that it is not segregated, the unthinkability of racial intermixing still compels her to notify 'the white community to Pat's "unnatural" position'.[21] He is subsequently removed from his Chinese immigrant family to be raised as 'an American boy should be raised' in a white middle-class family (p. 164). A year later, Pat's language is anglicized and his views are Americanized, to the point that he, in the company of white friends, drives away Pat with taunts of 'the China kid!' (p. 166).

Although critical of American journalistic and missionary discourses for their sensationalist and Orientalist rhetoric, Edith does nevertheless use this same rhetoric in a number of her short stories, albeit ironically and, arguably, strategically consistent with 'trickster stylistics' (p. 170). Often the focus of her trickster stylistics is the middle-class, English-speaking and Americanized couple, Mr and Mrs Spring Fragrance. In 'The Inferior Woman' (1912), Mrs Spring Fragrance Orientalizes Americans: 'Ah, these Americans! These mysterious, inscrutable, incomprehensible Americans!' (p. 33). In 'Mrs Spring Fragrance' (1912), she is so exhilarated by a lecture on 'America, the Protector of China!' that she informs her husband that this 'expression of benevolence' should override discrimination within the USA. Mrs Spring Fragrance begs him to forget the anti-Chinese policies of a barber and the immigration system. Mr Spring Fragrance's brother 'on a visit to this country, is detained under the roof-tree of this great Government' or, more properly, 'protected under the wing of the Eagle, the Emblem of Liberty'. Mrs Spring Fragrance goes on to imply that even excessive temporal and financial losses brought about by such protection are worth incurring (p. 21).

However, Mr Spring Fragrance does not forget racial discrimination, an unlikely prospect anyway given his wife's hyperbole. He focuses on American principles, specifically mobility and nobility for all, excluding, of course, his detained brother, in a conversation with an American journalist neighbour. However, the contradiction between democratic political rhetoric and dictatorial political reality is lost on the neighbour: 'understand, old fellow, we that are real Americans are up against that – even more than you. It is

against out principles.' Mr Spring Fragrance responds by offering
'the real Americans . . . [his] consolation that they should be compelled to do that which is against their principles' (p. 23). The
Spring Fragrances' rhetorical analyses not only problematize a
literal reading of this great government whose principals are
revealed to be unprincipled and undemocratic with respect to
Americans presumed unreal, but it also reinforces Edith's preoccupation with the fact of mediation.

The Eatons' different yet related emphasis on mediation is figuratively represented by American tourists, journalists and missionaries, who, even when their limited viewpoint is challenged, are still
unable to see the way in which 'the Oriental' owes more to dominant American ideologies than it does to the reality of life in China
and Chinatown. In addition to de-naturalizing the American way of
looking by exposing its racism, its limitations with respect to biraciality, and its constructedness, the Eatons offer a further challenge
to American Orientalism and the rigid hierarchies and categories on
which it is based through their depiction of interracial relationships. In these relationships, the Eatons resist Orientalist stereotypes by representing their Asian characters with, as Edith's editor
observes, 'insight and sympathy which are probably unique. To
others the alien Celestial is at best mere "literary material": in these
stories, he (or she) is a human being.'[22]

This humanity is emphasized by the capacity for love in particular, which is not, as many of the Eatons' white American characters
assume, a specifically Western emotion. Public displays of affection
are less common among the Eatons' Asian characters, although this
does not mean that, as Jamy explains to Spring-morning, there is
'no word in the Japanese language to express it, but in my land we
call it – Love!' (p. 698). Although often concerned simply with
sexual desire in their consideration of heterosexual relationships,
the Gold Mountain poets still mention love in the letters sent by the
'Estranged Wives' to 'Stranded Sojourners': 'Letters of love,
soaked in tears, all sent to you, / my dear' (p. 124).

The love between a white man and an Asian woman, as depicted
most famously in *Madame Butterfly*, does not threaten white patriarchy to the same extent as the relationship between an Asian man
and a white woman. As Pat Shea explains:

The motivation behind most anti-miscegenation laws was not to limit the sexual selections of white men, but to 'protect' white women and ensure the racial homogeneity of their children. This distinction was evident in states such as South Carolina, where a white man was allowed to marry a Chinese woman though the opposite combination was a crime.[23]

Winnifred focuses on both combinations in her fiction, although, admittedly, bestsellers like *A Japanese Nightingale* (1901) and *Tama* (1910) focus on the more acceptable combination of a white man and an Asian or Eurasian woman. In her first novel, *Miss Numè of Japan* (1899), she does, however, depict a relationship between Japanese Orito and American Cleo. Granted, the feminized and emasculated Orito commits suicide, this end tallying with anti-miscegenation fiction, but the novel resists the ideology it advocates when Cleo is subsequently betrothed to her brother-like cousin, Tom.[24] According to Shea, Winnifred 'seems to suggest that the obsession with the perpetuation of a "pure" white blood line will eventually foster incestuous couplings in American society.'[25]

Edith, too, represents this combination of Asian man and white woman in 'The Story of One White Woman Who Married a Chinese' and in its sequel 'Her Chinese Husband' (1912). After the working-class narrator leaves her American husband, James Carson, for his attempted infidelity, Minnie contemplates suicide and infanticide. Liu Kanghi intervenes in this double drowning and Minnie later becomes his wife. In her words: 'I followed him, obeyed him, trusted him from the very first. It never occurred to me to ask myself what manner of man was succoring me. I only know that he was a man' of numerous qualities that 'do not all belong to the whites' (pp. 72, 74). Kanghi may be manlier than Winnifred's Orito, but he still lacks Carson's passion. However, this hierarchy of increasingly masculine men is questioned when Minnie suspects that Carson's passion is contrived, if not predatory – in keeping with white patriarchy – as he fails to win her back from Kanghi. With the evil Carson gone, the story ends happily – almost:

For my boy . . . stands between his father and myself, like yet unlike us both, so will he stand in after years between his father's

and his mother's people. And if there is no kindliness nor understanding between them, what will my boy's fate be?

(p. 77)

Minnie's worst fears for her family's future are realized in the
sequel when Kanghi is murdered by some Chinese men 'who hate
with a bitter hatred all who would enlighten or be enlightened'
(p. 83). In addition to suggesting a feminist sensibility, Edith's critique of Chinese and American patriarchies, both of which privilege
racial purity, compels her to acknowledge that the Chinese are as
prejudiced as the English, Canadians and Americans. For the most
part, however, Edith's, as well as Winnifred's, romances focus on
the prejudice suffered by Asian and Asian American characters.
Granted, this suffering emerges from individual acts of passing –
over class, gender and racial boundaries – and, more frequently, from
cross-cultural relationships, but, to recall Edith's question: 'Are not
those who compel them . . . more to be blamed than they?' (p. 228).

Three of Edith's stories alert to this compulsion are 'The Prize
China Baby', 'The Wisdom of the New' and 'The Americanizing of
Pau Tsu' (1912). In these stories, a tension exists between American
and Chinese cultures, as acutely experienced by a Chinese immigrant
wife. While her forced Americanization leaves Pau Tsu contemplating death and divorce, the wives in the other two stories experience
death at first hand. Whether Americanization is regarded as advan-
tageous or disadvantageous, the outcome is the same in 'The Prize
China Baby' and 'The Wisdom of the New'. In both stories, children
die, arguably because their Chinese immigrant parents too single-
mindedly pursue Americanization. Assimilationism, thus pursued,
results in the destruction of the 'connecting link' between white and
Chinese Americans. Edith defines this link in terms of a shared individuality, although it could also be applied to a shared humanity that
exceeds national and racial boundaries (p. 230).

CONCLUSION

Euro-American ways of looking at 'the Oriental' are shown to be
unwise by all the writers in this chapter, whether categorized by

Asian American critics as ideologically good (Edith), bad (Lee and Winnifred) or in between (the Gold Mountain poets). Most unwise are Orientalist stereotypes that show Asians to be lacking humanity, their so-called slave labour and heathen traits – specifically in relation to sexuality and, with it, racial and national purity – apparently imperilling the USA. As Mrs Tyrrell puts it: 'I have always believed in the yellow peril, and I think we white people should stand together and do everything in our power to keep these horrible heathens – away from us', especially since, to her, interracial relationships are 'abominable – against nature [and] God' (p. 700). Not surprisingly, this racialized and Christianized them-and-us belief is questioned, if not de-naturalized, in Lee's and the Eatons' prose, as well as in *Songs of Gold Mountain*.

Indeed, Lee's autobiographical 'I' makes 'you' dependent, thus shifting 'you' into a less powerful position, which, he observes, is no less peculiar than the 'Orientals' that white American readers and tourists have come to see. This linguistic and ideological shift not only highlights the way in which people 'happen . . . to be born into the[ir] . . . condition of life' (p. 38), but it also foregrounds the fluidity of this and other conditions. Even the men in the Gold Mountain songs demonstrate this fluidity with respect to identity in their adoption of stereotypically feminine personas, as does Winnifred in her adoption of a Japanese persona. Here, men perform women, and Eurasians perform Chinese, Japanese and whites, suggesting a connecting link between them based on shared humanness. This humanness is less easily conveyed in the formulaic forms used by Winnifred, Lee and the poets. Edith's less conventional prose, which combines realism and romance, with a certain degree of irony, enables the depiction of individualized Chinese Americans who have souls, emotions, desires, capabilities, limitations and, finally, democratic rights.

Thus represented, this individual should also have rights, despite their denial by a power that exceeds Mrs Tyrrell and was inscribed in the very document that made the USA so appealing for immigrants: a constitution promising religious, political and economic freedom to its citizens and to some would-be citizens. This discrepancy likewise affected other racialized groups, most obviously Indians, Mexicans and enslaved Africans, but for Asian immigrants and their American-born children it applied well beyond the Nationality Act (1790), the Fourteenth Amendment (1868) and the Naturalization Act (1870) that permitted white and black Americans naturalized and birthright citizenship. For the Chinese American writers in this chapter, such discriminatory legislation with respect to immigration and naturalization in particular is, more than the received image of 'the Oriental', antithetical to Americanness.

In their critical analyses of white power, Lee, the Eatons and the Gold Mountain poets, variously explore the contradiction between democratic political rhetoric and dictatorial political reality, at times subtly by asserting cross-cultural similarities and by reversing nativist, racist and Orientalist binary oppositions, at other times more openly: 'So, liberty is your national principle; / Why do you practice autocracy?' (p. 85) and 'No Nation can afford to let go its high ideals'.[26] According to Hom, such an appeal to equality and freedom is 'the first crude sign of . . . Americanization' (p. 73). Moreover, these writers draw attention to the limitations of 'the Oriental' in contrast to the complexity of Asian and Eurasian identities, as they become American in ways that do not simply endorse assimilationism. All in all, then, theirs, too, is an *American* way of looking.

SUMMARY OF KEY POINTS

- The 1880s–1920s were marked by anti-Asian discrimination and violence, generally after sojourners and immigrants participated in nation-building in terms of their labour in the gold mines and in other industries.
- The yellow-peril stereotype circulated throughout American culture. Asians were regarded as naturally inferior consistent with biological racism.
- Asian immigrants protested discrimination and violence through strikes, legal cases and critical articles in newspapers and journals.
- Early poetry and prose also questioned dominant American ideologies by appealing to American democratic rhetoric, stressing cross-cultural similarities and reversing nativist, racist and

Orientalist binary oppositions. At times, this questioning was direct, at others subtle, for some later critics, so subtle as to be consistent with assimilationism. In Edith's prose, however, assimilation or Americanization risks death.

- Early poetry and prose emphasized realism, both formally and thematically. For example, autobiographical texts sought to represent life in Asia and the USA apart from American stereotypes. Romance also preoccupied early writers, more typically as a theme rather than a genre.

NOTES

1. Winnifred Eaton, *Miss Spring Morning*, in *The Blue Book Magazine* 20: 3 (Chicago: The Story-Press Corporation, 1915), pp. 679–80, p. 700. This story comes from 'The Winnifred Eaton Digital Archive', ed. Jean Lee Cole at http://etext.lib. virginia.edu/eaton/ [Accessed January 2007]. Hereafter references to this story are given in the text.

2. 'Digital Archive': 'Count Oguri's Quest', p. 144; 'Daughter of Two Lands', p. 33, p. 35. References to other stories from this archive are given in the text.

3. Edith Eaton/Sui Sin Far, *Mrs Spring Fragrance and Other Writings*, ed. and intro. Amy Ling and Annette White-Parks (Urbana: University of Illinois Press, 1995), p. 19. Hereafter references to this edition and the introductions are given in the text.

4. Angelo N. Ancheta, *Race, Rights, and the Asian American Experience* (New Brunswick, NJ: Rutgers University Press, 1998), pp. 23–6.

5. William F. Wu, *The Yellow Peril: Chinese Americans in American Fiction, 1850–1940* (Hamden, CT: Archon Books, 1982), p. 208, p. 10, pp. 12–13.

6. Marlon K. Hom (ed. and intro.), *Songs of Gold Mountain: Cantonese Rhymes from San Francisco Chinatown* (Berkeley: University of California Press, 1987), pp. 8–9. Hereafter references to the poems and the introductions are given in the text.

7. *New York Times* and Dr Arthur B. Stout, quoted in Stuart Creighton Miller, *The Unwelcome Immigrant: The American Image of the Chinese, 1785–1882* (Berkeley: University of California Press, 1969), p. 140, pp. 161–3, p. 158.

8. Miller, *Unwelcome*, pp. 152–3.

9. Sucheng Chan, *Asian Americans: An Interpretative History* (New York: Twayne Publishers, 1991), p. 81.

10. Sucheta Mazumdar, 'Through Western Eyes: Discovering Chinese Women in America', *A New Significance: Re-envisioning the History of the American West*, ed. Clyde A. Milner II (Oxford: Oxford University Press, 1996), pp. 163–4.

11. Wu, *Yellow*, pp. 30–1, p. 41, p. 126, p. 28.

12. Bret Harte, 'The Heathen Chinee', http://etext.lib.virginia.edu/railton/roughingit/map/chiharte.html [Accessed January 2007].

13. Alexander Saxton, quoted in Annette White-Parks, 'A Reversal of American Concepts of "Otherness" in the Fiction of Sui Sin Far', *MELUS* 20: 1 (Spring 1995), 27.

14. Yan Phou Lee, *When I Was a Boy in China*, ed. and intro. Richard V. Lee (Philadelphia, PA: Xlibris, [1887] 2003), p. 31, p. 38. Hereafter references to this edition and the introduction are given in the text.

15. Sau-ling Cynthia Wong, 'Autobiography as Guided Chinatown. Tour? Maxine Hong Kingston's *The Woman Warrior* and the Chinese-American Autobiographical Controversy', *Multicultural Autobiography: American Lives*, ed. James Robert Payne (Knoxville: University of Tennessee Press, 1992), pp. 262–3. Also see her comments on autobiography, p. 256: 'Some of the generalizations . . . such as the exclusively Western and Christian origin of autobiography, may be called into question by existing scholarship.'

16. Elaine H. Kim, *Asian American Literature: An Introduction to the Writings and their Social Context* (Philadelphia: Temple University Press, 1982), pp. 24–5.

17. Yan Phou Lee, 'The Chinese Must Stay', *North Atlantic Review* 148: 389 (April 1889), 476.

18. S. E. Solberg, 'Sui Sin Far/Edith Eaton: First Chinese-American Fictionist', *MELUS* 8: 1 (Spring 1981), 27.

19. Stephen Foster, quoted in Graham Huggan, *The Postcolonial Exotic: Marketing the Margins* (London: Routledge, 2001), p. 202.

20. Judith Butler, quoted in Vanessa Holford Diana, 'Biracial/Bicultural Identity in the Writings of Sui Sin Far', *MELUS* 26: 2 (Summer 2001), 172.

21. Diana, 'Biracial', 171.

22. William Purviance Fenn, quoted in Solberg, 'Sui Sin Far', 33

23. Pat Shea, 'Winnifred Eaton and the Politics of Miscegenation in Popular Fiction', *MELUS* 22: 2 (Summer 1997), 22.

24. See, for example, Wu, *Yellow*, p. 69: 'All the stories of miscegenation make violence, disease, and often death the fate of the main characters.'

25. Shea, 'Winnifred', 24.

26. Lee, 'The Chinese', 476.

CHAPTER 2

We are America, 1930s–50s

CONTEXTS AND INTERTEXTS

Euro-American ways of looking at Asians and Asian Americans according to the binary logic of good and bad 'Orientals' continues into the mid-twentieth century, again, for the most part, in relation to Japanese Americans and Chinese Americans. With the Japanese bombing of Pearl Harbor on 7 December 1941, however, Americans reversed their opinions of China and Japan, along with adhering to a logic that conflated the two cultures on either side of the Pacific. Indeed, 'the Chinese, once regarded as subhuman, were now fellow sufferers from Japanese aggression; the Japanese, once seen as charming and noble, were now regarded as treacherous and despicable.'[1] However, American sinophobia soon re-emerged in relation to Chinese communism in the Cultural Revolution (1949) and the Korean War (1950–3). Communist suspicions stimulated by unionizing Filipinos meant that they, too, were seen as contributing to 'the new peril [that] was seen as yellow in race and red in ideology', which in part necessitated their exclusion from the USA via the Tydings-McDuffie Act of 1934.[2]

The reversal of opinion with specific reference to Japanese Americans is described in a number of the short stories and novels discussed in this chapter. For example, in John Okada's 1957 Bildungsroman *No–No Boy* the eponymous character observes: 'There was a time when . . . it was all right . . . to be Japanese and feel and think all things that Japanese do even if we lived in America.'[3] Two other second-generation, or Nisei, writers, Toshio Mori and Hisaye Yamamoto, also contributed to this prewar Japanese American sensibility in their short story collections *Yokohama, California* (1949) and *Seventeen Syllables and Other Stories* (1988). The fact that they produced Japanese American literature by combining Japanese and American literary forms, for Yamamoto the seventeen-syllable poetic form *haiku*, and, for Mori, 'the time-honored *shibai* tradition of folk drama and humorous skits', further suggested that Japanese Americans in Yokohama California and elsewhere 'quite obviously believed in themselves, in what they could do, were doing, in America.'[4]

Such self-belief was particularly the case for the Issei, or first generation, whose ineligibility for citizenship did not diminish their hopes for their American-born children. Of the latter, Mori's Papa Noda proclaims: 'I have seven strong plants in my family. They'll root in the rich California soil and grow big. Maybe some day a fine blossom' (p. 113). Similarly, the second generation celebrate their parents. In 'The Woman Who Makes Swell Doughnuts', Mori's Nisei narrator observes of the eponymous archetypal mother figure:

> But what of a woman who isn't a mama but is . . . just sitting, just moving, just alive, planting the plants in the fields, caring for the children and the grandchildren and baking the tastiest doughnuts this side of the next world.
>
> (pp. 23–4)

These horticultural and culinary images of nurturing suggest that 'the lineage . . . counts. It means something, everything: the tradition, the heritage: Japanese America' (p. x).

Japanese America, thus described, proved remarkably resilient so that not even disasters of the kind described in some of Yamamoto's short stories seem able to disturb this generally 'pleasant outlook' – excluding, of course, ten-year-old Yoneko Hosoume in 'Yoneko's Earthquake' (1951). Set in 1933, this postwar short story is about a catastrophe that leaves the Hosoume family not only homeless but also divided:

The others soon oriented themselves to the catastrophe with philosophy . . . going so far as to regard the period as a sort of vacation from work, with their enforced alfresco existence a sort of camping trip. They tried to bring Yoneko to partake of this pleasant outlook, but she, shivering with each new quiver, looked on them as dreamers who refused to see things as they really were.[5]

While 'Yoneko's Earthquake' straddles the Second World War in terms of its setting and publication, the story nevertheless gestures by analogy towards the things that happened to Japanese Americans during the war, specifically their enforced existence in rural camps that severely disrupted intraracial and interracial relationships. The war meant that their lives in Yokohama and other places in the American West no longer rolled 'on regularly, just as in Boston, Cincinnati, Birmingham, Kansas City, Minneapolis, and Emeryville' (p. 71).

In February 1942, ten weeks after the Japanese attacked Pearl Harbor, President Franklin D. Roosevelt signed Executive Order 9066. For reasons of so-called military necessity to do with protecting the USA against sabotage and espionage, this order forced over 120,000 Japanese Americans – Issei, Nisei and Sansei, or third generation – into inland 'evacuation camps . . . of wind, sand, and heat' where 'circumstances made it unnecessary . . . to earn a competitive living' (pp. 20, 32). Here, Yamamoto's narrator in 'The Legend of Miss Sasagawara' (1950) describes the War Relocation Centre in Arizona as an evacuation camp, whereas other writers and critics refer to this camp and nine others in Utah, Colorado, Arkansas, Idaho, California and Wyoming as concentration camps. This latter label suggests an altogether less pleasant or dreamy reading of the Japanese American internment experience during and after the Second World War.

In February 1943, a year after Executive Order 9066 and, with it, several months of resistance within the camps in the form of strikes and uprisings, the US Army began to recruit volunteers on the mainland and in Hawaii to form the 442nd Regimental Combat Team. The internees in this team and other adult internees were forced to answer a loyalty questionnaire. Depending on their responses to two questions in particular, this questionnaire exacerbated already difficult wartime relationships within the Japanese American community:

> 27. Are you willing to serve in the armed forces of the United States on combat duty wherever ordered?
> 28. Will you swear unqualified allegiance to the United States of America and faithfully defend the United States from any or all attack by foreign or domestic forces, and forswear any form of allegiance or obedience to the Japanese emperor, to any other foreign government, power, or organization?

Negative responses to these questions by draft-age Japanese American males, labelled 'no–no boys', saw them segregated for disloyalty and some were sent to prison.[6]

Far from a camping holiday, then, the Japanese American internment and draft experiences testified to continuing racial inequalities in the USA based on biological racism. Apparently, Issei 'racial affinities are not severed by migration' and Nisei and Sansei 'racial strains are undiluted' by citizenship and Americanization, which made all Japanese Americans 'potential enemies'.[7] In the 1940s, these racial stains had other affinities as well, specifically to unionizing Filipinos whose cheap labour had helped to fill the gap created by the exclusionist Immigration Act of 1924. An advertisement in a Californian newspaper elaborates this affinity in the context of older nativist and racist concerns about protecting white women, labour and land:

> While Americans are dying to free their countrymen from Japanese slavery, the lavish expenditures of money by Filipinos on white women instead of assisting their countrymen is not promoting goodwill among Americans . . . Filipinos want America to build up their homeland and protect them, while their people conduct themselves as strikers . . . If the Filipinos act as they have recently, they should be classified with the Japanese; denied renting of land and such, as the Japanese were who also did not act properly as guests in America.[8]

Improper acts by white Americans, not Asian Americans, are the primary focus here, as they were in the previous chapter. With the exception of Filipino writer, Carlos Bulosan, the writers responding to such improprieties are Japanese Americans who experienced the internment first hand – Mori in Topaz, Utah, Yamamoto in Poston, Arizona, and yes–yes boy Okada, in the desert, perhaps Wyoming, like the Japanese American soldier in his Preface. Monica Sone's autobiography *Nisei Daughter* (1953) elaborates her family's evacuation to Camp Harmony and Minidoka Camp.

Generally speaking, these writers demonstrate an increasingly politicized aesthetic in Asian American literature that is only subtly and, for some critics, too subtly conveyed in the early literary texts by the Gold Mountain poets, Yan Phou Lee and the Eaton sisters. Compared to the earlier period, the 1930s onwards saw radical political movements within and beyond the USA directly protesting against class, gender and racial discrimination. Most obviously, Bulosan's semi-autobiography *America Is in the Heart* (1946), and Okada's novel directly contribute to antiracist critique, with their narrators questioning discrimination, if, at times, somewhat inarticulately. Despite ethnic and generic differences, both writers adhere to a social realist style. They also focus on the experiences of disenfranchized men, their female characters functioning as little more than foils, enough to suggest to critics like Viet Thanh Nguyen and Jinqi Ling that their narratives anticipate an androcentric, cultural nationalist sensibility.

In the mid-twentieth century, it was easier for a Filipino American than a Japanese American to criticize 'vandalism' by 'the broad white universe', and to insist that 'They can't silence me any more! I'll tell the world what they have done to me!'[9] While *No–No Boy* also resists silence, particularly at the end of the novel when a male character resorts to 'loud, gasping, beseeching howls' to convey his feelings of anger and frustration (p. 250), Mori's, Yamamoto's and Sone's characters are not always as outspoken. But, this said, all three writers do critically analyze white patriarchy as it is most violently articulated in war. For example, Mori's war story, 'Tomorrow is Coming, Children' ([1943] 1949), depicts an aged internee offering advice to his children: 'war is terrifying. It upsets personal life and hopes. But war has its good points too . . .

You become positive. You cannot sit on the fence, you must choose sides . . . to find out where [your] heart lay' (p. 21), even if that choice is radically compromised by the internment and draft experiences.

Like their mid-twentieth century fictional peers, Mori's internees hold American values close to their hearts, but not without first critically engaging with what and where America is and who Americans are. In the words of one of Bulosan's character's:

> America is not a land of one race or one class of men . . . America is not merely a land or an institution. America is in the hearts of men that died for freedom; it is also in the eyes of men that are building a new world . . . We are all that nameless foreigner, that homeless refugee, that hungry boy, that illiterate immigrant and that lynched black body. All of us, from the first Adams to the last Filipino, native born or alien, educated or illiterate – *We are America!*
>
> (p. 189)

CARLOS BULOSAN, *AMERICA IS IN THE HEART* (1946) AND TOSHIO MORI, SELECTED SHORT STORIES (1949)

For Carlos Bulosan (1911–56) and his narrator, Allos, America is understood in terms of a brotherhood, which is made particularly apparent in wars. *America Is in the Heart* begins with the return of Allos's oldest brother, Leon, to the Philippines from the First World War. It ends with two other brothers, Amado and Macario, leaving to join the US military to fight in the Second World War following Japan's attacks on Pearl Harbor and the Philippines. After Macario's departure, Allos is left to settle his 10-cent debt with a 'Negro bootblack' named Larkin whose hand, Allos observes, 'was like my brother's – tough, large, toil-scarred'. The two men share a beer, bought with the dime. Touched by the brothers' sense of responsibility, Larkin says as he also leaves to join the armed forces: 'I know I'll meet your brother again somewhere, because I got my dime without asking him. But if I don't see him again, I'll remember him every time I see the face of an American dime. Goodbye, friend!'

(pp. 324–5). This larger concept of 'universal brotherhood' clearly exceeds racial differences, even becoming something of a transcendental or 'mysterious force' (pp. 238, 122). This force could also explain how Allos meets up with his biological brothers, usually without prior communication, when they, like him, are constantly moving in and between the Philippines and the USA in search of work.

Larkin's connection between the face of a dime and, by implication, the face of Macario also reiterates the narrative's complex negotiation of the relationship or 'war between labor and capital' (p. 186). On the one hand, such a connection gestures towards the reification of Filipino immigrant labourers, or Pinoys, whom many Americans considered unworthy of a face, even the face of and on a coin: 'It must be realized that the Filipino is just the same as the manure that we put on the land – just the same.'[10] If not manure, Filipinos, particularly in the prewar years of 'the great hatred' were regarded as 'dogs' and 'brown monkeys' (pp. 143, 136). They were typically valued in terms of body parts, often hands, to be exploited in Alaskan fish canneries, Manila dance halls and Californian farms. On the other hand, however, Larkin's memorial to Macario lends itself to a more radical reading since he invests the coin with a significance that exceeds its monetary value. Thus understood, the coin signifies a system of beer-sharing brotherhood as opposed to an exploitative capitalist system. For Larkin to de-face the dime, replacing its white face (before 1946, the Liberty Head) with a Filipino face, further reinforces Macario's vision of a new world also populated on an equal basis by nonwhites and the poor.

This new world that values people equally (or, more precisely, men) and puts them above profit is arguably informed by Allos's mother's bartering business in the Philippines:

> My mother gave even to those peasants who had nothing to barter in the hope that when we came round again they would be ready to pay. We were not always able to collect everything we had loaned, but my mother kept on giving our products to needy peasants.
>
> (p. 33)

She barters in this way even though her family also suffers during the 'predatory years' (p. 14).

Similar business transactions by altruistic mothers also occur in the USA, particularly in Yokohama, California, during its predatory years of the Great Depression. For instance, Toshio Mori's (1910–80) doughnut-making Mama functions as an archetype or, as Stan Yogi phrases it, 'a metaphor for overarching values among Japanese Americans: sensitivity and obligation . . . based in empathy and interdependence.'[11] While Mama's 'little world' seems secure, a refuge even, 'when . . . spirit wanes, when hell is loose' (pp. 23–4), the Japanese American mother in another of Mori's stories sees her sensitivity and obligation more directly challenged by economic insecurity.

In 'My Mother Stands on Her Head', a long-serving food peddler named Ishimoto-san repeatedly overcharges a family for groceries they could have bought more cheaply elsewhere. His so-called profiteering has an adverse affect on his business, and his customers drop him. Because the family's nursery business is also struggling, they pressurize the mother to drop him as well. After all, 'at the Safeway . . . you could buy a Salinas lettuce three for a nickel. And you buy an apple-size lettuce from him for a nickel apiece' (p. 35). Presumably, this larger company sources vegetables from an agricultural industry that renders small Japanese American grocery and nursery businesses unprofitable through its exploitation of cheap Asian labour. In this war between labour and capital, however, the mother's sense of obligation prevails and 'Ishimoto-san began coming as before' (p. 38). Her empathetic viewpoint helps to contextualize his overcharging, which is less about profiteering as surviving economic and racial inequality and exploitation.

The mothers in Mori's and Bulosan's narratives are similarly altruistic, although it is worth noting that their business transactions generate different readings, one privileging race, the other, gender. Mori's mothers conduct their business according to Japanese American principles, whereas Bulosan's mother conducts her business according to maternal principles. As Rachel C. Lee observes, her 'labor is overridden by her symbolic potential as Mother', which in turn suggests to another feminist critic, Patricia Chu, the limitations of Bulosan's socialist education and, arguably, his colonial education as well.[12] His androcentric stance is even more discernible in his representation of other Filipinas. These women are associated with imprisonment via their attempts to secure husbands. In so doing, they remove Filipinos from brotherhood in both the Philippines and the USA.

For example, the fraternal reunion that opens *America Is in the Heart* is soon disrupted by war-veteran Leon's marriage to a woman who fails a virginity test. Her apparent sexual impropriety necessitates the couple's punishment – shackling, stoning, whipping and exile (pp. 6–8). Similarly, Allos and his cousin are forced to leave their village after dancing with two sisters determined to enforce marriage. Filipinas seem intent on trapping Allos and his brothers, snaring them as if they were birds. Through a marriage that hinders his career aspirations, Luciano, of all the brothers, most resembles the birds he once caged: 'I knew that he would have a child every year. I knew that in ten years he would be so burdened with responsibilities that he would want to lie down and die' (p. 89). In all these cases, then, Filipinas are foils to male labour and by extension brotherhood, if not freedom *per se* by virtue of imprisonment in their sex.[13]

However, *America Is in the Heart* does gesture toward the political and economic context of Filipina behaviour. Like Luciano, who snares birds and is ensnared by women and children, predatory Filipinas are trapped by patriarchal traditions and the Philippines' predatory years. For this reason, then, they are not 'inherently dissolute' or the 'true exploiters', and neither are Filipinos in the USA.[14] In anti-Filipino California, for instance, Filipinos are stereotyped as 'sex-crazy' for white women, 'same as the niggers' and 'same as the Chinamen, with their opium' (p. 141). Even respectable people like businessmen and policemen presume that 'every Filipino is a pimp' (p. 121). Stereotyped thus, one businessman says to Allos that 'you bring it on yourself . . . prostitution and gambling', as if such dissolute activities are inherent to Filipinos. Allos responds by pointing out that 'the gambling and the prostitution are operated by three of this town's most *respectable* citizens' (p. 163). By virtue of a citizenship withheld from Filipino immigrants by the Tydings–McDuffie Act of 1934, the town's pimps cannot be Filipinos. Denied citizenship until

1946, and, with it, the apparent respectability of upward class mobility, Filipinos were forced 'into a filthy segment of American society', hardly a situation that they brought on themselves (p. 121).

This racist, patriarchal nation-state comprising respectable citizens like businessmen and policeman who are not adverse to dissolute activities, including vigilantism, also helps to explain the persistence of Bulosan's symbolic view of women, particularly white American women. In their nurturing temperanent many of these women resemble Mary the mother of Jesus as Christian tradition depicts her. For example: Miss Mary Strandon tells Allos about Abraham Lincoln's vision of American equality, as well as giving him access to books; Marion provides food, rest and warmth after Allos escapes near-castration by vigilantes; Mary is 'a symbol of goodness' and 'an angel molded into purity' (p. 301). Alongside these and other Marys is the symbolic woman *par excellence*. Of Eileen Odell, Allos asserts: 'She was undeniably the *America* I had wanted to find in those frantic days of fear and fright, in those acute hours of hunger and loneliness. This America was human, good, and real.' And, moreover, this is 'her great tradition' to which Allos wants to contribute, not that racist, patriarchal nation-state (pp. 235, 327).

Allos takes care to point out that his gendering of America exceeds or 'annihilated all personal motives' in a way that endows it with a wider significance. This annihilation is important ideologically, enabling Allos to interpret his experiences alongside 'dynamic social forces'. He takes 'an historical attitude. I was to understand and interpret this chaos from a collective point of view, because it was pervasive and universal' (pp. 236, 143–4). While Marxist concepts and concerns clearly inform Bulosan's text, it is also possible to read the annihilation of the personal, particularly with regard to the feminizing of America, as 'stemming from, in Frantz Fanon's term, the colonial complex'.[15] This complex involves interracial relationships between nonwhite men and white or light-skinned women in a power relation consistent with nativist, racist and imperialist ideologies.

In Asian American literature, from the Gold Mountain poets to Bulosan, John Okada, Louis Chu and Frank Chin, Asian

American male characters consider such 'Girls . . . all superbly / beautiful and charming; / By all means, have a taste of the white scent while / there's time' (p. 257). Of this interracial relationship, Sheng-mei Ma observes that 'the imagination of the dispossessed projects the craving for self-empowerment onto the body of Caucasian women.' Although Allos's craving lacks a certain eroticism, as when, for example, he describes one white woman's body in terms of its 'onionlike whiteness' (p. 141), he is nevertheless fixated on it in 'an essentialist manner', not least because it functions as 'a political symbol within which lies the promise of power yearned by the ostracized'.[16] Interracial relationships thus seem to promise Allos and other Asian American male characters masculinity denied to them by both white vigilantes and anti-miscegenation laws. These relationships also promise a minimal sense of Americanness, albeit at the expense of women and, for that matter, Filipinos since the promise of self-empowerment is necessarily deferred.

More so than the interracial relationships, the end of *America Is in the Heart* 'ostensibly affirms the American system seemingly to the point of urging acquiescence to colonial co-optation.'[17] In Allos's words: 'the American earth was like a huge heart unfolding warmly to receive me . . . It came to me that no man – no one at all – could destroy my faith in America' (p. 326). This pro-American ending thus contradicts much of the narrative, which, for the most part, depicts the USA as a heartless place for Filipinos and other minority groups. Rather than simply affirming dominant American ideologies, the narrative arguably promotes critical analysis of the ending by problematizing Allos's reliability as a narrator. His tendency towards 'illusion' and 'sentimentality' with respect to women, the Philippines and the USA undercuts the realism of the ending without detracting from the harsh reality of Filipino immigrant life (pp. 234, 198). More than this, Marilyn Alquizola asserts, Allos's 'idealistic Americanism functions as a survival strategy', not only for him but also for Bulosan 'by keeping hope alive'. Along with aiding immigrant survival, the heart-warming ending ensured the survival of the antiracist and anti-imperialist message in *America Is in the Heart*, even beyond Bulosan's blacklisting during the Red Scare in the 1950s.[18]

MONICA SONE, *NISEI DAUGHTER* (1953), JOHN OKADA, *NO–NO BOY* (1957) AND HISAYE YAMAMOTO, SELECTED SHORT STORIES (1949–51)

Similarly to *America Is in the Heart*, *Nisei Daughter* by Monica Sone (1919–) and *No–No Boy* by John Okada (1923–71) end with the 'false ring' of assimilationism that is most obviously problematized by Executive Order 9066 and the subsequent internment of Japanese Americans.[19] While the autobiographical *Nisei Daughter* charts the narrator's life before and during internment, with only the last two chapters dealing with her relocation to Chicago to work and Indiana to study, Okada's Bildungsroman more or less begins where Sone's ends: no–no boy, Ichiro Yamada 'had been gone for four years, two in camp and two in prison' (p. 1). Despite these historical differences, the young Seattleites occupy a similar geography, around Main Street, and a similar class of small business owners. They also articulate a similar preoccupation with the ' "terrible" Japaneseness' of the Issei mother and the impact that this has on the Nisei child.[20] The war and intergenerational relationships are also addressed by Hisaye Yamamoto (1921–) in several of her short stories from the late 1940s and early 1950s.

In *Nisei Daughter*, the Issei mother, although fun loving, if only on the outside, is depicted as 'destroyer of an Edenic pre-racially corrupted childhood'.[21] In these few years of 'amoebic bliss', her daughter did not know 'whether [she] was plant or animal'. Kazuko Itoi continues, 'One day when I was a happy six-year-old, I made the shocking discovery that I had Japanese blood. I was a Japanese. Mother announced this fact of life . . . in a quiet, deliberate manner one Sunday afternoon.'[22] This fact disrupts Kazuko's sense of identity: 'I didn't see how I could be a Yankee and Japanese at the same time. It was like being born with two heads. It sounded freakish and a lot of trouble' (p. 19).

And, it is a lot of trouble, not only on and after the family's evacuation to the concentration camps, but also before it. Going back to 1904 when her father arrived in the USA determined to study law, his labour ensuring that 'his dream of Ann Arbor grew dimmer', Kazuko describes how he earned enough money to buy a hotel in 'Skidrow . . . with its shoddy stores, decayed buildings, and shrivelled men' (pp. 5, 8). In this part of town, where 'being Oriental had never been an urgent problem', the family are still harassed by the police and other uniformed men (p. 113). Kazuko's father or, to his racist arresting officers, 'Shorty' and 'l'il Tokyo', is unsuccessfully framed for bootlegging, while Kazuko's mother is harassed by two uniformed men – presumably, because she is to them the sexually available Japanese geisha (pp. 35–9, 63–4).

Whether it is articulated in or beyond the USA, the 'Japan versus America' opposition, particularly when understood in the context of the Second World War sends 'tempers skyrocketing' within Japanese Americans families. As Kazuko observes:

I used to criticize Japan's aggressions in China and Manchuria while Father and Mother condemned Great Britain and America's superior attitude towards Asiatics and their inter-ference with Japan's economic growth. During these argu-ments, we had eyed each other like strangers, parents against children. They left us with a hollow feeling at the pit of the stomach.

(p. 148)

The parents also articulate scepticism, in Ichiro's mother's case, an irrational scepticism, about the progress and even outcome of the war. In their defence of Japan, and maintenance of Japaneseness through, for example, the smuggling of Japanese food into the camps and the unwavering belief in Japan's strength, Issei mothers deteriorate physically and psychologically. Kazuko's interned mother no longer looks happy, but aged and pensive. Ichiro's mother is found dead in her own bath after having apparently committed suicide. Moreover, Rosie's mother in Yamamoto's 'Seventeen Syllables' (1949) also adheres to Japaneseness by writing *haiku* poetry, which, although not exactly terrible, does nevertheless transform her into 'an earnest, muttering stranger' (p. 9).

Another point of comparison between characters that pursue Japaneseness too singularly is the image of a rock. Of her Japanese American peers, Kazuko says they 'sat like rocks . . . I began to think of the Japanese as the Silent People', almost to the point of '*rigor mortis* . . . no noise, no trouble, no back talk' (pp. 131, 25). Of his

Japanese mother, Ichiro says that she was 'only a rock of hate and fanatic stubbornness and was, therefore, neither woman nor mother' (p. 21). In her semi-autobiographical poem, Yamamoto's Miss Sasagawara also describes a saintly man who, like her Buddhist father, seeks Nirvana and stifles within himself 'all unworthy desire and consequently all evil'. To his companion in the poem, as well as to the daughter–poet, his unbending devotion is 'a sort of madness, the monstrous sort which, pure of itself, might possibly bring troublous, scented scenes to recur in the other's sleep' (pp. 32–3). All three stories thus depict characters who are too Japanese, in some cases, fatally so, which, in turn, contrasts with the lively freedom available in the USA – if mainly to white Americans.

This affirmation of Americanness is conveyed in Okada's novel through the opposition between two women: Ichiro's Issei mother and Nisei lover. Ichiro's immigrant mother is 'a small, flat-chested, shapeless woman' whose 'awkward, skinny body . . . had dried and toughened'. She stands in contrast to Emi whose 'heavy breasts' and 'long legs were strong and shapely like a white woman's' (pp. 10, 83). Like Allos, Ichiro's views of women are informed by the colonial complex, and he 'shuns his unintegrated mother and embraces Emi who em-bodies Americanness'.[23] In *Nisei Daughter*, the Japanese mother is not so overtly shunned by either her child or the narrative. Instead, as Shirley Lim observes, erasure is gradually achieved through 'the destruction of the mother's language possessions and . . . internment', until she apologizes to Kazuko, now named Monica, for her Japanese identity: 'We felt terribly bad about being your Japanese parents' (p. 236). Monica also seems to adopt this apologetic stance when, for example, she seems a little too understanding of her exclusion from a sorority at Wendell College, Indiana, because of continuing racial restrictions.[24]

In Yamamoto's 'The Legend of Miss Sasagawara' (1950), two Nisei internees also seem a little too understanding with respect to racial discrimination. After a conversation about the outside world, they, as the narrator puts it:

> ended up as we always did, agreeing that our mission in life, pushing twenty as we were, was first to finish college somewhere when and if the war ended and we were free again, and

then to find good jobs and two nice, clean young men, preferably handsome, preferably rich, who would cherish us forever
and a day.

(p. 21)

The girls' romanticized mission mitigates internment to the point
of erasure – almost. Indeed, Miss Sasagawara's experiences, the
death of her mother in another camp and the fanaticism of her
father, never mind her own institutionalization in a sanatorium,
stands in ironic contrast to the girls' mission.

Compared to Miss Sasagawara's experiences, particularly the
death of her mother, Ichiro and Kazuko seem somewhat liberated
by their mothers' disappearances. With Mrs Yamada dead, Ichiro
feels 'a little bit freer, a bit more hopeful'. These feelings had for
so long eluded him because her rock-solid racial distinctions,
which, to some extent, resemble those of the US government,
forced the family to 'conform to a mold that never existed'
(pp. 196, 186). Such feelings are less easily achieved by Kazuko,
who gives up her family life in the camp for work and study. In
both cases, then, it seems that Japanese American identity
and relationships can only properly develop in a motherless
household – ideally, the sort of baseball-watching, pie-eating and
cheerful household of yes–yes boy Kenji Kanno. Kenji may have
lost a leg in the war, an injury that leaves him with an incurable
stump, but at least his Pop is his buddy (pp. 128–9, 123).
These signifiers of Americanness, when coupled with loving
family relationships, would seem to suggest that *No–No Boy* advocates assimilationism.

The binary opposition between terrible Japaneseness and wonderful Americanness also seems to be affirmed at the end of both
No–No Boy and *Nisei Daughter*. Monica no longer claims to think
of her bicultural identity as monstrous: 'I used to feel like a two-
headed monstrosity, but now I find that two heads are better than
one' (p. 236). For Sone, like Bulosan, America is gendered, and her
feminine dimension, specifically 'her ideas and ideals of democracy', is opposed to and takes precedence over 'the government as
a paternal organization' (p. 237). Once feminized, it becomes much
easier for Monica to reintegrate:

I was going back into its main stream, still with my Oriental eyes, but with an entirely different outlook, for now I felt more like a whole person instead of a sadly split personality. The Japanese and the American parts of me were now blended into one.

(p. 238)

Significantly, however, Monica's sense of oneness is not simply assimilationist. During the conversation in which her mother apologizes for being Japanese, Monica says: 'I don't resent my Japanese blood anymore. I'm proud of it, because of you and the Issei who've struggled so much for us' (p. 236). This struggle has given the Nisei a 'clearer understanding of America and its way of life', which, interestingly, Monica refrains from describing in anything other than abstract terms consistent with idealistic Americanism. Similar to *America Is in the Heart*, *Nisei Daughter* promotes an ironic reading of this ideology: 'I thought, in America, many things are possible', not just happiness, but also internment and its accompanying physical and psychological suffering (p. 237). The gaps in the narration are significant here, 'articulate silences', perhaps, that contrast with Monica's generally upbeat and at times apologetic narrative.[25]

The ending of *No–No Boy* also resists the assimilationism it apparently advocates, albeit in a much more dramatic way. The Nisei men, some of whom are brothers, others, acquaintances and friends, come together in a climatic and violent end when yes–yes boy Bull confronts no–no boy Freddie. A fight ensues, and Freddie escapes in his car, only to crash it: 'What a mess! Didja see it? Poor guy musta been half way out when the car smacked the building. Just about cut him in two. Ugh!' Phatic utterances of this kind, as well as silences marked by ellipsis, recur on the final pages of the novel. Bull's 'Agggggggghh', as well as his crying and howling, occurs alongside Ichiro's inability 'to put it into words' or speak (pp. 249–51).

These linguistic gaps may suggest political gaps in the sense that androcentric cultural nationalism of the late 1960s and early 1970s, which would empower more explicit confrontation with American society, was either unavailable or minimally available. These linguistic gaps may also suggest other personal and political gaps between Ichiro and Bull, as well as between Japanese America and mainstream American society. Like Bulosan's Allos and Sone's Monica,

Ichiro gestures towards idealistic Americanism at the end of the narrative, only to immediately question it: 'A glimmer of hope – was that it?' He chases this glimmer of hope, despite the obstacles, here, a list of adjectives that get in his way and collect around a promise, as opposed to anything more immediate or substantial: 'he chased that faint and elusive insinuation of promise' (pp. 250–1).

This promise, arguably the American democratic promise of equality, is deferred. Also deferred is the reconciliation between no–no boy Ichiro and yes–yes boy Bull on the occasion of Freddie's death. The physical and psychological gap between these two men persists. Indeed, while Ichiro may seem to share Bull's feelings of sadness and isolation, the language used to describe their new-found relationship is remarkably impersonal: 'He gave the shoulder a tender squeeze, patted the head once tenderly, and began to walk slowly . . . away' (p. 250). In its use of the definite article rather than personal pronouns, the ending of the novel suggests the impossibility of personal and political resolution at the time of the narrative and beyond for both no–no boys (Freddie and Ichiro) and yes–yes boys (Bull, Kenji and Okada).

The notion that to certain Americans, Japanese Americans are 'Japs' or even, in the context of the developing Cold War, 'coolies' and 'Chinks', is critically addressed in Yamamoto's 'Wilshire Bus' (1950). In this short story, a Japanese American woman, Esther Kuroiwa, takes a bus ride to the hospital at a soldiers' home in order to visit her injured Nisei husband. On this bus is a red-faced drunken man who loudly proclaims to an elderly Chinese American couple 'get off this bus, why don't you go back where you came from? Why don't you go back to China?' Esther's ethnicity – 'she was Japanese, not Chinese' – apparently makes her exempt from the drunk's comments, even allowing her to gloat momentarily over the fact that he 'had specified the Chinese as the unwanted'. But how could she rely on this drunk to distinguish between Asian Americans, particularly in light of the fact that changing wartime relationships between the USA and East Asian countries necessitated the wearing of 'I AM KOREAN', 'I AM CHINESE' and 'I AM JAPANESE' badges (pp. 35–6)?

After the drunk disembarks from the bus, another man speaks to the elderly couple and possibly to Esther. He reassures them that white Americans 'aren't all like that man. We don't all feel the way he does. We believe in an America that is a melting pot of all sorts of people.' He even insists that the white girl behind Esther should get a Purple Heart for putting up with the drunk. The irony of his misdirected speech, alongside the fact that the elderly couple also disembark from the bus at the soldiers' home, reveals the hypocrisy of American melting pot ideals in relation to Asian Americans. This hypocrisy destabilizes Esther:

> she was filled once again in her life with the infuriatingly help-less, insidiously sickening sensation of there being in the world nothing solid she could put her finger on, nothing solid she could come to grips with, nothing solid she could sink her teeth into, nothing solid.
>
> (p. 37)

Like Ichiro, then, Esther seeks but does not find anything substantial in the USA, especially not in its democratic promise. 'Wilshire Bus' thus draws attention to the gap between political rhetoric and political reality, specifically with respect to the American melting pot. Even when she is confronted with a ward of injured soldiers, including her yes–yes boy husband, which should be proof enough of Japanese American loyalty to democracy versus fascist dictatorships abroad, Esther is unable to articulate her sense of racial and national dislocation. She instead almost dismisses it as a gender limitation: 'yes, weren't woman silly?' (p. 38).

CONCLUSION

'We are America' is variously proclaimed by all the writers in this chapter in circumstances not unlike those described in the preceding chapter. Most obviously, exclusionist legislation persists in, for example, the 1934 Tydings–McDuffie Act. The yellow–peril stereotype also persists, again with particular reference to Asian immigrant labour and sexuality. As Bulosan's Allos observes:

> I came to know . . . that in many ways it was a crime to be a Filipino in California. I came to know that the public streets

were not free to my people . . . We were suspect each time we were seen with a white woman.

(p. 121)

Moreover, Pearl Harbor, which, as Sone and Bulosan respectively describe it, 'hit like a blockbuster' and 'blared into . . . consciousness' (p. 145; p. 315), forced all Americans to confront the fact that 'Tomorrow is Coming, Children'. As Mori's internee puts: 'You cannot sit on the fence, you must choose sides . . . to find where [your] heart [lies]' (p. 21). For Asian immigrants and their American-born children, America lay in their hearts, more so than in political reality, despite their fight for democracy in employment and in the Second World War. The war also compelled the USA to choose between democratic and dictatorial political systems. It more or less made this choice through changes to the anti-Asian legislation in the 1940s and 1950s. A clause in the McCarran–Walter Act of 1952 granted naturalization rights and a small immigration quota to the Japanese, thus ending racial discrimination with respect to naturalized citizenship.

All the writers in this chapter respond to these historical and political changes, Bulosan most forcefully since his Filipino identity put him in a better position than his Japanese American peers to 'tell the world what they have done' to him and to others like him (p. 180). In contrast, Japanese America seems more to resemble Kazuko's school in that it is marked by *'rigor mortis . . .* no noise, no trouble, no back talk' (p. 25). Not surprisingly, writing is difficult under such circumstances, not least when either interned or at war. This struggle with writing and language generally is articulated in the texts selected here via the representation of 'there being . . . nothing solid' in American melting pot rhetoric (p. 37). Here, Yamamoto's protagonist, like Okada's protagonist, is left in a position where questions about continuing racial inequality in the USA go officially unanswered, even after the war has ended: 'weren't women silly?' and 'a glimmer of hope – was that it?' (p. 38; p. 250).

SUMMARY OF KEY POINTS

- The 1930s–50s were marked by anti-Asian discrimination, typically in relation to the USA's changing relationships with Asian countries in the Second World War. In 1952, anti-Asian discrimination with respect to naturalized citizenship ended, notwithstanding the continuation of a discriminatory quota system.

- The yellow-peril stereotype circulated throughout American culture. Asian Americans were assumed to imperil the USA sexually, economically and, under communism in China and Korea, ideologically.
- Asian Americans protested against discrimination and stereotypes in legal cases, as well as in uprisings in Japanese American concentration camps.
- Mid-twentieth-century prose realistically described the lives of ordinary Asian Americans as they were disrupted by economic insecurity and the war. Such disruptions adversely affected both familial and sexual relationships, sometimes resulting in madness and death. To this extent, the texts were critical of the USA, although antiracist critique is, for some later critics, difficult to discern in texts that ended in support of American democratic values.
- Mid-twentieth-century literature combined American and Asian literary forms. For example: *Yokohama, California* references Sherwood Anderson's *Winesburg, Ohio* (1919) along with the Japanese tradition of *shibai*, or humorous folk drama; *No–No Boy* references the Japanese children's story, 'Momotaro', in a Bildungsroman replete with American slang.

NOTES

1. Amy Ling, *Between Worlds: Women Writers of Chinese Ancestry* (New York: Pergamon Press, 1990), p. 56.
2. Ronald Takaki, *Strangers from a Different Shore: A History of Asian Americans* (Boston: Back Bay Books, 1998), p. 415, pp. 331–2.
3. John Okada, *No-No Boy* (Seattle: University of Washington Press, [1957] 1979), p. 15. Hereafter references to this edition are given in the text.
4. Toshio Mori, *Yokohama, California*, intro. Lawson Fusao Inada (Seattle: University of Washington Press, [1949] 1985), p. vi,

p. x. Despite its postwar publication date, most of the stories were written before the Second World War. Hereafter references to this edition and the introduction are given in the text.

5. Hisaye Yamamoto, *Seventeen Syllables and Other Stories* (New Brunswick, NJ: Rutgers University Press, [1988] 2001), p. 51. Hereafter references to this edition are given in the text.

6. Stephen H. Sumida, 'Japanese American Moral Dilemmas in John Okada's *No–No Boy* and Milton Murayama's *All I Asking For Is My Body*', *Frontiers of Asian American Studies*, ed. Gail M. Nomura, Russell Endo, Stephen H. Sumida and Russell C. Leong (Pullman: Washington State University Press, 1989), pp. 225–6. Of 'the contradictions inherent in the questions and their context', Sumida asks:

> How can I be drafted into the U.S. Army when my citizenship has already been revoked and the Selective Service has classified me 4-C, 'enemy alien'? Can the U.S. government unilaterally revoke the U.S. citizenship which is mine by birth? If my citizenship was not revoked or has been restored, why am I imprisoned in this camp without ever having been charged with a crime or given a fair trial? . . . How can the issei be asked to renounce their Japanese citizenship when the U.S. denies them any other? And how can I 'forswear' . . . allegiance to the Japanese emperor unless I have such allegiance in the first place, and what if I never had it?

7. General DeWitt, quoted in Takaki, *Strangers*, p. 391.

8. Advertisement, quoted in Takaki, *Strangers*, p. 363.

9. Carlos Bulosan, *America Is in the Heart: A Personal History* (Seattle: University of Washington Press, [1946] 1973), p. 47, p. 164, p. 180. Hereafter references to this edition are given in the text.

10. A secretary, quoted in Takaki, *Strangers*, p. 324.

11. Stan Yogi, 'Japanese American Literature', *An Interethnic Companion to Asian American Literature*, ed. and intro. King-kok Cheung (Cambridge: Cambridge University Press, 1997), p. 132.

12. Rachel C. Lee, *The Americas of Asian American Literature: Gendered Fictions of Nation and Transnation* (Princeton: Princeton University Press, 1999), pp. 27–8; Patricia Chu, *Assimilating Asians: Gendered Strategies of Authorship in Asian America* (Durham, NC: Duke University Press, 2000), p. 47.

13. Lee, *Americas*, pp. 27–8.

14. Cheryl Higashida, 'Re-Signed Subjects: Women, Work, and World in the Fiction of Carlos Bulosan and Hisaye Yamamoto', *Studies in the Literary Imagination* 37: 1 (Spring 2004), 50.

15. Sheng-mei Ma, 'Postcolonial Feminizing of America in Carlos Bulosan', *Ideas of Home: Literature of Asian Migration*, ed. Geoffrey Kain (East Lansing: Michigan State University Press, 1997), p. 129.

16. Sheng-mei Ma, *Immigrant Subjectivities in Asian American and Asian Diaspora Literature* (New York: SUNY Press, 1998), pp. 66–7.

17. Marilyn Alquizola, 'Subversion of Affirmation: The Text and the Subtext of *America Is in the Heart*', *Asian Americans: Comparative and Global Perspectives*, ed. Shirley Hune, Hyung-chan Kim, Stephen S. Fugita and Amy Ling (Pullman: Washington State University Press, 1991), pp. 199–200.

18. Ibid., p. 207.

19. Lisa Lowe, *Immigrant Acts: On Asian American Cultural Politics* (Durham, NC: Duke University Press, 1996), p. 49.

20. Shirley Geok-lin Lim, 'Japanese American Women's Life Stories: Maternality in Monica Sone's *Nisei Daughter* and Joy Kogawa's *Obasan*', *Feminist Studies* 16: 2 (Summer 1990), 298.

21. Ibid., 295.

22. Monica Sone, *Nisei Daughter* (Seattle: University of Washington Press, [1953] 1979), p. 3. Hereafter references to this edition are given in the text.

23. Ma, *Immigrant*, p. 74.

24. Lim, 'Maternality', 298–9.

25. King-kok Cheung, *Articulate Silences: Hisaye Yamamoto, Maxine Hong Kingston, Joy Kogawa* (Ithaca, NY: Cornell University Press, 1993), p. 1.

CHAPTER 3

Noise, Trouble and Backtalk, 1960s–70s

CONTEXTS AND INTERTEXTS

Arguably taking off from the howl of 'Agggggggghh' of John Okada's yes–yes boy, the Asian American writers in this period also resort to phatic utterances: 'when wounded, sad, or angry, or swearing, or wondering whined, shouted, or screamed, "aiiieeeee!"' Between the late 1950s and the early 1970s, 'AIIIEEEEE!!!' became more than a howl. For cultural nationalist critics Frank Chin, Jeffery Paul Chan, Lawson Fusao Inada and Shawn Hsu Wong in their anthology *Aiiieeeee!* (1974) it became 'more than a whine, shout, or scream. It is fifty years of our whole voice.'[1] While the wholeness of this voice is debateable, mainly because it comes from Chinese American, Japanese American and Filipino American men, it does nevertheless convey the defiant determination of this newly racialized constituency to coalesce for political reasons – as Asian Americans in the newly emerging Asian American movement and Asian American studies. Both the political movement and the academic field arose in the late 1960s in order to protest against American racism and imperialism in, for example, 'Hiroshima / Vietnam / Tule Lake' concentration camp and throughout American culture consistent with other minority movements.[2]

From the mid-1960s onwards, these movements helped to ensure that at least on a legal front the USA could no longer segregate and discriminate on the basis of race. Congress outlawed racial discrimination via the Civil Rights Act (1964) and the Voting Rights Act (1965), but, for a short while, this discrimination persisted in immigration. The annual quota system established in 1924 and reinforced in 1952 allowed approximately one hundred people from each Asian country to immigrate. In 1965, however, immigration legislation was liberalized and democratized, with Asian countries achieving equality with other countries through the allocation of 20,000 visas per year. As a result, the Asian American population increased dramatically.

The move from racial dictatorship towards racial democracy was also advocated throughout culture, most directly in oral, street-orientated forms such as poetry and drama. While early Asian American literature tended to be dominated by romantic and realistic prose, which indirectly and, at times, inarticulately criticized American dominant ideologies, later texts are noticeably more experimental in terms of genre and form. Poetry and drama became more visible in the 1960s and 1970s, with poets like Ai, Meena Alexander, Lawson Fusao Inada, Joy Kogawa, Janice Mirikitani, Al Robles, Merle Woo and John Yau, and playwrights like Frank Chin, Philip Gotanda, David Henry Hwang and Momoko Iko publishing their first texts at this time. Poetry and drama also became more 'democratized in terms of subject matter, and characterized by informal diction and direct reference in the service of class-, race-, or gender-based oppositional politics.'[3]

The prose of this period also emphasized the importance of orality in speech and song. Similar to the prose of Hisaye Yamamoto and John Okada, for example, which combined informal diction with Asian poetry and song, specifically *haiku* and the Japanese folk tale and song 'Momotaro', later prose experimented with rigid generic boundaries. For instance, Maxine Hong Kingston's *The Woman Warrior: Memoirs of a Girlhood Among Ghosts* (1976) and *China Men* (1980) take the form of Chinese talk-story, as well as referencing folk songs. Although talk-story is a conservative communal form comprising references to Chinese lore, myth and tradition, as well as to historical sources and events, Kingston uses it to radical effect in keeping with the oppositional politics of cultural nationalism.[4]

Generally speaking, cultural nationalism focused on three related concerns to do with resisting silence, questioning stereotypes and revising cultural history. More precisely, it involved the expression of 'yellow' voices and by extension Asian American identities against racial stereotypes such as the threatening yellow peril and the controllable model minority. As a phrase, the model minority was used in popular culture in the mid-1960s, although assimilationist Asian Americans were represented earlier. In 1925, for example, Earl Derr Biggers created the model-minority figure *par excellence* in the form of the compliant Chinese Hawaiian detective Charlie Chan. Cultural nationalism also highlighted the ways in which Asian Americans contributed to the cultural historical formation of the USA in excess of assumptions of compliancy and invisibility. In short, cultural nationalism was an aesthetico-political project concerned with 'claiming America', to employ Kingston's oft-cited phrase. At the same time, however, claiming America also involved rejecting 'the notion of assimilation into . . . the spiritual bankruptcy, cultural sterility, imperialism, materialism, and racial self-denial of the Anglo-American ideal.'[5]

In, for example, Janice Mirikitani's activist poetry from the 1970s (and later) there emerges 'a loud, yellow noise', often from generations of women who refuse to be destroyed by 'civilized America'. This civility is undone by the violent domination of Asians and Asian Americans, specifically, as the poem 'We, the Dangerous' (1978) highlights, in terms of labour in 'the sweat shops / the laundries' and wars in Asia (pp. 94, 26–7). A similar politics is articulated in the poem 'Ms.' (1977), although, here, Mirikitani's unnamed yellow woman implicates a white woman, 'miss ann/ hearst/rockerfeller/hughes', in this violence: 'Her lips pressed white / thinning words like pins / pricking me' and 'stop calling ME *gook*'. Both women experience the violence of language, although the white woman's preoccupation with the 'Miss–Ms' debate hardly makes her a victim. As the yellow woman observes: 'I said / it was a waste of time / worrying about it' because this white woman is privileged in terms of race and class. Her privilege depends on the exploitation of others – Indians for their land, Africans for their natural and human resources and Asians for their labour. While 'never soiled by / sexism', Ms. is nevertheless soiled by nativism, racism and imperialism. Not even her idealized image, articulated in terms of dazzling whiteness, can conceal the underlying violence of these ideologies: 'quit / killing us / for democracy' (pp. 95–6).

While this one-to-one encounter suggests a personal struggle over democracy, Mirikitani politicizes this struggle by her use of 'us' in the historical context of genocide, slavery and wars in Asia. She thus reinforces new models of racial identity in relation to state institutions as articulated in the civil rights and the power movements. Indeed, activists in the late 1960s and 1970s

> understood that racism operated not primarily through the acts of prejudiced individuals, against individuals of color, but through the subordination and exploitation of . . . communities. They understood that institutional racism operated by denying economic resources, education, political power and self-determination to communities of people defined by race.[6]

Mirikitani and other activist Asian American students formed various political groups between the autumn of 1967 and the summer of 1968, including, for example, the Intercollegiate Chinese for Social Action (ICSA), Philippine–American Collegiate Endeavour (PACE) and the Asian American Political Alliance (AAPA) to address institutional racism within the educational system and beyond. Many members of these groups also joined the multiracial Third World Liberation Front (TWLF), which organized the longest student strike in American history beginning in November 1968 at San Francisco State College. This strike sought to make the curriculum, as well as student and staff recruitment, 'serve the people' through the development of ethnic studies programmes. As the activism by students and others intensified, so did the actions of the state's 'internal army': 'Like maybe you break a window. But what about the inequity, the psychological damage inflicted on an individual and [the destruction] of their history. What about that kind of violence?'[7]

Such a question indicates that racial discrimination did not simply end with the introduction of new democratic laws in the mid-1960s but actually persisted afterwards. And, it is the history of these different forms of violence that preoccupies many of the Asian American writers in this period, and in more defiant terms than previously. In addition to criticizing racism, Asian American cultural nationalists embarked on a 'pen war' between androcentric and feminist writers, specifically Frank Chin and Maxine Hong Kingston. Crucial to androcentric cultural nationalist Chin, along with fellow *Aiiieeeee!* editors, was the status of Asian American masculinity in relation to a violent history of institutional racism.

In their essay 'Racist Love' (1972) Frank Chin and Jeffery Paul Chan discuss the ways in which exclusion, deportation and anti-miscegenation laws ensured that Chinese immigrant men 'would not reproduce. And eventually they would die out.' 'The Concept of the Dual Personality' exacerbated this 'cultural extinction' by dividing Chinese American masculinity into 'two incompatible segments', one orientated towards America, the other, towards China. Chin and Chan argue that both segments fuel self-hatred to the point of schizophrenia since neither recognizes 'Chinese-American cultural integrity' and 'style of Chinese-American manhood'. Without these hyphens, then, Asian Americans risked becoming Americanized Asians, rather than Asian-Americans.[8] In *The Big Aiiieeeee!* (1991), Chin clarifies his argument, with particular reference to literature by fake, not real, Asian American writers. Two Chinese American texts in particular stand out in this regard: Jade Snow Wong's autobiography *Fifth Chinese Daughter*, regarded as fake or assimilationist in its stance, as opposed to the real *Eat a Bowl of Tea*, Louis Chu's Bildungsroman, which Kingston and Chin respectively identify as influential on their own literary development.

JADE SNOW WONG, *FIFTH CHINESE DAUGHTER* (1950) AND LOUIS CHU, *EAT A BOWL OF TEA* (1961)

According to Chin, *Fifth Chinese Daughter* contributes to cultural extinction both formally and thematically, not only of Chinese Americans but also of Japanese Americans:

During World War II . . . patriotic Chinese-Americans wrote anti-Japanese propaganda disguised as autobiography . . .

Though *Fifth Chinese Daughter* was published in 1950, it fits th[is] mold perfectly. There is reason to believe work on it actually began during the war. Chapters of it appeared in magazines in 1947.[9]

More generally, Chin contends, autobiography is propaganda because it is a Christian form. It is akin to confession and prayer in that it expresses 'perpetual self-contempt and redemption, self-hatred and forgiveness'.[10] While autobiography is typically written in the first person singular, Jade Snow Wong's life story, thus far (1926–46; she died in 2006), is told in 'the third-person-singular style . . . rooted in Chinese literary form (reflecting cultural disregard for the individual)' or 'the submergence of the individual'.[11] For Chin, this self-disregard verges on self-contempt, particularly as Wong's autobiography reinforces the ideological underpinnings of its form thematically through adherence to 'the acceptable stereotype' of Christianized Chinatown societies: 'The Chinese, in the parlance of the Bible, were raw material for the "flock," pathological sheep for the shepherd . . . We are meek, timid, passive, docile, industrious . . . A race without sinful manhood, born to mortify our flesh.'[12]

Jade Snow's father best represents this pathological sheep. Not only is he a local preacher but he also preaches 'New-World Christian ideals', particularly about women: 'You do not realize the shameful and degraded position into which the Chinese culture has pushed its women. Here in America, the Christian concept allows women their freedom and individuality. I wish my daughters to have this Christian opportunity' (pp. 5, 246). Here, the USA is superior to China, while at other times this Orientalist hierarchy is reversed, albeit in a way that continues to associate Chineseness with restriction. Again, Jade Snow is the focus of her father's remarks: 'You are shameless. Your skin is yellow. Your features are forever Chinese. We are content with our proven ways. Do not try to force foreign ideas into my home. Go. You will one day tell us sorrowfully that you have been mistaken' (p. 130). Not surprisingly, Chin and the *Aiiieeeee!* group find in these speeches and in the rest of *Fifth Chinese Daughter* a stereotypical view of Chinatown comprising unhyphenated Chinese Americans quietly suffering from dual personality that makes them too Chinese or, more accurately, Americanized Chinese.

In contrast to Wong's 'snow job' is Louis Chu's (1915–70) *Eat a Bowl of Tea* about a non-Christian and male-dominated New York Chinatown in the late 1940s. According to the *Aiiieeeee!* group, 'Chu's book honestly and accurately dramatizes the Chinese-American experience from a Chinese-American point of view, and not from an exclusively "Chinese or Chinese-according-to-white" point of view.'[13] For the most part, Chu's male characters lead insular lives in 'slumlike' apartments, basement clubs and barbershops. This insularity notwithstanding, these men do exceed the acceptable stereotype linguistically, experientially and ideologically: theirs is a Chinatown that 'instead of flying the flag of excellence, flew the multi-colored washes of its inhabitants.'[14] Indeed, the colourful language of the old bachelors and the younger generation of men, a language that is neither English nor Chinese-according-to-whites, tallies well with their interest in sex, money and tong politics. The relationships between these men tend to be verbally or physically violent, particularly when it comes to women. Indeed, misogynist terms like 'Goddamsonovabitch!' alongside various other phrases, from the oft-repeated 'Wow your mother' to 'Nowadays women are not trustworthy', indicate that this is a patriarchal Chinatown, albeit a fading one (pp. 11, 15–22, 110).

Chu's bachelor fathers, Wong Wah Gay and his old friend, Lee Gong, represent, in Ruth Y. Hsiao's words, 'the authoritarian father reduced to a pathetic parody' by assertive wives in China and by 'the social and historical conditions of the Chinese emigrants in America'.[15] Wah Gay's Chinese-born son, Ben Loy, is similarly reduced via his apparent obedience to a proprietorial father who proudly proclaims that he has 'kept him on the straight path'. Unbeknown to Wah Gay, however, Ben Loy has strayed from this path in his relationships with white prostitutes. Too much manliness as a bachelor accounts for 'his lack of manliness' as a husband to Mei Oi (pp. 26, 77). Impotent men, not only sexually impotent Ben Loy but also socially impotent characters like Wah Gay, Lee Gong and handsome, though lazy, Ah Song, are common in Chu's decaying New York Chinatown. In many respects, this setting is responsible for male impotency since it disrupts Chinese American patriarchy by rendering sexual and patrilineal relationships dysfunctional. The most obvious disruption to these relationships is when Ben Loy's wife, Mei Oi, has a son, Kuo Ming, with her seducer and rapist, Ah Song.

Towards the end of the novel, the act of eating the bowl of tea from a San Francisco Chinatown herb store proves curative with regard to these dysfunctional relationships: 'This time Ben Loy responded with a blind thrust of passion and his wife's urging, melting body was there to claim it.' Following this sex scene, the couple agree to invite their fathers to Kuo Ming's second haircut party (p. 250). According to Chan, Chu sends Ben Loy to San Francisco to 'reclaim his virility, his paternity, and his wife . . . [in] the city where Chinese-America first began' in order to bring up the first native-born Chinese American in the novel (p. 5). San Francisco is certainly a city of 'New frontiers, new people, new times, new ideas' and 'a new golden mountain', although this newness does not extend to Mei Oi (p. 246). At the end of the novel, she still resembles the walking, talking and smiling China doll that Ben Loy first met. 'What else did he need to know?' (p. 51)

Such a question is not only applicable to Ben Loy but to Chu's other male characters as well. However, their misogyny is not merely personal prejudice. Given that Chinese women's immigration was restricted by both China and the USA, and that racial purity was privileged by both Chinese American and American patriarchies, it is hardly surprising that Chinese American gender and sexual identities are represented in such limited terms. Moreover, anti-immigration and anti-miscegenation legislation contributed to the stereotype of emasculated Chinese American men. Chu's novel tackles this stereotype by exposing its historical and ideological underpinnings in a language and style that, although considered 'tasteless and raw' in its day, is, for this very reason, identifiably masculine (p. 2). It is no small wonder, then, that Chu, writing both 'with love' and 'with all the warts showing' is generally regarded as the originator of a new Chinese American masculine sensibility that finds further expression nearly a decade and a half later in 'AIIIEEEEE!!!' – both the anthology and the sentiment.[16]

FRANK CHIN, *THE CHICKENCOOP CHINAMAN* (1972),
THE YEAR OF THE DRAGON (1974) AND *THE CHINAMAN
PACIFIC AND FRISCO R.R. CO.* (1988)

In the tradition of Chu, Frank Chin (1940–) describes Chinatown
inhabitants without compromise in his literary texts from 'Food for
All his Dead' (1962) to the short stories in *The Chinaman Pacific and
Frisco R.R. Co.*, many of which were originally published in the
1970s at the time his plays *The Chickencoop Chinaman* and *The Year
of the Dragon* were first staged. In all three texts, Chin's Chinatown
inhabitants, particularly the older generation, are described as
'living corpses'.[17] He elaborates this condition in 'The Chinatown
Kid' (1973): 'The Chinese in America . . . live beyond endurance,
beyond the limits of interest and curiosity and die slowly like cities
blacking out a light bulb at a time, and even then not dead' (pp. 35–6).

Into this decaying Chinatown, the younger generation are, in
the words of *The Chickencoop Chinaman*'s eponymous character
Tam(pax) Lum, 'made, not born . . . Out of junk-imports, lies, railroad scrap iron, dirty jokes, broken bottles, cigar smoke, Cosquilla
Indian blood, wino spit, and lots of milk of amnesia.' Continuing
his conversation with the Hong Kong Dream Girl, Tam refuses to
euphemize the violence of his multiplicitous and magical making
when he proclaims: 'Born: No! Crashed! Not born. Stamped! Not
born! Created! Not born. No more born than the heaven and earth.
No more born than nylon or acrylic. For I am a Chinaman! A
miracle synthetic!'[18] He goes on to describe himself as an orphan
since he is unable to imagine his birth as anything other than a
miracle when 'the laws didn't let our women in' and his own crazy,
dishwashing father always wore underpants, even in the bath
(pp. 26, 17). The Chinese father's emasculation is more pronounced in Chin's short stories, among them, 'Give the Enemy
Sweet Sissies and Women to Infatuate Him, and Jades and Silks to
Blind Him with Greed' (1970), 'A Chinese Lady Dies' (1970) and
'Railroad Standard Time' (1978). As another character called
Tampax puts it in this last story: 'my father . . . was captured in
total paralysis from a vertebra in the neck on down' (p. 4).

A San Francisco Chinatown herb store like those visited by
Chu's and Wong's protagonists would perhaps offer the most

obvious antidote to this condition. Although proclaimed by Chin real and fake respectively, *Eat a Bowl of Tea* and *Fifth Chinese Daughter* both depict their protagonists' empowerment through herbal remedies prescribed for conditions related to their gender and sexual identities. Most obviously, herbal tea restores Ben Loy's masculinity. Jade Snow's empowerment is more convoluted. She uses the Chinese brushes bought from the herb store to decorate her pottery, which she then sells. Her pottery business is so successful that 'after three months, she was driving the first postwar automobile in Chinatown . . . For the first time in her life, she felt contentment . . . She had found herself and struck her speed' even in 'a man's world' (pp. 244, 246, 234).

Eat a Bowl of Tea and *Fifth Chinese Daughter* both end with their protagonists successfully overcoming the racist conditions imposed on their gender and sexual identities after visiting herb doctors, but is such an ending possible for Chin's characters, specifically his young male characters? Can they too achieve success in a man's world and, in the process, find themselves and strike their own speed? Unlike these earlier writers, Chin's Chinatown Kids are not able to find themselves in such a straightforward manner because they are orphans and, for this reason, lack a self parented in the normal way through biological reproduction. However, two other forms of reproduction are available to them, both involving paper sons. Exploiting the loss of San Francisco's municipal records in the 1906 earthquake, the first kind of paper son was an illegal immigrant who fraudulently claimed that he was either an American-born citizen or another Chinese American man's son.[19] The second kind of paper son is Tam who 'figuratively fathers himself by describing his creation as a verbal and volitional act rather than a physical birth.' Tam, Patricia Chu continues, is 'an ethnic verbal construct made of cultural debris, cultural forgetfulness (milk of amnesia), and language.' This self-fathering on paper also makes the character an author, if not 'the Asian American artist-hero' who struggles to father, to write and to author(ize) texts and a canon that are 'inextricably linked to concerns about creating a descent line of one's own, in this case, an Asian American line.'[20] Tam says as much near the beginning of the play, albeit in the context of discussion about his children: 'I should have done some THING. One thing I've done alone, with all my heart. A gift. Not revenge' (p. 27).

The task for Tam and his peers is to construct a Chinese American identity and tradition apart from white racist stereotyping. Tam begins this task not by following Chinese-identified traditions, such as herbal tea or 'I Ching' (p. 23), but by searching for a strong masculine identity in two American heroes: the Lone Ranger and the black boxer Ovaltine Jack Dancer. As a child, Tam fantasized that the Lone Ranger was Chinese American, his mask hiding his Asian eyes. Tam's view changes when the now ailing ranger shoots him in the hand, sits on his butt, and proceeds to stereotype him as 'honorary white . . . China boys, you be legendary obeyers of the law, legendary humble, legendary passive. Thank me now and I'll let ya get back to Chinatown preservin your culture!' Tam concludes that the Lone Ranger so dominated or 'deafened' his boyhood that he became 'them three Chinee monkeys, Hear no Evil, See no Evil, Speak no Evil' (pp. 35–7).

Clearly, the white American hero does not provide Tam with a positive identity and tradition. He thus turns to another boyhood hero for a solution to his honorary whiteness. Repeatedly referred to by both Tam and his friend Blackjap Kenji as a champion and a hero, Ovaltine affirms their masculinity via 'the greatest piss . . . ever'. As Tam describes it, in the style of a buddy film:

we took Ovaltine for a ride, went out riding with Ovaltine . . . and, we all got out of the short, the car, and under the stars, we stood next to the car, and on the road, you know, we pissed all together into the bushes.

(p. 41)

Tam hopes that this great moment of interracial brotherhood will be repeated on his trip to see Ovaltine's trainer and so-called father, Charley Popcorn: 'This trip's going to make me well. I'm going to see again, and talk and hear' (p. 23). Heroic blackness thus seems to offer Tam (and Kenji) the possibility of a solution to honorary whiteness, as it also did for Asian Americans influenced by the Black Power and the Black Arts Movements of the 1960s and 1970s.

For Chin and the *Aiiieeeee!* editors, black cultural nationalism and the black power movement enabled insights into Asian American experiences. For example, they criticized an Americanized Chinese vision that 'reinforces white racist stereotypes and falls short of the vision Malcolm X and other blacks had for their "minority".'[21] Tam and Kenji's respect for black masculinity is clear, although, unlike Chin, they uncritically idealize blackness in a way that is satirized or, at least, exposed by other characters in the play, most notably Popcorn. On first meeting Tam, Popcorn emasculates Tam, not by maiming his hand, like the Lone Ranger (arguably a symbolic castration), but by calling him 'queer'. Popcorn thus reinforces the stereotype that 'in American eyes we don't appear as he-men types . . . We look like queers!' (pp. 39, 59). Tam's emasculation is further reinforced when Popcorn avoids his punch – incidentally, a punch that 'couldn't crack piecrust' – and Tam falls flat on his face. In a later scene, Tam is seen carrying Popcorn, bearing his weight, not on his butt this time, but on his back (p. 50).

Whether white racist or 'black white racist', both American heroes fail to provide a positive identity and tradition for Tam; even Ovaltine fails him when it is revealed that he 'done bullshit you and the whole world' (pp. 42, 49). Tam responds first with hysteria to Ovaltine's 'faking up a father' (p. 62), specifically a southern slave father, who, as Chu contends, serves 'to authenticate his blackness'.[22] When Ovaltine also promotes this fake story in a book (perhaps the kind of profit-making book wealthy white Americans demand from black sporting champions), Tam responds with legendary passivity, silently accepting towards the end of the play the role of 'Chinaman cook'. For Chin, this role falls under the white racist category of 'ornamental Oriental' (pp. 63, 59).

A similar end is discernible in *The Year of the Dragon*, a play that sees members of a Chinatown family, the Engs, particularly the three children, profiting financially from 'Oriental Ornamentalia'.[23] While the daughter owns a successful business in Boston writing Chinese cookbooks, or 'food pornography', her older brother Fred is a guide for 'Eng's Chinatown tour'n' travoo' in San Francisco (pp. 86, 71). Their impressionable gun-carrying younger brother Johnny seems to resist these ornamental Oriental stereotypes, although he also wants to contribute to the family business, despite

Fred's protestations. As Fred says to Johnny, 'I am shit. This family is shit. Chinatown's shit. You can't love each other around here without hating yourself' (pp. 124–5). The Eng parents reinforce racial self-hatred, especially dying Pa, who refuses to see Fred as an individual, let alone a hero-artist, forcing him towards the end of the play to become '*a shrunken Charlie Chan, an image of death. He becomes the tourist guide*' (p. 141).

The cook and the guide involve, in Chin's words, 'a Chinaman, playing a white man playing Chinese . . . [in] a minstrel show' (p. xxii). This show is so powerful with respect to Chinese American masculinity that it is difficult to imagine an alternative. Asian American critics tend to agree that Chin's 'preoccupation with death and decay, his sexism, cynicism, and sense of alienation', never mind his homophobia, 'have prevented him from creating protagonists who can overcome the devastating effects of racism on Chinese American men.'[24] And, yet, as Daniel Y. Kim observes, Chin's masochism on these counts also proves strangely liberating, arguably like the 'sore loser' in the short story 'Railroad Standard Time' who goes down fighting as he rides 'a mass of spasms and death throes' (pp. 3, 7).[25]

In the plays, Tam and Fred in particular suffer from self-loathing for adhering to white stereotypes (cook and guide), and for, in Tam's case, 'faking up a father, not knowing your past, and the killer instinct' (p. 62). Although Tam is referring to Ovaltine here, these comments are also relevant to him since he too has the killer instinct in the sense that he participates in love–hate interracial relationships with a white woman (Barbara) and, perhaps more crucially, a white older man (the Lone Ranger). In this latter relationship, Tam (and, arguably, Chin) becomes 'a disfigured, disfiguring copy of the man he loves, the man he hates, the man he is, "the mythic Westerner," who – as he himself tells us – is "no good".' However, this no-good man does serve as a negative example to Asian American men. In Daniel Kim's words: 'while Chin's writings are indeed *descriptive* of a kind of self-loathing that I feel is part of our legacy, we must resist the *prescriptive* pull that his writings exert.'[26]

Tam tries to resist this pull when he asserts: 'I should have done some THING. One thing I've done alone, with all my heart. A gift.

Not revenge' (p. 27). The gift Tam bequeaths is difficult to fathom since, towards the end of the play, he offers to cook for the other characters, now called children: 'keep my mouth shut slicin greens and meat, and be gone tomorrow', hardly the backtalking '*word magician*' that began the play (pp. 63, 3). However, his silence does finally allow Tam to hear – his grandmother, who instructs him to ' "Listen!" . . . And we'd listen in the kitchen' about the Old West and about her father who came back from the Sierra Nevada mountains after tunnelling through it for 'a Chinaman borne, high-steppin Iron Moonhunter' train and railroad (p. 65). As Tam develops 'an ear for trains', along with the heroic Chinese American tradition that the railroad represents, he encourages his children (now, presumably, the audience as well) not only to ride with him but also to 'Listen in the kitchen for the Chickencoop Chinaman slowin on home' (p. 66). Here, then, Tam has found his own speed, as well as a version of the Old West that includes Chinese immigrant men. This identity and history is arguably the hero-artist's gift to the ever-increasing number of children he has fathered, not only his biological children, peers, audience and readers, but also himself. In this way, then, Tam 'effectively reverses what Chin calls the "pen[ned] up" position of being the ineffective other.'[27]

For Chin 'life is war' and 'writing is fighting', as it is for 'The Eat and Run Midnight People' (1978) comprising 'the badasses of China, the barbarians . . . the dregs, the bandits, the killers, the get out of town eat and run folks . . . Murderers and sailors. Rebel Yellers and hardcore cooks' (p. 11).[28] This militant stance has not gone uncriticized, at least not by Asian American feminists. The debate or pen war between androcentric and feminist critics, as much as it has energized Asian American literary studies, has also proved divisive and reductive with respect to the relationship between gender, race and dominant ideologies. The binary logic of this debate, argues King-kok Cheung, bypasses the fact that 'genuine heroism' involves claiming cultural traditions 'without getting bogged down in the mire of traditional constraints', attacking 'stereotypes without falling prey to their binary opposites', and charting 'new topographies for manliness and womanliness'.[29]

MAXINE HONG KINGSTON, *THE WOMAN WARRIOR* (1976) AND *CHINA MEN* (1980)

Apart from Wong's *Fifth Chinese Daughter*, along with a whole host of other fake books from the 1940s to the 1960s (for example, Pardee Lowe's *Father and Glorious Descendent* (1943), Virginia Lee's *The House Tai Ming Built* (1963) and Betty Lee Sung's *Mountain of Gold* (1967)), Maxine Hong Kingston's *The Woman Warrior* is the target of Chin's and the *Aiiieeeee!* group's critique. Chin and Kingston (1940–) are often viewed as oppositional figures because of their respective political commitments to androcentrism (Chin) and feminism (Kingston) and because of their respective aesthetic commitments to 'raging satires, polemic and slapstick comedies' (Chin) and semi-autobiography (Kingston).[30] There are, nevertheless, a number of similarities in their writings from the 1970s in that both question dominant American ideologies as well as seeking to construct a specifically Chinese American literary tradition. In this way, then, both Chin and Kingston differently contribute to cultural nationalism.

Like Tam in *The Chickencoop Chinaman*, Kingston's characters attempt to formulate Chinese American identity apart from the Orientalist stereotypes perpetuated in the mainstream media, specifically films, magazines and cartoons. Again like Tam, whose grandmother insists he turn off the radio so that he can listen to the 'Old West when Chinamans was . . . all the thunder in the mountains' (p. 65), Kingston's characters turn to their families and ancestors for help with self-understanding. *The Woman Warrior*'s narrator 'listened to the adults talk-storying', whereas the narrator in *China Men* stands 'at the edge of the sugarcane and listened for the voices of the great grandfathers.'[31] Chin's and Kingston's characters thus develop an ear for Chinese American history against a double marginalization in history and by historical discourse. In other words, they highlight legislative and vigilantist anti-Asian acts made even worse by the exclusion of Chinese immigrants and Chinese Americans from 'the American grand historical narrative'.[32] Granted, the terms are different, but their characters grapple with the sort of scenario that so maddens one of narrator's aunts in *The Woman Warrior*: 'The real punishment was not the raid swiftly inflicted,' although this is bad enough, 'but the family's deliberately forgetting her' (p. 22).

While both Chin and Kingston remember Chinese American history in forms that foreground orality – typically a noisy orality, Chin in backtalking, masculine language, and Kingston in talk-story – they do so in markedly different ways. As David Leiwei Li observes of Kingston's memoir and Chin's essay, 'Confessions of the Chinatown Cowboy' (1972), 'Unlike . . . Chin, who clears murky grounds by looking into "hard" history, excavating the remains of Chinese American written documents and interviewing living heroes . . . Kingston solicits "ancestral help" by tapping into the resources of familial oral stories.'[33] These oral stories and, more generally, popular, communal and empowering talk-stories combine autobiography and memoir, as well as history and mythology. Kingston's narrator repeatedly emphasizes her inability to separate these different genres or, more accurately, 'what is peculiar to childhood, to poverty, insanities, one family, your mother who marked your growing with stories, from what is Chinese. What is Chinese tradition and what is the movies?' (p. 13). It is perhaps surprising, then, that the multiple and at times contradictory stories she tells in her memoirs of a girlhood among ghosts are often read as hard Chinese history by American reviewers – to Chin's and, for that matter, Kingston's consternation.

In her essay, 'Cultural Mis-readings by American Reviewers' (1982), Kingston, effectively acknowledging Chin's worst fear, insists many of the reviews of *The Woman Warrior* 'praise the wrong things' using the 'false standard' of 'the exotic, inscrutable, mysterious oriental'. She continues:

> I had not calculated how blinding stereotyping is, how stupefying. The critics who said how the book was good because it was, or was not, like the oriental fantasy in their heads might as well have said how weak it was, since it in fact did not break through that fantasy.

This Oriental fantasy meant that these American reviewers did not 'hear the American slang', 'see the American settings . . . and the way the Chinese myths have been transmuted by America'. With

Americanness going unheard and unseen, these reviewers margin-
alize Chinese American history and, with it, 'a battle for recognition as Americans; we have fought hard for the right to legal
American citizenship'. For this reason, Kingston advocates remov-
ing the hyphen from 'Chinese-American', as Chin also does
between *Aiiieeeee!* and *The Big Aiiieeeee!* While a Chinese-
American gives the impression of 'double citizenship', observes
Kingston in a way reminiscent of Chin's critique of the dual personality concept, a Chinese American is 'a type of American' – but,
unfortunately, not the type of American discernible to certain
reviewers.[34]

This failure of *The Woman Warrior* to 'translate well' for certain
American reviewers and Chin seems to hinge on one particular
chapter (p. 186). Of the chapter, 'White Tigers', Kingston insists
that it represents a 'childish myth . . . not a Chinese myth but one
transformed by America, a sort of kung fu movie parody'. Whether
'White Tigers' is favoured or not, albeit for the same reasons to do
with 'the women's lib angle and the Third World angle', the chapter
generates such divided responses because of its depiction of a powerful female figure from a well-known Chinese legend, Fa Mu
Lan.[35] As the Chinese equivalent to well-known European stories
and legends, 'The Ballad of Mulan' is, at least for Chin, easily told
and remembered.[36] This story and its heroine thus provide a stark
contrast to the forgotten Chinese women in the rest of Kingston's
memoir, particularly the unnamed American-born narrator's two
aunts: 'The No Name Woman' and Moon Orchid 'At the Western
Palace'.

For conceiving an illegitimate child from an adulterous relationship, pursued either by choice or, more likely, by force, while her
husband is sojourning in the USA in the early 1920s, the no-name
aunt is chased by a group of angry villagers and subsequently
commits suicide and infanticide simultaneously by drowning. The
young narrator comments that the aunt's punishment 'was not the
raid swiftly inflicted by the villagers, but the family's deliberately
forgetting her' (p. 22). The impact of such a deliberate act is also
the focus of a later chapter when Moon Orchid travels to the USA
in the early 1970s to be reunited with her sojourning husband
whose new life, specifically his career and family, leaves no room for

her. He informs her that she is to him a person from 'a book I had read a long time ago' (p. 139). Although he has supported her financially for thirty years he has deliberately erased Moon Orchid from his new life, which is a contributing factor to her madness. Whether regarded as loyal or disloyal, both of the narrator's aunts are effectively forgotten, deliberately erased not only from life through death and madness but also from memory, which is enough to make them mad.

The differences between these forgotten Chinese women and the unforgettable Chinese heroine aside, Chin argues that Fa Mu Lan is also depicted according to 'the specs of the stereotype of the Chinese woman as a pathological white supremacist victimized and trapped in a hideous Chinese civilization', not least when Kingston deliberately fakes this legendary history to emphasize 'ethical male domination or misogynistic cruelty' consistent with the women's liberation movement. For Chin, then, Western feminism is wrongly imposed on Fa Mu Lan, just as the tattoo from another legend is wrongly carved on her back.[37] Thus prepared for battle, this cross-dressing heroine takes her father's place and leads a peasant army against the emperor and his representatives. When confronted by Fa Mu Lan, a self-proclaimed female avenger, a baron quotes two Confucian maxims – 'Girls are maggots in the rice . . . It is more profitable to raise geese than daughters' – after which he is beheaded. Unlike the foot-bound women in the baron's house, who, so unverifiable legend has it, became an Amazonian army, Fa Mu Lan settles into domestic servitude. She kneels at the feet of her parents-in-law and proclaims: 'I will stay with you, doing farmwork and housework, and giving you more sons', perhaps because they are more profitable to raise than girls (pp. 45–7).

Both Chinese and Chinese American civilizations seem hideous, particularly with respect to their treatment of girls and women. Apparently regardless of context, then, these girls and women are considered essentially bad on both economic and filial levels: 'There's no profit in raising girls . . . When you raise girls, you're raising children for strangers.' Misogyny thus seems little transformed by the USA: 'Even now', in the narrator's 'American life', 'China wraps double binds around [her] feet' (pp. 47–9). China is thus established as the origin of misogyny, but, importantly, this is not exclusively the case. Indeed, American culture determines that women should grow up not as 'wives or slaves', but as cheerleaders (p. 25). This 'American-feminine' (p. 18) role seems to require nothing more than straight knees and the odd shout of 'rah-rah', hardly a change from the subordinate role allocated to women in Chinese history.[38]

Along with misogynistic Chinese, Chinese American and American patriarchies, Kingston's narrator confronts the violence of racism and capitalism with respect to her identity, family and community. These two ideologies come together most obviously in the form of urban renewal or the commercial destruction of Asian American communities in the early 1960s. At this time, these communities were already in decline because of a history of Asian exclusions and quotas. Urban renewal destroys local buildings and businesses, including the narrator's parents' laundry, which is replaced with a car park for profit-seeking executives connected to the building industry, land development and real estate. While her parents are financially compensated, the money they receive is insufficient for them to start a new business. The narrator's mother does poorly paid farm work, while her father quietly fades away, 'the brown . . . going out of his eyes. He has stopped talking . . . he eats leftovers. He doesn't cook new food' (pp. 96–7). Their children are also mistaken for beggars by the local druggist who, out of sympathy, provides them with free out-of-date candy.

Capitalism is further critiqued in relation to the narrator's employers, who are to her 'the enemy . . . I easily recognize them – business-suited in their modern American executive guise, each boss two feet taller than I am and impossible to meet eye to eye.' Their height, along with other physical features such as a 'bossy stomach opulent', suggests that these men put themselves above others, specifically racially marked groups, not even deigning to provide explanations for their overt racism. While one boss uses the term 'nigger yellow', another boss hosts a business dinner in a restaurant precisely because black political groups – the Congress of Racial Equality (CORE) and the National Association for the Advancement of Colored People (NAACP) – are picketing it as part of organized efforts to address racial inequality at work. The narrator concludes her critique of American capitalism, also making the hideousness of American civilization apparent via references to economic asymmetry that is organized along racial lines: 'It's not just the stupid racists that I have to do something about, but the tyrants who for whatever reason can deny my family food and work' (p. 50).

Although the narrator regards racism as an individual problem, the fault of racists and tyrants, *The Woman Warrior* invariably contextualizes these individual acts through 'the hide-and-seek game of naming'. According to David Leiwei Li, this game generates several interpretative possibilities. Not only does it enable movement from individual to collective identities but it also brings 'into consciousness the cultural ignorance that surfaces in cross-cultural exchange', along with re-producing this history – of silence and silencing.[39] The unnamed tyrants and racists thus become representative of a white racist identity, and their power to verbally abuse, unfairly dismiss and generally antagonize non-whites becomes representative of the USA's dictatorial history. From exclusion and internment to the Red Scare in the 1950s, this history silenced Chinese Americans. Thus contextualized, silence is, as Li argues, 'a strategic response to institutional racism, an act of survival, and not at all an immutable Asian cultural trait', as Kingston's narrator momentarily assumes.[40]

A date on the first page of *The Woman Warrior* begins this hide-and-seek game of history: 1924 is the year of the no-name aunt's 'hurry-up wedding' to, presumably, a hurry-up sojourner who needs to leave for the USA before the passing of an immigration act that is to end virtually all Asian immigration (p. 11). The Immigration Act of 1924 thus provides the hidden context for the abandoned aunt's extramarital relationship, along with linking her, and, by extension, Chinese women's, oppression to American discriminatory legislation.[41] A conversation about racial deportations in the context of the anti-communist Confession Program provides another hidden context, the namelessness of those involved again drawing attention to their representativeness: 'So-and-so trusted them, and he was deported. They can deport his children too.' As this deportation conversation continues it provides the hidden context that contributed to the model-minority stereotype popularized in the mid-1960s and later: 'Lie to Americans', the narrator's parents advise. 'Tell them we have no crimes and no poverty . . . and say we have no unemployment. And, of course, tell them we're against Communism' (p. 165).

The notion that the USA, more than China, restricts Chinese Americans is also explored in *The Woman Warrior*'s companion text, *China Men*. The first Chinese man represented is Tang Ao whose experience of immigration to North America involves a process of feminization. His ankles are chained together so that the women in this female-dominated land can transform him into a courtesan: 'She's pretty, don't you agree?' (pp. 9–10). Clearly, Tang Ao's manliness is at issue here, although not necessarily in keeping with the (China)man-hating version of feminism Chin attributes to Kingston. Indeed, male and female critics alike argue that this opening story functions more broadly as a 'double-edged antiracist, antisexist sword . . . "pointing not only to the mortification of Chinese men in the new world but also to the subjugation of women both in old China and in America." '[42]

In addition to Tang Ao, *China Men* features other men, many of whom are related to the narrator, again a daughter, who is older than her counterpart in *The Woman Warrior*. Kingston's narrator again tells multiple and at times contradictory stories about different generations, this time, different generations of men from her great grandfather to her brother. In so doing, she revises American history to include the fundamental role Chinese immigrant men played in the material production of the USA. However, *China Men*'s revisionism does not stop here since simply replacing the American hero and history with a Chinese American hero and history presents little challenge to white patriarchy. Already, Frank Chin's *The Chickencoop Chinaman* has highlighted the limitations of Chinese American men simply asserting themselves according to a version of white masculinity that necessarily excludes them. For this reason, his-story is no good for both Kingston and Chin – at least as no good as the Lone Ranger whose mask could never hide Asian eyes because white masculinity is historically defined against nonwhite men (and women).

Rather than affirming his-stories or, in Jinqi Ling's terms, 'the American grand historical narrative', *China Men*'s revisionism involves 'the double displacement of two interrelated linear meta-narratives informing the Asian American identity politics' of the late 1960s and 1970s: 'that of Western historicism and that of the male-oriented Asian American nationalist imagination'. The displacement of these metanarratives and their accompanying racist and sexist hierarchies enables Kingston's narrator to tell his-stories about a past that 'the available history is unable to tell' because a history of violence and the violence of history have effectively rendered China Men (and Warrior Women) subalterns: 'No stories. No past. No China' (p. 18).[43] These men cannot speak, at least not in ways that the available history can hear – without this history bringing itself into crisis. In many respects, this history is as blind to subaltern 'wild men' as the black man is to the white police in the slough of the narrator's childhood: 'The newspaper . . . said the police had been on the lookout for him for a long time, but we had seen him everyday' (p. 219).

The wild men in the narrator's family are also seen and heard by her, their silences proving particularly productive in the sense associated with the plantation working great grandfather of the Sandalwood Mountains in Hawaii: 'He withstood the hours; he did the work well, but the rule of silence wrought him up . . . He suddenly had all kinds of things to say' (p. 101). Similarly, as King-kok Cheung notes in *Articulate Silences* (1993): 'just as the father's taciturnity . . . provokes the daughter to invent his life, so the exclusion of China Men from white American history goads the narrator to create an alternative history by extrapolating from the meagre sources available.'[44] The narrator also extrapolates from other less meagre sources such as newspapers, cartoons and films, as well as ancient myths and scholarly texts. Moreover, she also uses her imagination, which to hard historian Chin destroys unalterable facts of both Chinese and Chinese American histories. Like her childish contemporary in *The Woman Warrior*, 'for lack of adult explanations we children made up what was happening' (p. 184). In this way, then, *China Men*'s narrator claims to resemble her Cantonese relatives and others: 'Cantonese . . . have always been revolutionaries, nonconformists, people with fabulous imaginations, people who invented the Gold Mountain.' She continues: 'I want to discern what it is that makes people go West and turn into

Americans. I want to compare China, a country I made up, with what country is really out there' (p. 89).

For example, three mountain men – the great grandfathers of the Sandalwood Mountains, Bak Goong and Bak Sook Goong, and the grandfather of the Sierra Nevada mountains, Ah Goong – reinforce the narrator's claim about the Cantonese by 'fucking the world', in contrast to the emasculated Tang Ao (p. 132). Although their work is hard and literally involves remaking the Hawaiian and the Californian landscapes respectively, Bak Goong's and Ah Goong's sexualized relationships with the land arguably 'underscores both the insufferable deprivation of China Men and their strategies of survival through grandiose imagination.'[45] The other great grand-father, Bak Sook Goong, is less titanic in his strategy for survival: 'He became the godfather of many Hawaiian children' and, later, his sojourn over, he 'brought his Sandalwood Mountain wife back' to China (pp. 109, 119). All three men experience some form of slavery in their work, with Bak Goong and Ah Goong in particular using alternative means of communication in the form of coded coughs, coded cakes and a shout party to protest and improve their oppressive conditions. Granted, Ah Goong ends up 'a fleaman', but, as the narrator highlights, he is also 'an American ancestor, a holding, homing ancestor of this place' (p. 150). His claim on the USA is achieved through sexual relationships, contrary, then, to the stereotype of emasculated Chinese American men.

Sexuality is also discussed in relation to the narrator's father, BaBa or Ed, after the 'cunning, resourceful, successful inventor, Edison'. Ed, too, then, has an inventive imagination, not properly served in China where he fails as a Mandarin scholar and becomes a village teacher. Apparently, 'America – a peaceful country, a free country. America. The Gold Mountain. The Beautiful Nation' is where 'everything's possible', especially as it has 'no manners, no traditions, no wives' (pp. 72, 45, 62). Ed's Chinese wife does join him eventually, but not before he has claimed America in various ways. Whether Ed's claim is legal or illegal remains ambivalent, although, his immigrant status aside, he does claim America by starting a business. This claim is reinforced by land ownership, which, in a way similar to his grandfather's, involves a relationship with the 'pregnant earth' through horticulture (pp. 105, 249). Ed's final means of claiming America is through relationships with blonde women consistent with the colonial complex. His desire for them, if thwarted by their economic exploitation of him, nevertheless represents an attempt to gain Americanness.[46]

With its privileging of whiteness *per se*, white men for their power and white women for their ability to give nonwhite men access to this power, the colonial complex necessarily generates racial self-hatred. Its impact is strongly felt by Kingston's narrator. Ed is given to silence, screams and obscenities, to which his daughter responds: 'What I want from you is for you to tell me that those curses are only common Chinese sayings. That you did not mean to make me sicken at being female' (p. 18). Perhaps this is what Kingston also wants from other similarly misogynist fathers, most obviously, the 'self-fathering' Frank Chin. Such a possibility is enabled by *China Men*'s hide-and-seek game of naming with respect to fathers. Granted, the narrator's father is (re)named, but the chapters concerning him also gesture towards his representativeness, particularly given Kingston's two-paragraph chapter 'On Fathers'.

In this chapter, some children excitedly greet a man: 'But I'm not your father. You've made a mistake' (p. 11). Here, the daughter misidentifies her father, just as the father misidentified her daughter, which *China Men* helps to explain historically. In the context of Tang Ao's feminization and emasculation within the USA, a father's misogyny with respect to his daughter makes some sense in that he restores his masculinity by disparaging femininity. In the context of anti-Asian exclusion laws, it makes sense that a daughter made a mistake about a father whose origins are so obscure that even his birth year is difficult to fathom: 'My father was born in a year of the Rabbit, 1891 or 1903 or 1915' and 'in 1903 my father was born in San Francisco, where my grandmother had come disguised as a man. Or . . . [she] gave birth at a distance . . . Or the men of those days had the power to have babies' (pp. 19, 231).

In another chapter, 'The Wild Man of the Green Swamp', the consequences of misnaming and misidentification are further explored. The eponymous character is misidentified on the basis of his looks. To the police, 'he looked Chinese', despite the fact that he is Taiwanese (pp. 217–8). This misidentification ultimately proves fatal when he commits suicide for fear of being sent back to China.

As well as being assigned the wrong national identity, this family man is rendered a wild man by the police, presumably because Asianness and wildness are assumed to be akin in the sense described by Mirikitani in her poem, 'We, the Dangerous' (1978). With specific reference to the Second World War and the Vietnam War, Mirikitani writes, 'And they commanded we dwell in the desert / . . . We, closer to the earth' and 'We, akin to the jungle' (p. 26). The Taiwanese father's wildness exceeds habitat, however, with *China Men* also suggesting that he is wild because he exceeds official categories, which, if they are not immediately obvious – say, in the form of 'an enemy person' – can at least be listed on something the size of a dog tag (p. 260).

This dog-tag approach to identification was employed during the Second World War and the Korean War. In the chapter about war, 'The Brother in Vietnam', the narrator describes her dog tag:

> So our dog tags had *O* for religion and *O* for race because neither black nor white. Mine also had *O* for blood type. Some kids said *O* was for 'Oriental', but I knew it was for 'Other' because the Filipinos, the Gypsies, and the Hawaiian boy were *O*s.
>
> (pp. 269–70)

Clearly, 'O' does not fulfil the purpose of the dog tag. Asian American identity thus exceeds its conceptualization in a racially bipolar formation that has historically rendered it invisible (nothing, or zero) since it is neither black nor white. More than this, the otherness of 'O' unmasks the arbitrariness of official categories with respect to race: 'O' includes Asian Americans, here, Chinese Americans and Asian Pacific Islanders, as well as Gypsies. Presumably, then, 'O' means 'other than Anglo Saxon', unless that WASP is also a hippy. In the context of the Vietnam War, 'the rumour . . . went that the brother's draft board was channelling hippies and blacks into the infantry. And 'Orientals belonged over there in Asia fighting among their own kind . . . They'd send a gook to fight the gook war' (pp. 271, 276). Despite racial categorization based on skin colour, these so-called problem groups demonstrate the arbitrariness of official categories with regard to race and nationality.

With school children wearing dog tags during the Korean War, and even hippies and pacifists going to the Vietnam War, *China Men* makes it clear that nobody can escape war: the USA is 'a country that operates on a war economy . . . Everything was connected to everything else and to war'. For example, the brother in Vietnam enlists as 'a Pacifist in the Navy rather than in gaol, no more or less guilty that the ordinary stay-at-home citizen of the war economy' (pp. 277–8). Inescapability is also at issue in 'An Elegy', the chapter that immediately precedes and provides a context for reading 'The Brother in Vietnam'. In 'An Elegy', an exiled prince, presuming himself incorruptible, moralistically bemoans a bad world and commits suicide. Of this prince, Jinqi Ling argues, his 'detached discourse' proves inappropriate as a model for critique in that it 'fails to acknowledge the inescapability of the harsh world he must not only face but also work to change.'[47]

This inescapability or connectedness renders everyone and everything complicit in the harshness of the world, for the prince, a 'corrupt world' and, for the brother, 'a war economy' (pp. 252, 277). At the same time, however, the acknowledgement of complicity does afford critical possibilities. This critical insight is as terrifying as the brother's nightmare in which he 'hacks into the enemy, slicing them . . . cutting whatever human meat comes within range', only to discover that the enemy are 'the victims too, who are his own relatives' (p. 284). The violence of this nightmare is terrifying enough, not least when it becomes a reality, as in, for example, Mirikitani's war poem, 'Jungle Rot and Open Arms' (1977). In this poem, an Asian American soldier, again a brother, tells his sister that, after a raid, he awoke to find his Vietnamese lover's 'arm / still clasping mine / I could not find / the rest of her', not even 'Her hair' that was 'long and dark – like yours / he said' (p. 24).

Also terrifying is the fact that to certain Americans the racial similarities between 'a gook' and a 'gookish' American renders them all potential enemies and by extension targets (pp. 276, 272). According to Elaine Kim, 'the racial character' of US wars in Southeast Asia proved difficult for many Asian Americans to ignore, particularly in view of the extreme attitudes of American military leaders.[48] As the narrator in *China Men* notes, these leaders, somewhat routinely and indiscriminately, identify an Asian country as 'the enemy of the world', justification enough, apparently, to bomb that country 'into the Stone Age' (pp. 278, 270). Mirikitani takes this Orientalist logic further, emphasizing its underlying racism, when she notes in her poem 'Japs' (1978) that 'if you're too dark / they will kill you'. As with 'Ms.' (1977), Mirikitani's poems 'We, the Dangerous' and 'Japs' highlight the violent consequences of homogeneity, not just for Asians and Asian Americans in 'Hiroshima / Vietnam / Tule Lake' (p. 27) but also for those considered too dark by white America: 'They are coming / to nail you to boxes'.[49]

More terrifying than killing an enemy that looks like family is the kin-versus-foe violent hierarchy that enables the former to imagine the latter as absolutely Other. For Kingston's and Mirikitani's soldiers respectively, these others are imagined as 'meat' that 'they would dress . . . in napalm' (p. 284; p. 27). The soldier in Mirikitani's poem 'Jungle Rot' responds with hate and rage to this violence, which, as his sister notes, also violently impacts on him: 'his breath sapped by B-52s / his eyes blinded by the blood of children / his hands bound to bayonets / his soul buried in a shallow grave' (p. 25). Like his Vietnamese lover, then, this American soldier is obliterated by the Vietnam War that exceeds the boundaries between kin and foe, civilian and soldier and, finally, Vietnam and the USA. In his sister's words, 'i stood amidst / his wreckage and wept for myself', their different yet related experiences of war ensuring that the siblings 'sat in a silence / that mocks fools' (pp. 24–5). This notion of silence, as Mirikitani proposes in her poems from the 1980s, is so destructive that it leaves Japanese American women in particular 'Without tongue, / a dead boat on the bottom of the sea / a wingless beetle waiting for descending shoe' (p. 55). Perhaps the sister in 'Jungle Rot' is not fooled by the power of silence since she emphasizes the importance of words at the end of the poem. Crucially, these words are not the insubstantial words of a *political education*', but 'words / . . . like / the stone, / the gravemarker' (p. 25).

Similarly, *China Men* is not silenced by war and the terrifying insights it generates. The narrative continues, just as the brother in Vietnam continues: 'He had not gotten killed, and he had not killed anyone' (p. 297). After 'The Brother in Vietnam' are Kingston's final chapters, 'The Hundred-Year-Old Man' and 'On Listening'. The old man, named Tu Fu, resembles the great grandfather of the Sandalwood Mountains in his connection to Hawaii, opium and farming. With this opium reference in particular, alongside the fact that there is also mention of the Vietnam War, the penultimate chapter also recalls the great grandfather's epiphany and the brother's nightmare. The epiphany reveals the importance of loving strangers as much as family, with the nightmare revealing the way in which killing destroys self, family and strangers. Like his pacifist great grandson, Bak Goong concludes that 'wars are laughable; how could a human being remember which side he was on?' Instead of thinking in terms of sides, he resolves to 'embrace opposing thoughts at the same moment' (p. 97). Tu Fu's resolution is much simpler: 'What I like best is to work in a cane field when the young green plants are just growing up.' Presumably, these are the same plants that the narrator hears on her visit to Hawaii: 'I . . . search for my American ancestors by listening in the cane' (pp. 299, 92). Kingston's narrator, much like Chin's character in *The Chickencoop Chinaman* and Mirikitani's character in her poem 'Prisons of Silence' (1983), survives by speaking and listening: 'From this cell of history / this mute grave, / we birth our rage. / We heal our tongues./ We listen to ourselves' (p. 64).

The fact that survival is for these Asian American writers linked to both listening and speaking is further reinforced by Kingston's final chapter from *China Men*, 'On Listening'. In this chapter, a Filipino scholar speaks about the Gold Mountain to a group of young Chinese American men. Crucially, his speech does not take the form of a monologue but instead involves multiple speakers and listeners interrupting each other in their telling of multiple stories about the Gold Mountain. The stories range from fantasy, of mandarins in gold chairs and in hot-air balloons, to drudgery, of Chinese in chains. One of these men in chains indirectly criticizes Chinese sojourners and immigrants when he remarks that 'all they saw was gold'. To see only gold and, by extension, to see only the Gold Mountain, is to limit Asian American history. Hence Kingston's narrator responds with 'good' when the Filipino scholar goes 'on to

something else', presumably something more than 'just' gold
(p. 301). 'On Listening' arguably puts into question a singular view
of Asian American history in a way that refuses to see speakers and
listeners, 'as either sacrosanct or necessarily oppositional'; rather, as
Li asserts, Kingston 'regards them as mutually constitutive relations that need perpetual interruption'.[50]

Indeed, perpetual interruption informs both *The Woman
Warrior* and *China Men* when the narrators discuss enlarging the
mind 'so that there is room for paradoxes' and 'opposing thoughts'
(p. 34; p. 97). Exchanges between speakers and listeners, as well as
ancestors and children, provide the most obvious context for
perpetual interruption. In *The Woman Warrior*, for example,
the narrator ends the narrative with a story her mother told her,
not when she was young but recently, when she told her she was
also a story-talker. 'The beginning is hers, the ending, mine'
(p. 184). *China Men* follows a similar logic, albeit in terms of a
father–daughter exchange: 'I'll tell you what I suppose from your
silences and few words, and you can tell me that I'm mistaken.
You'll just have to speak up with the real stories if I've got you
wrong' (p. 18).

These interrupted stories also have a larger target: the hard
history of legislative racism represented in 'The Laws'. Beginning
in 1868, the year that the USA and China affirmed their friendship
via the Burlingame Treaty, this chapter goes on to list over a
hundred years of anti-Chinese legislation. This list undermines
American democratic rhetoric and, in so doing, reinforces the point
made throughout *China Men* that the American grand historical
narrative privileges white American men over Chinese American
men through racism. Kingston's texts therefore emphasize the
importance of interrupting this androcentric and Eurocentric narrative. If left uninterrupted by Chinese American men, this narrative, although it promises to restore their long-denied masculinity,
only does so on its own terms and by denigrating women. However,
Kingston's feminist stance with respect to this denigration has been
criticized by Frank Chin, who argues that her political beliefs make
her texts fake and assimilationist. In the binary logic that underlies
this assessment, fact is privileged over fiction, realism over myth,
and androcentrism over a version of feminism that is attentive to

the complex relationships between gender, race and dominant ideologies.

CONCLUSION

'Noise, trouble and backtalk' undoubtedly mark Asian American literature in the 1960s and 1970s, not surprisingly given that the narrators and protagonists in the texts selected here are effectively outlaws with respect to American mainstream culture. They are ousted from this culture into sloughs, deserts and swamps, their marginalization also recalling an older history of exclusion that still continues to resonate. Moreover, they are rendered outlaws, their tongues liberated like Kingston's 'outlaw knot-maker', when, following Chin's '*outlaw army*' in 'A Chinese Lady Dies', they '*mount up*' against racism as it operates institutionally in education, employment and politics (p. 147; pp. 111, 113). In addition to promoting a critique of racism and other dominant American ideologies, the texts in this chapter reconstruct Asian American historical and literary traditions, along with asserting Asian American identity, in forms of writing at once critical, dramatic, filmic, folkloric, historical, poetic and prosaic.

Such assertions necessarily involve a struggle over identity politics, as best demonstrated by the pen war. The focus of this war was a limited definition of Asian American identity that uncritically reiterated dominant discourses. Of this identity, Elaine Kim observes that it is 'fixed, closed, and ready-made – a desperate attempt to render [Asian Americans] voiced and visible.'[51] The writers in this chapter, the Woman Warriors, the China Men and even the Chinatown Cowboys critically negotiate in their literary texts the impact of adhering to dominant discourses, specifically when reversing binary oppositions for the purposes of self-empowerment. While voiced and visible, this form of self-empowerment ultimately proves no good since the dominant discursive context ensures it is neither heard nor seen. As much as noise, trouble and backtalk, then, listening is crucial for these writers – listening to their American ancestors and to others with whom they are connected in multiple ways via epiphanies, nightmares, writing and talk-storying. Even if these stories do not add up to one whole voice at least they ensure a future: 'he . . . went on to something else. / Good' (p. 301).

SUMMARY OF KEY POINTS

- The 1960s–1970s saw the end of racial discrimination with respect to voting, civil rights and immigration. However, Asian Americans still encountered discrimination, as in, for example, racist slurs like 'gook'.
- The model-minority stereotype was popularized in the mid-1960s. Racist stereotypes were understood as more than personal prejudice: they operated on an institutional level, in the case of the model-minority stereotype by permitting some Asian Americans cultural and economic mobility not granted to other Asian Americans and other racial minorities.
- Asian American cultural nationalism developed in the late 1960s. It gained expression in student strikes calling for ethnic studies programmes.
- As an aesthetico–political project, cultural nationalism, whether androcentric or feminist in emphasis (the pen war) was committed to resisting silence, questioning stereotypes and revising cultural history.
- Asian American texts combined American and Asian literary forms, particularly oral forms like poetry, drama and talk-story. In addition to this emphasis on speech, Asian American texts highlighted the importance of listening for the purposes of self-understanding and antiracist critique.

NOTES

1. Frank Chin, Jeffery Paul Chan, Lawson Fusao Inada and Shawn Hsu Wong (eds), 'Preface', *Aiiieeeee! An Anthology of Asian-American Writers* (Washington, DC: Howard University Press, 1974), pp. vii–viii.
2. Janice Mirikitani, 'We, the Dangerous' (1978), *We, the Dangerous: New and Selected Poems* (London: Virago, 1995),

p. 27. Hereafter references to this edition are given in the text.

3. Sunn Shelley Wong, 'Sizing Up Asian American Poetry', *A Resource Guide to Asian American Literature*, ed. Sau-ling Cynthia Wong and Stephen Sumida (New York: MLA, 2001), p. 291.

4. King-kok Cheung, *Articulate Silences: Hisaye Yamomoto, Maxine Hong Kingston, Joy Kogawa* (Ithaca: Cornell University Press, 1993), p. 85, p. 124.

5. Elaine H. Kim, *Asian American Literature: An Introduction to the Writings and their Social Context* (Philadelphia: Temple University Press, 1982), p. 209, p. 224.

6. Charles R. Lawrence, 'Beyond Redress: Reclaiming the Meaning of Affirmative Action', *Amerasia Journal* 19:1 (1993), 4.

7. Mao Zedong and student activists, quoted in Karen Umemoto, ' "On Strike!" San Francisco State College Strike, 1968–1969: The Role of Asian American Students', *Contemporary Asian America: A Multidisciplinary Reader*, ed. Min Zhou and James V. Gatewood (New York: New York University Press, 2000), p. 49, p. 54, pp. 71–2. In this same anthology, also see Glenn Omatsu, 'The "Four Prisons" and the Movements of Liberation: Asian American Activism from the 1960s to the 1990s', p. 81. Omatsu also discusses the activism of others, p. 85: 'It is commonly believed that the movement involved only college students. In fact, a range of people, including high-school youth, tenants, small-business people, former prison inmates, former addicts, the elderly, and workers, embraced the struggles.'

8. Frank Chin and Jeffery Paul Chan, 'Racist Love', *Seeing Through Shuck*, ed. Richard Kostelanetz (New York: Ballantine Books, 1972), pp. 70–4, p. 76.

9. Chin et al., 'Preface', p. xiv.

10. Frank Chin, 'This is Not an Autobiography', *Genre* 18 (Summer 1985), 112.

11. Jade Snow Wong, *Fifth Chinese Daughter* (Seattle: University of Washington Press, [1950] 1989), p. vii, p. xiii. Hereafter references to this edition are given in the text.

12. Chin and Chan, 'Racist', p. 67, p. 69.
13. Chin et al., 'Preface', p. xv, p. ix.
14. Louis Chu, *Eat a Bowl of Tea*, intro. Jeffery Chan (New York: Lyle Stuart Books, [1961] 2002), p. 10. Hereafter references to this edition and the introduction are given in the text.
15. Ruth Y. Hsiao, 'Facing the Incurable: Patriarchy in *Eat a Bowl of Tea*', *Reading the Literatures of Asian America*, ed. Shirley Geok-lin Lim and Amy Ling (Philadelphia: Temple University Press, 1992), p. 153, p. 156.
16. Chu, quoted in Elaine H. Kim, 'Defining Asian American Realities through Literature', *Cultural Critique* 6 (Spring 1987), 97.
17. Frank Chin, *The Chinaman Pacific and Frisco R.R. Co.* (Minneapolis: Coffee House Press, 1988), p. 36. Hereafter references to edition are given in the text.
18. Frank Chin, *The Chickencoop China and The Year of the Dragon*, intro. Dorothy Ritsuko McDonald (Seattle: University of Washington Press, 1981), p. 6, p. 8. Hereafter references to this edition and the introduction are given in the text.
19. Jennifer Ting, 'Bachelor Society: Deviant Heterosexuality and Asian American Historiography', *Privileging Positions: The Sites of Asian American Studies*, ed. Gary Y. Okihiro, Marilyn Alquizola, Dorothy Fujita Rony and K. Scott Wong (Pullman: Washington State University Press, 1995), p. 277.
20. Patricia Chu, *Assimilating Asians: Gendered Strategies of Authorship in Asian America* (Durham: Duke University Press, 2000), pp. 71–2.
21. Chin et al., 'Preface', p. xiii.
22. Chu, *Assimilating*, p. 73.
23. Chin, 'Autobiography', 111.
24. Kim, *Asian American*, p. 189.
25. Daniel Y. Kim, 'The Strange Love of Frank Chin', in *Q & A: Queer in Asian America*, ed. David L. Eng and Alice Y. Hom (Philadelphia: Temple University Press, 1998), p. 296.
26. Ibid., p. 296, p. 294.
27. David Leiwei Li, 'The Production of Chinese American Tradition: Displacing American Orientalist Discourse', Lim and Ling (eds), *Reading the Literatures*, p. 324.

28. Frank Chin, 'Come All Ye Asian American Writers of the Real and the Fake', *The Big Aiiieeeee! An Anthology of Chinese American and Japanese American Literature*, ed. Jeffery Paul Chan, Frank Chin, Lawson Fusao Inada and Shawn Wong (New York: Meridian, 1991), p. 6, p. 35.

29. King-Kok Cheung, 'The Woman Warrior versus The Chinaman Pacific: Must a Chinese American Critic Choose between Feminism and Heroism?' *Conflicts in Feminism*, ed. Marianne Hirsch and Evelyn Fox Keller (New York: Routledge, 1990), p. 235, p. 246.

30. Chin, 'Autobiography', 125.

31. Maxine Hong Kingston, *The Woman Warrior* (London: Picador, 1976), p. 25; Maxine Hong Kingston, *China Men* (London: Picador, 1980), p. 89. Hereafter references to these editions are given in the text.

32. Jinqi Ling, *Narrating Nationalisms: Ideology and Form in Asian American Literature* (Oxford: Oxford University Press, 1998), p. 119.

33. Li, 'Production', p. 328.

34. Maxine Hong Kingston, 'Cultural Mis-readings by American Reviewers', *Asian and Western Writers in Dialogue*, ed. Guy Armirthanayagam (London: Macmillan, 1982), pp. 55–60.

35. Ibid., p. 57.

36. Chin, 'Come All Ye', p. 3.

37. Ibid., p. 3, p. 6.

38. David Leiwei Li, 'The Naming of a Chinese American "I": Cross-Cultural Sign/ifications in *The Woman Warrior*', in *Criticism* 30:4 (Fall 1988), 509.

39. Ibid., 500, 503.

40. David Leiwei Li, *Imagining the Nation: Asian American Literature and Cultural Consent* (Stanford: Stanford University Press, 1998), pp. 58–9.

41. Ibid., p. 61.

42. King-kok Cheung, quoted in Donald C. Goellnicht, 'Tang Ao in America: Male Subject Positions in *China Men*', Lim and Ling (eds), *Reading the Literatures*, p. 194.

43. Ling, *Narrating*, p. 119, p. 111.

44. Cheung, *Articulate*, p. 114.

45. Ibid., p. 104.
46. Sheng-mei Ma, 'Postcolonial Feminizing of America in Carlos Bulosan', in *Ideas of Home: Literature of Asian Migration*, ed. Geoffrey Kain (East Lansing: Michigan State University Press, 1997), p. 129.
47. Ling, *Narrating*, pp. 125–6.
48. Kim, *Asian American*, p. 221.
49. Mirikitani, quoted in Kim, *Asian American*, p. 222.
50. Li, *Imagining*, p. 75.
51. Elaine H. Kim, 'Foreword', Lim and Ling (eds), *Reading the Literatures*, p. xv.

CHAPTER 4

Between Worlds, the 1980s

CONTEXTS AND INTERTEXTS

The Civil Rights Act (1964) and the Voting Rights Act (1965) would seem to suggest that the defiant voices of racial minorities in the USA did have a responsive audience in Congress. For Asian Americans, the 1965 Immigration Act signalled the end of overt anti-Asian discrimination, along with the transformation of the Asian American population. Between 1965 and 1985, this population increased dramatically, from one million to five million. By the end of the decade, it had reached over seven million, an upward trend that continues into the 2000s. In addition to growing, the Asian American population became more diverse. While immigrants from East Asia and South Asia generally immigrated for economic reasons, refugees from Southeast Asia, specifically from the Vietnam War (1959–75), immigrated for political reasons, 'ranging from fear of repression or imprisonment in reeducation camps to past associations with the former regime and ideological opposition to communism.'[1]

Whether brought about by law or war, this second, larger wave of Asian immigration meant that by the 1980s the Asian American population was predominantly immigrant. This changing demographic complicated Asian American self-understanding, heretofore defined according to the *Aiiieeeee!* group's ideal of English-speaking Chinese and Japanese American heterosexual men. These men typically lived in California, sometimes Hawaii and New York, and they, like the Filipino scholar's audience in Maxine Hong Kingston's *China Men*, were preoccupied with the Gold Mountain, 'railroads, "bachelor societies," and internment'.[2] The representativeness of this androcentric cultural nationalist ideal, although questioned by feminist writers, was most radically challenged by a rising population that was not only demographically but also ideologically diverse.[3]

This diversifying of Asian America coincided with a reactionary political climate. The move towards racial democracy, as evidenced in the outlawing of racist legislation in the 1960s, was seriously challenged by the Republican view of American culture. In the 1980s, Republican politicians, including the newly elected president, Ronald Reagan, tended not to discuss race, or, at least, not overtly. Race was considered extraneous to state matters, if it mattered at all in the newly developing colour-blind society. What was a state matter, however, were 'career criminals', 'welfare queens', 'illegal aliens' and other groups who failed to conform to traditional American values, best represented by self-reliant individuals who were part of a nuclear family and a Christian community. These identities are not raced as such, but they are racialized with, for example, the illegal alien referring to Asian and Latino/a undocumented migrants workers. With race so well codified, it is hardly surprising that racial hegemony proved, and continues to prove, particularly effective at undermining oppositional politics.[4]

The role of Asian Americans in this hegemonic process is complex, if not ambiguous. The constituency is sharply divided, with some living in 'a comfort zone' where neither racism nor classism affects them, from which others, specifically recent immigrants, refugees and the poor are excluded.[5] Also excluded are the victims of rising numbers of anti-Asian hate crimes. In the 1980s, then, Asian America was caught between worlds, one of suffering and the other of success, with the successful exacerbating suffering by also participating in 'immigrant-bashing' and, more widely, opposing affirmative action more or less in keeping with the model-minority stereotype.[6]

The Asian American literary texts selected in this chapter critically negotiate relationships between these worlds within the

USA, typically in terms of family and other personal relationships. These relationships are frequently marked by conflict, the immigrant and the refugee characters often being demonized by their American-born counterparts and others as they struggle with the 'colossal obstacle course' of immigration and acculturation.[7] Immigrant bashing does make the characters ideologically suspect, and, for some critics, the writers too particularly if privileged in terms of class and caste. Even if these characters refrained from immigrant bashing by praising and idealizing immigrants, this reversal in opinion does not escape the essentialist logic that underpins these apparently opposite views of immigrants. In both cases, the figure of the immigrant is stereotyped as essentially foreign, following a logic that also informs the yellow-peril and model-minority stereotypes. The novels and plays discussed in this chapter promote this insight with respect to the inescapability of dominant American ideologies, not least when immigrant and refugee characters bash each other. Through their characters, these texts formulate a complicated relationship with ideology by demonstrating that even successful ideology critique is liable to appropriation, but, crucially, not to the extent that oppositional politics are completely undermined.

One of the most obvious examples of Asian American success with respect to antiracist critique was the winning of redress and reparations for Japanese American internment during the Second World War. From the late 1960s onwards, Japanese Americans had campaigned for redress. In 1981, the Commission on Wartime Relocation and Internment of Civilians recommended redress and reparations. On 10 August 1988, the Civil Liberties Act was passed and the USA formally apologized for internment, as well as paying each surviving internee $20,000. This political advance forms a complicated relationship with 'America's Super Minority' and 'America's Greatest Success Story', so celebrated in the press and in politics during the 1980s.[8]

Of this relationship, Don T. Nakanishi asks why, if Asian Americans were the greatest success story, Japanese Americans would 'resurrect, visibly identify with, and seek redress and reparations for an event which remained controversial and emotion-ladden even after many decades.' Japanese American 'guilt, shame, repression, and vulnerability' kept the experience buried, but, particularly for cultural nationalist critics, its resurrection was necessary because it contributed to 'the common history of racial oppression which Asian Americans shared with other racial minorities.' The threat of internment camps for African Americans in the late 1960s and, more recently, Chinese Americans and Arab Americans, ensures that the Japanese American internment was not merely a past mistake, which, once uncovered, was finally resolved through verbal apology and financial compensation. For Nakanishi and others, the internment exceeds not only its historical moment but also individual mistakes and misfortune.[9] Indeed, its legacy serves to highlight the fundamental instability of democracy with respect to the civil rights and human rights of Japanese Americans, Japanese Canadians and other racial minority groups in and beyond North America.

JOY KOGAWA, *OBASAN* (1981)

In her Bildungsroman *Obasan*, Japanese Canadian writer Joy Kogawa (1935–) focuses on the internment experience and its legacy. The racism legitimated by the War Measures Act, the Canadian version of Executive Order 9066, was, in many respects, worse than its American equivalent because Japanese Canadian families were separated. Along with other able-bodied men, the narrator's father was sent to an interior labour camp, while her mother was prevented from returning to Canada from Japan. The narrator, Naomi Nakane, sums up Canada's 'short harsh history' in a pamphlet entitled 'Racial Discrimination by Orders-in-Council': 'Seizure and government sale of fishing boats. Suspension of fishing licences. Relocation camps. Liquidation of property . . . Deportation. Revocation of nationality.'[10] In addition to these losses, Naomi recounts many deaths – of animals, family and community members. Such 'outright race persecution' (p. 101) was not merely a domestic matter since it also extended to the USA and beyond North America to Japan through the atomic bombings of Nagasaki and Hiroshima in August 1945. Naomi's Japanese Canadian mother serves to connect these acts of aggression as she was trapped in Japan by Canadian foreign policy and then fatally injured in Nagasaki as a result of American foreign policy.

For those who do survive death brought about by both national and transnational racisms, the experience of the Japanese Canadian internment continues to impact on their lives in harmful ways. In addition to having a near-death experience during childhood, Naomi's childhood nickname is 'Nomi, a homophone for "no me," no self'.[11] Her self-denigration continues into adulthood when she describes herself as an 'old maid', with her childlessness at thirty-six being part of the 'crone-prone syndrome' from which her two childless aunts, Aya Obasan and Aunt Emily, also suffer (pp. 9–10). Naomi frequently discusses the living death of the wartime evacuation to 'chicken coop' accommodation on the Alberta prairie. For example: 'I have been invaded by dust and grit from the fields and mud is in my bone marrow. I can't move anymore . . . and there is no escape' (pp. 232–3). Naomi remains in this state for thirty years, right up until 1972.

Her activist aunt and 'word warrior' offers her a possibility of escape: 'You have to remember. You are your history. If you cut any of it off you're an amputee. Don't deny the past. Remember every-thing. If you are bitter, be bitter. Cry it out! Scream! Denial is gan-grene' (pp. 39, 60). According to Aunt Emily's logic, then, escape in the form of witness statements in which the truth of internment shines through, ultimately, for the purpose of redress, stimulates Naomi to 'write the vision and make it plain' (p. 38). While *Obasan* and Kogawa's 1992 novel *Itsuka* do write the vision, these narratives of internment and its legacy are hardly plain. Not only is *Obasan*'s narrative non-linear, beginning and ending in 1972, with flashbacks to the 1940s, 1950s and 1960s, but it is also multi-generic in its use of letters, historical documents, (semi-)autobiography, fairytales and fiction. On this count, then, it is, as King-kok Cheung and other critics point out:

'historiographic metafiction,' a genre that . . . 'inscribes and then subverts its mimetic engagement with the world. It does not reject [mimesis] . . . but it does irrevocably change any simple notions of realism or reference, by confronting the dis-course of art with the discourse of history.'[12]

This change is most readily apparent in *Obasan*'s formal and thematic preoccupations with interrelated unspeakable events variously perpetuated by white racism: white racist north American governments and a white paedophile, Old Man Gower. This traumatic history is unspeakable in the sense that Naomi does not fully know it and so cannot fully tell it, at least not in a way familiar to the traditional historian. Of her childhood, prior to internment, Naomi only recalls 'bits . . . I can only skirt the edges . . . Fragments of fragments . . . Segments of stories' (p. 64). Given that the truth for her is 'murky, shadowy and gray' and that, again for her, the 'crimes of history . . . can stay in history', it is hardly surprising that Naomi 'cannot speak' and 'will not speak' it (pp. 38, 50, x).

Yet, crimes of history do not stay in history; they may not come into history in quite the way assumed or desired by activist Aunt Emily, but, as Naomi's other aunt silently implies, they do still come into history. In her discussion of silence in *Articulate Silences* (1993), Cheung questions the Eurocentric privileging of speech as necessarily active and silence as necessarily passive. With respect to this assumption about speech, Naomi reveals that activism risks jeopardizing the safety of some Japanese Canadians: 'I can only see a dark field with Aunt Emily beaming a flashlight to where the rest of us crouch and hide, our eyes downcast as we seek the safety of invisibility' (p. 38). Also commenting on this problematic opposition, as it impacts differently on factions within the Japanese Canadian community, Kogawa states: 'the struggle against the government was a big struggle, but the community's struggle inside itself was, I think, even harder . . . But even worse are the struggles within the family.'[13]

These different yet related struggles are exacerbated by the fact Japanese Canadians are divided over their views of Canada. In *Obasan*, Naomi's aunt and uncle articulate this division:

'Why in a time of war with Germany and Japan would our government seize the property and homes of Canadian-born Canadians but not the homes of German-born Germans?' she [Aunt Emily] asked angrily. / 'Racism,' she answered herself. 'The Nazis are everywhere.'

(p. 45)

For Uncle, however, 'this country is the best. There is food. There is medicine. There is pension money. Gratitude. Gratitude' (p. 50). At this point, Naomi sides with her uncle against her aunt, although, ultimately, her understanding of the Japanese Canadian internment is complicated by the insight that both alternatives are simultaneously empowering and disempowering. Thus attuned to the way in which 'words can liberate but . . . also distort and wound', and 'silence may obliterate . . . [but] also minister, soothe, and communicate', Kogawa's novel offers a model of critique that acknowledges the inescapability of dominant ideologies.[14] It thus draws attention to the fact that escapability is an ideological assumption, most directly when Aunt Emily's argument also has the potential to oppress despite the fact that it is politically just and historically true.

Such contradictory views of Canada and antiracist critique are difficult to live by, which is arguably the reason why Naomi's narrative ends with closure. Although healing images of reconciliation between speech and silence, land and sea, earth and sky, humanity and nature do end Naomi's narrative, they, crucially, do not end the novel. In addition to the natural images of, for example, 'water and stone dancing' in 'a quiet ballet, soundless as breath' (p. 296), are consolatory Christian images that also seem to offer the possibility of personal and cultural healing. This healing is possible even when the Christian symbolism is reversed, as when, for example, the yellow Easter chicks are killed rather than nurtured by the white hen. The colour imagery helps to racialize and historicize this anomaly of nature, along with suggesting that so-called anomalies of culture during the Second World War can also be transcended through Christian love.

However, this 'appeal for transcendental Christian love', argues Scott McFarlane, functions to displace the historical reality of the Japanese Canadian experience during and after the war, as does the naturalization of asymmetrical racial relationships via the white hen and yellow chick story. According to him, this double displacement is consistent with a national Bildungsroman that imagines 'Japanese Canadians as already interned and already internable', and Canada as a mistaken or 'fallen yet redeemable nation'. Similarly to its American counterpart, this story of redress serves to redeem Canada of past racism without radically engaging the way in which racism persists even in a progressive Canada: 'For Japanese Canadians then, Canadian cultural identity continuously signifies their own *alieNation*.'[15]

McFarlane's important point about *Obasan's* appropriation as national Bildungsroman – an appropriation that displaces the fact that redress and racism are ongoing issues – makes sense with respect to Naomi's narrative. Although Naomi's narrative ends with closure, the novel does not. 'Excerpt from the memorandum sent by the Co-operative Committee on Japanese Canadians to the House and the Senate of Canada, April 1946' actually ends the novel. In describing the actions of the Canadian government as 'wrong and indefensible' in a way comparable to Nazism (p. 297), this memorandum underlines the fact that the wartime treatment of Japanese Canadians has not achieved closure. Even in the early 1990s the National Association of Japanese Canadians (NAJC) was still seeking redress for Japanese Canadians excluded from the Canadian government's redress settlement of September 1988. The government claimed that Japanese Canadians trapped in or deported to Japan during the war were not entitled to redress, despite the fact that their experiences also affected the Japanese Canadian community.[16]

On this matter, *Obasan*'s Naomi observes,

> I pictured her trapped in Japan by government regulations, or by an ailing grandmother . . . By the time this country opened its pale arms to you, it was too late. First you could not, then you chose not to come. Now you are gone . . . Young Mother at Nagasaki, am I not also there?
>
> (pp. 283, 290)

Between 1941 and 1949, Japanese Canadians like Naomi's mother were prohibited from retuning to Canada. Between 1945 and 1949, Naomi's mother was hospitalized for the horrific injuries she sustained in the atomic bombing of Nagasaki. Presumably, these injuries prevent her return, and she dies in Japan. She also makes the decision not to return in order to protect her children: 'I am praying that they may never know' (p. 290). The reasons for her non-return are various, but, despite the Canadian government's claims in the early 1990s that not all those who were trapped in Japan were entitled to redress, the actions of this government implicate it in the suffering of both her and her children.

In a 1996 interview with Ruth Y. Hsu, Kogawa discusses Canadian racism beyond redress. Both women agree that some lessons had been learnt in North America because of the redress movements, although clearly not enough. As Hsu remarks, 'it seems as if we're not learning the lessons because the same sort of brutal and violent imagination' that enabled internment 'still exists'. She cites five different attacks on Asian Americans, including the murder of Vincent Chin in 1982, to support her argument. Rather than focusing on physical violence, Kogawa cites a newspaper's coverage of violence in Vancouver following a hockey game: 'a newspaper cartoon presented the violence as being caused by Asian gangs. That form of media discrimination is terribly violent against the people, and different from an individual being so demented that they would actually shoot somebody.'[17]

Though different, these acts of violence both involve scapegoating whereby racism is rendered anomalous rather than integral to North American cultures consistent with the rise of racial reaction in the 1980s. The link between individual and institutional acts of violence is particularly apparent in the murder cases of Chinese American Vincent Chin and, five years later, Indian American Navroze Mody. The differences between these two cases aside, neither Chin nor Mody was regarded as American by their assailants or by a reactionary legal system: 'They Ain't Americans', but rather a 'Jap' and a 'dot-head' respectively. The country and the constituency they were assumed to represent were thought to be a threat to the livelihoods of 'real' Americans. Mody was also disliked for his Indian identity, 'as defined by the symbols of Indian culture', including smell and dress. Finally, the authorities also participated in 'lynching' Chin and Mody. The judge allowed Chin's assailants to plead guilty to manslaughter, for which they received three years probation and a $3,780 fine, and the police hindered Mody's murder investigation.[18]

By highlighting the larger significance of these acts of racial violence – literal immigrant bashing, along with its institutionalized legitimation – Asian Americans resist the view that racial attacks are anomalous and not deeply embedded in American culture. Indeed, nativism, racism and Orientalism are so pervasive that these ideologies, as Sheng-mei Ma highlights, 'infiltrate . . . every segment of the American society, specifically amongst Chinese Americans themselves'. For example, Chinese American writers such as Maxine Hong Kingston and Frank Chin, as well as other writers inside and outside the *Aiiieeeee!* group, 'frequently take on the white gaze at their nonwhite object' for their own self-empowerment.[19] Whether this immigrant bashing is interpreted literally or ironically, foreign-born Asians are Orientalized in certain Chinese American texts apparently consistent with a normalized American 'we': 'You know they shouldn't have the smell they have, dress the way they do . . . and walk around in tribes.'[20]

MAXINE HONG KINGSTON, *TRIPMASTER MONKEY* (1989) AND DAVID HENRY HWANG, *FOB* (1979) AND *M. BUTTERFLY* (1988)

While not commenting on smell, David Henry Hwang (1957–) in his play *FOB* does identify the way new immigrants, Fresh off the Boat, offend the other senses of Americans: not white Americans, but Chinese Americans. As one ABC or American-born Chinese sees them: 'Clumsy, ugly, greasy FOB. Loud, stupid, four-eyed FOB. Big feet. Horny.'[21] As it stands, this description of loathsome Chinese immigrant men would support Frank Chin's view that Hwang, alongside Kingston and, in the late 1980s, Amy Tan, uncritically perpetuates white racism. Yet, Chin is not immune to immigrant bashing when he indirectly compares Chinese immigrants to animals, as well as 'Albinos', 'dwarves' and 'midgets'. These comparisons, observes Ma, serve to differentiate FOBs from ABCs:

> Such aliens are then conceived as having a certain kind of corporal deformity as the locus of their difference. To distance himself and other Asian Americans from immigrants is, to Chin, to avoid weaknesses intrinsic to the bodily makeup of that foreign group.[22]

In short, it seems that all four of these Chinese American canonical writers proclaim like *The Woman Warrior*'s narrator that 'Chinese people are very weird' on account of their bodies and behaviours (p. 143).

Kingston's satirical and polemical novel, *Tripmaster Monkey: His Fake Book*, begins with the cowboy-booted, suicide-contemplating, draft-dodging Chin-inspired protagonist, Wittman Ah Sing, encountering various characters in the San Francisco of the late 1960s. These characters include a decrepit white woman, a pigeon 'disgorging milk', 'a vomiting drunk' and 'Immigrants. Fresh Off the Boats out in public'.[23] This last and closest encounter receives the most attention. As Wittman, the ABC, walks into a tunnel, he meets an immigrant family – 'a Chinese dude from China', followed by his family – none of whom know how to walk properly, presumably because of their deformed legs. Instead they 'scrabble' along, 'spitting seeds. So uncool' in their FOB clothes and with their FOB smell (pp. 4–5). Wittman's senses are also offended by two 'fellow ethnicks' whose bodies are, for him, too short and too flat. The flat-chested woman also smells 'like hot restaurant air that blows into alleys', thus joining her other equally unattractive Asian American peers, whom Wittman compares to animals (pp. 73–4). Although immigrant bashing is empowering in that it enables Wittman to differentiate his ABC self from FOB other, differentiation thus pursued also functions to bash him. In short, it is an expression of racial self-hatred.

As *Tripmaster Monkey* progresses, however, Wittman in his 'One-Man Show' directs his critique towards white racists, 'Mr. And Mrs. Potato Head', and white-dominated institutions, particularly the American culture industry. According to Wittman, this industry 'brainwashes' Asian Americans into various forms of enslavement and suicide. He advises his audience not to kill themselves since this would 'play into their hands' (pp. 317, 319). His solution to brainwashing involves practising peace and love, not war. 'Unbrainwashing' is advocated in two staged events. The first event is a kissing contest, which is meant to dispel the stereotype that 'we're a people who don't kiss and don't hug' (p. 329). The second event is a play, which involves acknowledging the limitations of war and, by implication, violent Chinese American masculinity:

He had staged the War of the Three Kingdoms as heroically
as he could, which made him start to understand: The three
brothers and Cho Cho were masters of war . . . And they *lost*.
The clanging and banging fooled us, but now we know – they
lost. Studying the mightiest war epic of all time, Wittman
changed – beeen! into a pacifist.

(p. 340)

Similar to *Obasan*, then, love is something of a transcendental force
in *Tripmaster Monkey*.

However, this interracial peace-bringing love is limited to an
Asian American man and white American woman, specifically to
Wittman and Tana who apparently marry at the end of the novel.
Their interracial marriage effectively replaces, perhaps even displaces, intraracial relationships, whether between ABCs or between
ABCs and FOBs. According to David Leiwei Li, such a traditional
ending suggests that 'the dominant racial hierarchy . . . has not
entirely lost its grip on *Tripmaster Monkey*'s interracial imagination.'[24] Importantly, however, this ending is not exactly traditional;
rather Wittman's 'new clever wedding ritual [is] of his own
making', which his family and community 'took . . . to mean that he
was announcing his marriage to Tana' (p. 339). But Wittman is
already married to Tana, which makes the second marriage ceremony fake, despite wedding rituals such as rice throwing, photo
shooting, champagne drinking and conga dancing. *Tripmaster
Monkey: His Fake Book* thus ends with a fake marriage, which in
turn problematizes the novel's apparent commitment to narrative
and ideological closure via the interracial romance.

The interracial romance is also the focus of Hwang's later play, *M.
Butterfly*. On this occasion, however, the relationship is between 'the
submissive Oriental woman and the cruel white man'.[25] This play, as
Hwang explains in the afterword, is informed by two interracial relationships, one real, between a French diplomat (Bernard Bouriscot)
and a Chinese singer and spy (Shi Peipu), and the other, fictional,
between an American navy officer (Pinkerton) and a Japanese geisha
(Cho–Cho–San). Despite their differences, both relationships
exemplify ' "Yellow Fever" – Caucasian men with a fetish for exotic
Oriental women', at least on the surface. Crucially for Hwang,

however, the real relationship shifts from heterosexual 'Yellow Fever' to homosexual 'Rice Queen' fantasies when it is revealed that Bouriscot was deceived for a period of twenty years regarding the anatomical sex of his cross-dressing lover, Mr Shi Peipu (pp. 98, vii).

In *M. Butterfly*, Hwang's French diplomat, Rene Gallimard, is in a relationship with a male spy disguised as a Chinese actress, Song Liling. Gallimard's 'little one', or Madame Butterfly, is different from her Japanese female predecessor, although these differences hardly seem to matter since he operates in 'the world of fantasy', specifically Orientalist fantasy (pp. 86, 91). Song highlights the Orientalist underpinnings of the interracial romance when delivering his 'armchair political theory' to the court at the espionage trial: 'The West has sort of an international rape mentality towards the East' (pp. 82–3). His East is also Vietnam, and in support of this assertion he cites French colonialism, the French-Indochina War and the Vietnam War.

Song continues: 'You expect Oriental countries to submit to your guns, and you expect Oriental women to be submissive to your men' (pp. 82–3). Submissive Asian women, who take 'whatever punishment we give them, and bounce back, strengthened by love, unconditionally', represent to Gallimard 'the perfect woman', even when she is a man (p. 91). Gallimard's ignorance regarding his lover's sexual identity is also explained, again by Song, in terms of the stereotype of the emasculated Asian man: 'I am an Oriental. And being an Oriental, I could never be completely a man' (pp. 3–4, 90–1). Following this Orientalist logic, Asian men fail to measure up quantitatively in the sense that they are without the West's 'big guns, big industry, big money' and 'great big weeniehead' (p. 83). This measurement is also qualitative since an Asian man is not 'a real man', defined by Hwang's Pinkerton as a 'womanizing cad' (pp. 6–7).

Despite its armchair status, Song's theorizing reinforces the general point made throughout Hwang's play about the way in which 'our considerations of race and sex intersect the issue of imperialism' (p. 99). This is an issue that not even the transcendent force of (Christian) love is able to survive. Gallimard says as much at the end of the play when he acknowledges the reality of his relationship with Song and his own identity as Butterfly:

The love of a Butterfly can withstand many things – unfaith-
fulness, loss, even abandonment. But how can it face the one sin
that implies all others? The devastating knowledge that, under-
neath it all, the object of her love was nothing more, nothing less
than . . . a man. (*He sets the tip of the knife against his body*) . . .
My name is Rene Gallimard – also known as Madame Butterfly.

(pp. 92–3)

Gallimard-as-Butterfly promptly commits suicide, as did his
predecessor in *Madame Butterfly*. However, Cho-Cho-San has
arguably achieved retribution in the sense that the latest version of
her Western lover dies, but not before being emasculated.
Gallimard's emasculation is also achieved in his relationships with
assertive and submissive women alike, including 'screaming'
Isabelle, 'uninhibited' Renee, maternal Helga and, finally, Song,
to the point that when Gallimard looks in the mirror, he sees
'nothing but . . . a woman' (pp. 33, 54, 92).

Whether in relation to his personal or public life, Gallimard's
phallocentric assumption of power proves delusional, if not plain
wrong. Of his diplomatic skills, for example, an ambassador
observes: 'everything you predicted here in the Orient . . . just
hasn't happened' (p. 69). Gallimard is no more a real man than
either Pinkerton or, more generally, male world leaders. While
Pinkerton gets others to do errands for him, like ending his relationship with Cho-Cho-San, male leaders have 'pricks the size of
pins' (pp. 13, 56). In addition to reversing the Orientalist hierarchy,
principally by ensuring that the Western man is emasculated,
M. Butterfly is 'a deconstructivist *Madame Butterfly*' (p. 95) in the
sense described by Douglas Kerr: 'Song's submissiveness . . . is an
instrument of power' and 'Gallimard's dream of power was the
weakness that enabled Song to use him' for spying purposes with
respect to American troop movements in Vietnam.[26]

This deconstructivist *Madame Butterfly* challenges the
Orientalist binary opposition between complete Western men and
incomplete Eastern men, along with demonstrating the constructedness of gender, sexual and racial categories via the changing
appearances of its leading characters. But not all of Hwang's critics
are convinced by this challenge. For example, Frank Chin and other

critics argue that Song-as-Butterfly reinforces the Orientalist stereotype of emasculated Asian American men so as to strengthen the play's popular appeal. Its appeal to white Americans is further reinforced by the play's end and the dramatic attention accorded to Gallimard, which was always the case since he, much more than Song, directs his lines to his 'ideal audience' (p. 4). In so doing, *M. Butterfly* 'appropriates the pathos (Butterfly's last possession), taking it away from the Eastern and the female . . . and investing it finally in a Western voice' that is privileged in terms of class, gender and sexuality.[27]

The fact that this voice is male and heterosexual is further reinforced by Gallimard's suicide on becoming a woman, to which Song, on becoming a man, tenderly responds: '*Two words leave his lips.* / Butterfly? Butterfly?' (p. 93). Here, then, the heterosexist discourse of patriarchy appropriates homosexuality, not by proclaiming that 'there is no homosexuality' (p. 48) but, rather, by heterosexualizing it. Both Gallimard and Song desire women in their men, which hardly seems deconstructivist. However, this failure to deconstruct heterosexism does nevertheless generate critical interpretative possibilities. For example, Andrew Shin proposes that 'Rene Gallimard's failed construction of a gay identity through the stereotype of an Asian woman, the mask of a gay Asian opera singer in Communist China', highlights 'the prison-house of heterosexism . . . in the homophobic West.'[28]

AMY TAN, *THE JOY LUCK CLUB* (1989)

The romance has traditionally dominated representations of interracial relationships in Asian American literature, from the Eaton sisters onwards. The priority given to relationships between white Americans and Asian Americans also offers implicit commentary on intraracial relationships in terms of the colonial complex.[29] In interracial relationships, whiteness tends to be idealized, which leads to racial self-hatred that is then directed towards Asian immigrants and Asians. Alongside the interracial romance is the family romance, which increasingly dominated Asian American literature in the 1980s and later, so much so that critics note that the contemporary period is typified by 'Asian American mother/daughter sweet stories, your cross-generational stuff, your intercultural jive'.[30] Of the many Asian American women writing in this period, Maxine Hong Kingston and Amy Tan (1952–) are most readily associated with the matrilineal format, if not with Asian American writing *per se*. Their popular success is controversially regarded by some Asian American critics, who argue that Tan, more than Kingston, achieved fame and fortune by immigrant bashing and, more generally, by uncritically adhering to dominant American ideologies.

Tan's first novel, *The Joy Luck Club*, is criticized for its perpetuation of the Orientalist binary opposition between backward, enslaved and enslaving Chinese immigrant mothers and enlightened and free American-born daughters. Further, this family romance is typically assumed to move unproblematically towards narrative and ideological closure. *The Joy Luck Club* may not end with a marriage, not even a fake one as in Kingston's *Tripmaster Monkey*, but it does seem to end happily nonetheless. Its two generations of women narrators, seven in all, who take it in turns to recount their experiences, apparently reconcile the cultural differences that heretofore rendered them strangers. This reconciliation even seems to transcend death. Thus understood, Tan is, for Chin, part of 'the generation of converts that was a generation of spies' for white racism that is 'out to Happy End us'.[31]

Shifting the terms from racism to neo-racism, neo-Orientalism and neoconservatism in keeping with larger political shifts in American culture during the 1980s, other Asian American critics proclaim Tan's ideological balancing act in *The Joy Luck Club* so slick that she can bring together apparently oppositional discourses: 'neoconservative rhetoric' and dominant American ideologies on the one hand and 'poststructural and multicultural celebrations of diasporic subjectivity' on the other.[32] These ideological combinations ensure that her novels, not just *The Joy Luck Club* but also *The Kitchen God's Wife* (1992), have, in Sau-ling Cynthia Wong's words, 'a little bit of something for everyone', from the 'naïve voyeur' to the critical reader and, ultimately, the white racist.[33]

For example, *The Joy Luck Club*'s opening vignette 'Feathers from a Thousand *Li* Away' highlights familial and cultural practices that serve to limit women's development in a way that apparently coheres with the assumptions of white patriarchy. This vignette is about a Chinese woman, who, before emigrating to the USA, buys a duck that becomes a goose and, eventually, a swan. The bird's transformation serves to highlight the woman's aspirations with regard to immigration as a movement from oppression to freedom:

> *In America I will have a daughter just like me. But over there nobody will say her worth is measured by the loudness of her husband's belch. Over there nobody will look down on her . . . She will know my meaning, because I will give her this swan – a creature that became more than what was hoped for.*[34]

Clearly, this vignette implies that Chinese patriarchy limits Chinese women's development. On her arrival, however, American immigration officials take the swan, leaving the woman with only a single feather. This act, together with the many immigration forms she has to complete, suggests that the USA is also limiting, specifically with respect to its assimilationist demands: '*she forgot why she had come and what she had left behind*' (p. 17). Her Coca-Cola drinking and English-speaking daughter is similarly preoccupied, as her mother, now an old woman, waits for the time when she can finally inform her daughter about the swan feather's meaning. As an introduction to the rest of the novel, this vignette taps into feminist concerns about the lot of a housewife, by invoking, as well as questioning, the possibility of an improvement in women's circumstances through immigration.

Although this opening vignette emphasizes transformation, and to this extent coheres with the novel's emphasis on diversity, principally articulated on a formal level through its multiple narrators, Tan's more critical commentators point out that *The Joy Luck Club*'s postmodern engagement with identity is effectively fake. Its postmodern narrative is most directly compromised by biological essentialism, which, for David Leiwei Li, suggests 'Tan's active participation in the dominant privatization of social problems . . . The biological family is privatized as the essential unit of social coherence', specifically racial and national coherence.[35] Following Li's logic, it hardly matters that a duck becomes a swan (feather) since a Chinese American woman, despite being brought up on Coca-Cola and speaking only American English, is essentially Chinese: 'Once you are born Chinese, you cannot help but feel and think Chinese' (p. 267).

While Chineseness is explored by all of Tan's narrators, its most forceful theorization is articulated by the main narrator, Jing-mei 'June' Woo, on the trip her recently deceased mother, Suyuan Woo, was meant to take:

> The minute our train . . . enters Shenzhen, China, I feel different. I can feel the skin on my forehead tingling, my blood rushing through a new course, my bones aching with a familiar old pain. And I think, My mother was right. I am becoming Chinese.
>
> (p. 267)

These bodily responses anticipate the biological essentialism of the third from last paragraph of the novel when Jing-mei says 'now I also see what part of me is Chinese. It is so obvious. It is my family. It is in our blood. After all these years, it can finally be let go' (p. 288).

Thus understood, then, *The Joy Luck Club* privatizes, essentializes and naturalizes ideological and political matters by keeping them in both the body and the family, albeit in non-biological families comprising titular aunts and cousins. This extended family forms the stock market investing, mah jong playing and talk-storying San Francisco version of the Joy Luck Club. This move towards the domain of the club, with few explicit extra-familial references to American culture, seems to coincide with right-wing values concerning the family. In the 1980s, white Republican politicians proclaimed respect for Asian Americans because they also accorded primacy to the family, particularly the kind of family that is autonomous and successful on a socio-economic front.

However, this homogenized view of the Asian American family is as mistaken as Jing-mei's view of the familial club: 'I imagined Joy Luck was a shameful Chinese custom, like the secret gathering of the Ku Klux Klan or the tom-tom dances of TV Indians preparing for war. But tonight, there's no mystery' (p. 28). Formed in response to the Sino-Japanese War (1937–45), the Chinese club enables survival of 'unspeakable tragedies', whereas the American club forms in response to the different but nonetheless difficult experiences of immigration and diaspora (p. 20). Its reformation suggests to Wendy Ho 'insidious links' between past and present, China and the USA, mothers and daughters. She continues,

> It is important to read these women's stories as the complicated physical, psychological, cultural, and sociohistorical position-ings for personal and communal survival and resistance in the Chinese diaspora communities of the United States. In this light, these stories record . . . daily heroic actions of many of the Joy Luck mothers, who struggle to raise children under stressful political and sociohistorical conditions.[36]

A further reason for the club's formation relates to the Cultural Revolution (1949) and the anti-Communist Confession Program (1955–late 1960s), even after the Red Scare had subsided with resumption of diplomatic relations between the PRC and the USA in 1979. Reminiscent of *The Woman Warrior*'s anonymous deporta-tion conversation, *The Joy Luck Club*'s immigration conversation recounts how one of the aunties recently approached someone about the possibility of her brother immigrating:

> Who knows who? And that person told her she can get her brother in bad trouble in China. That person said FBI will put her on a list and give her trouble in the U.S. the rest of her life. That person said, You ask for a house loan and they say no loan, because your brother is a communist.

These concerns about lists and loans may be ungrounded, espe-cially since auntie An-mei Hsu already has a house, but they do, nevertheless, recall a history of economic and ideological difficulties that continues to generate fear: 'But still she was scared' (p. 30).

The links between the private clubs and various political crises, most notably, war, immigration and diaspora, call into question the claim that *The Joy Luck Club* uncritically privatizes social problems. Moreover, this claim is arguably underpinned by the patriarchal binary opposition between the private and the public spheres. With respect to both Chinese and American patriarchies, Tan's critique is harsh. The white American patriarch may seem like the 'big, important husband' or the 'angel of light', rescuing Chinese and Chinese American women from Chineseness, but the benevolence of this paternal act is revealed for its racial and imperial underpinnings when rescued women are subordinated, even in the USA (pp. 67, 250). An-mei articulates this subaltern condition of different generations of women when she observes that 'even though I taught my daughter the opposite, still she came out the same way! . . . All of us are like stairs, one step after another, going up and down, but all going the same way' (p. 215).

Far from undermining the Orientalist binary opposition between China and the USA, An-mei's simile seems to reinforce it because of an 'irrefutable generational destiny' – written in the body and elsewhere.[37] Whether achieved supernaturally in terms of astrology, the Five Elements and *feng shui*, or naturally in terms of blood and bones, this destiny is the main point of contention for Tan's critics. It grounds their assertions that writer and novel are neo-Orientalist and neo-racist, nowhere more so than when Jing-mei travels to China. Given that Chineseness has repeatedly been Orientalized by way of reference to the Chinese immigrant mothers, most outrageously when two American-born daughters describe them as enslavers, murderers and violently sinocentric, Jing-mei's essentialism on the China trip should hardly come as a surprise. After all, essentialism is a focus of *The Joy Luck Club* but, crucially, not its telos.[38]

Undoubtedly Tan's characters essentialize each other in a way that inhibits the intergenerational relationships in particular, so much so that they are 'unseen and not seeing, unheard and not hearing, unknown by others' and each other (p. 67). To some extent this situation is countered formally, through both the novel's multiple narrators and talk-story. It features talk-stories by and about different generations of women consistent with Kingston's *The Woman Warrior*: 'Here is a story my mother told me . . . The beginning is hers, the ending, mine' (p. 184). Quite literally, *The Joy Luck Club* is partly a story Tan's mother told her, as well as beginning with a mother's vignette and ending with a daughter's chapter.

Kingston's talk-story is also about translating well, which Tan's talk-story also attempts to do, albeit in terms of matrilineal relationships. For example, Waverly Jong re-translates her mother when she describes this potential child murderer as 'an old woman, a wok for her armor, a knitting needle for her sword, getting a little crabby as she waited patiently for her daughter to invite her in' (pp. 183–4).

All but Jing-mei benefit from improved intergenerational relationships since the fact of mother's death makes impossible the sort of scenario experienced by the Jongs and their peers. Yet, Jing-mei's trip to the Chinese motherland does function as a way for her to acquire cultural knowledge and self-understanding. On this trip, she moves from a state of becoming Chinese to partial belonging: 'I also see what part of me is Chinese. It is so obvious. It is my family. It is in our blood' (p. 288). Fundamental to Jing-mei's trip is the often-overlooked narrative context, which, contrary to her biological essentialism, repeatedly highlights how Chineseness depends on decidedly non-biological factors for its construction, including a travel guide, a shampoo and a family photograph. If it is possible to understand *The Joy Luck Club* teleologically, then, its telos is to demonstrate how essentialism is inescapably built into even the most private experiences. Tan's narrators cannot help but essentialize themselves and each other, although the novel does make possible a shift of focus not exactly beyond what is said (which would risk marginalizing the characters' ideologically suspect comments), but to how it is said. Indeed, how obvious is a racial essence if it depends on mediated forms, often overly mediated forms such as a travel guide and a shampoo, to bring this essence into being?

Here, then, Jing-mei discovers Chineseness, albeit from an inescapably Western vantage point, a mediated discovery Tan repeats in later novels, whether she returns the native to China in *The Hundred Secret Senses* (1995) or returns China to the native in *The Bonesetter's Daughter* (2001). Other texts from the 1980s also represent this movement from Asia to the USA in more overt ways through immigrant narratives that also reflect the changing demographics within the Asian American population. Already, it should be apparent that Asian Americans, specifically ABCs like Chin, Hwang, Kingston and Tan, depict Asian immigrants as physically and psychologically unappealing characters for reasons that are not always in keeping with racial self-hatred. In contrast to the texts discussed so far in this chapter, *Jasmine* and *The Coffin Tree* are written by immigrant women. Bharati Mukherjee (1940–) and Wendy Law-Yone (1947–) voluntarily left Asia, the first as an Indian immigrant and the second as a biracial Burmese exile.

BHARATI MUKHERJEE, *JASMINE* (1989) AND WENDY LAW-YONE, *THE COFFIN TREE* (1983)

Unlike cultural nationalist writers like Chin and Kingston, whose literary representations involve claiming America for Asian Americans without bypassing the Asian in American, Bharati Mukherjee claims America, '*not* [as] a minority', but rather, as an American. As she asserts in interviews and essays: 'I believe that some people were meant to be American even if they never leave their village in Punjab – at heart, they are American.'[39] By 'American', Mukherjee means being possessed of a spirit of adventurousness, an understanding that is most forcefully articulated in her immigrant novel, *Jasmine*.

For the most part, however, *Jasmine* is more in keeping with an adventure novel, even a fantasy novel, owing to the fact that its eponymous narrator (who also has at least five other names) achieves Americanness by obliterating the real conditions of immigration and diaspora. Admittedly, Jasmine's class positions are low in the sense that she is a village girl and an undocumented migrant who is raped on arrival in the USA – even before she has time to travel to the Florida Institute of Technology where her husband was meant to study before he was murdered, and where she had meant to burn his suit and herself in an act of self-immolation: 'I had planned it all so perfectly. To lay out the suit, to fill it with twigs and papers. To light it, then lie upon it in the white cotton sari I had brought from home.'[40] But, this said, Jasmine's class and national affiliations do bear an uncanny resemblance to Mukherjee's, whose higher status more accurately reflects post-1965 Indian immigration. These similarities become even more apparent when Mukherjee's and Jasmine's experiences of immigration and diaspora are contrasted with those of 'hard-to-place' (p. 14) Vietnamese and Burmese orphans in *Jasmine* and in *The Coffin Tree* respectively.

The profound differences of living with the colonial legacy of British rule in the Punjab and Burma (now Myanmar) aside, the opening chapters of Mukherjee's and Wendy Law-Yone's Bildungsromans do share a number of important similarities. Both *Jasmine* and *The Coffin Tree* begin with their narrators' childhoods prior to immigration in environments where older members of the community tyrannically determine their development. According to an astrologer, Jasmine's fate in widowhood and exile is written in the stars and on her face, if not in her mother's accursed history. In *The Coffin Tree*, the unnamed narrator's grandmother rules by fear, even from beyond the grave, as her ghost curses her granddaughter as a witch and a 'little mother killer' (pp. 5–6). In different ways, then, both girls are confronted with the fact that they are regarded on familial and cultural levels as curses.

Regardless of its many manifestations in the West and in Western beliefs, superstition is too easily proclaimed in Orientalist fashion as being something peculiar to the East. Notably, however, superstitious talk, in whatever society it originates, is accompanied by remarkably similar images of death. Of the Catholic Redemptorist priest in *The Coffin Tree*, Law-Yone's narrator criticizes 'his own brand of black magic', particularly his allegorizing of sin as '*a rotting corpse we drag around with us, until we confess and repent*' (pp. 26–7). In this novel and *Jasmine*, the bodies of 'living organisms', one, a Burmese grandmother, the other, a dog, fall apart when the 'glue' that binds their bodies together finally gives way (p. 3; p. 5). Scarred psychologically and, in Jasmine's case, literally, by these violent formative experiences, Mukherjee's and Law-Yone's narrators link these broken bodies with identity. After representing her scar as a third eye Jasmine sees in the dog's broken body a version of identity that stays with her into adulthood: 'I know what I don't want to become' (p. 5). This choice with regard to identity seems unavailable to Jasmine's Burmese contemporary whose grandmother's broken body becomes a precursor of an almost obligatory fate. Indeed, following the deaths of her half brother, Shan, and her revolutionary father, Law-Yone's narrator uncovers 'an identity I had never known . . . No one could deter me from the battle I was doing with myself, from my games of suicide . . . imagining my head blown apart and spattering the walls' (pp. 154–7).

Moreover, British colonialisms also provide a context for understanding Mukherjee's and Law-Yone's narrators' comments about broken and split identities. Both girls receive a colonial education that privileges the King's English, as well as imperial texts, over other Englishes, languages and literatures. In 'Immigrant Writing: Give Us Your Maximalists!' (1988), Mukherjee describes how colonization 'forced us to see ourselves as both the "we" and the "other"'. Of this split, she says in an interview,

> I had to . . . exercise sympathy for both the 'we', the British, who were doing the trashing and the natives, and identify with the natives who were being trashed and that I think destroyed the majority of people in my generation . . . that they saw themselves as broken in two.[41]

Significantly, neither narrator seems a particularly adept colonized subject. Indeed, Jasmine abandoned *Great Expectations* and *Jane Eyre* on account of their difficulty, while her Burmese contemporary recalls how a 'lapse into pidgin was punishable by one hundred corrective lines in the King's English' (p. 41; p. 9).

The experience of living between cultures is further reinforced by postwar partitions and divisions. In 1947, the Partition forced Jasmine's family to leave Lahore, to the detriment of her father in particular who is described as living in 'a bunker' (p. 42). His bunker lifestyle is explained by his privileging of an idealized Lahori past, which sets an impossible standard for his present impoverished circumstances in Hasnapur, India. From this village, he listened to Pakistani radio broadcasts from Lahore. 'Otherwise,' Jasmine continues:

> he detested Urdu and Muslims, which he naturally associated with the loss of our fortune. He refused to speak Hindi as well, considering it the language of Gandhi, the man who had approved the partition of Punjab and the slaughter of millions . . . He said the Punjabi you heard a beggar mutter by the trash

pits of Lahore was poetry compared to the crow-talk Punjabi
of the richest merchants in . . . Hasnapur.

(p. 42)

Postcoloniality also disrupts family life in *The Coffin Tree*,
although the narrator's father is more directly involved in radical
insurrections against the British colonial system in the 1930s and the
1940s. As a founder and general in the People's Army, he fought for
'Independence for the Hill States, Freedom from Oppression,
Liberation from the Tyranny of the Central Government' (p. 39).
Following the 1962 military *coup* by the new dictatorial government,
the narrator's father is forced underground. At this time, 'oppression became the only reality' and he sends his two children away
'because war and bloodshed were in the wind, and he wanted us
safely in America . . . "You'll be free in America"' (pp. 33, 43).

Along with (de)colonization, immigration contributes further to
the splitting of the narrators' and other characters' identities in
both *Jasmine* and *The Coffin Tree*. The narrators in both novels
describe their journeys from Burma and India respectively as
falling out of a 'groove' or into a 'loop' (p. 44; p. 102). They also
compare migration to other worldly experiences. In Jasmine's
words: 'a shadow world of aircraft permanently aloft that share air
lanes and radio frequencies with Pan Am and British Air and Air-
India, portaging people who coexist with tourists and businessmen.
But we are refugees and mercenaries and guest workers' (p. 100). If
fortunate enough to land at their chosen destination, for example,
New York (in *The Coffin Tree*), refugees typically find their
'footing . . . nearly as awkward as the astronauts' first steps in the
atmosphere of the moon' (p. 44). Less fortunate than Law-Yone's
refugees, Jasmine and her adopted Vietnamese stepson, Du Thien,
journey separately by boat to the USA. Both Jasmine and Du recall
clothes left for them by 'nigger-shipping' white men. These clothes
lay 'flat on the beach, as though the people inside had been zapped
by aliens' (pp. 111, 107). Whether from India, Vietnam or Burma,
immigration is described as a self-alienating experience.

Mukherjee's and Law-Yone's protagonists respond to this self-
alienation in different ways and, in so doing, contribute to an understanding of Americanness that complicates its presumed association

with freedom. Critics attuned to American Orientalism highlight the ways in which the East is stereotyped in *Jasmine* as backward and determined by 'ancient prescriptions' for both genders, for men, 'silence, order, authority' and, for women, 'submission, beauty, innocence' (p. 151). In *The Coffin Tree*, the narrator also describes her parents in terms compatible with this gendered binary opposition. Her father is God-like in his 'unanswerable' power and her mother is almost as 'perfect' in her beauty and death (pp. 28, 14). Thus represented, these third-world women in particular function as 'a foil to construct the free and independent "American woman".' This neocolonial opposition, Inderpal Grewal continues, makes India (and other Asian countries) 'a uniformly oppressive place for women. In contrast, the US becomes the land of hope, freedom, and independence for women.'42 *The Coffin Tree* and *Jasmine* reinforce this version of immigration and Americanization when their characters assume that they will be free in the USA. As Jasmine puts it: 'We could say or be anything we wanted. We'd be on the other side of the earth' (p. 85).

However, this movement from oppression to freedom is problematized, even in Mukherjee's more overtly pro-American novel, most obviously when Jasmine is violently raped within a few hours of her arrival. On this same night, she also murders her rapist, becoming, as she claims, Kali or 'Death incarnate' (p. 119). Similarly, Shan is raped in the USA, although his sister is not fully convinced of this. Brother and sister move from one temporary address to another, from cheap hotels occupied by drug addicts, prostitutes and pimps, to the basement of one of their father's political contacts for whom they work as caretakers to his children and pets. From New York the siblings move to South Carolina and Florida looking for work, temporally separating to Shan's detriment. His 'breach with reality' and his 'necessary lies – his need to paint the world in colors grim enough to justify his own crumbling will', 'his nostalgia for a past that never was', and 'his mistrust of strangers' – last for two years, until his death. In short, Shan is 'unanchored' by immigration and diaspora (pp. 72, 77, 74). After his death, his sister attempts suicide and is subsequently institutionalized.

Also working as a mobile caretaker, first to yuppie New York couple, Taylor and Wylie Hayes and their adopted daughter, Duff, and then to small-town banker and Iowan landowner Bud Ripplemeyer, Jasmine, unlike Shan, seems to thrive on the fact that the immigrant experience is unanchored. She 'shuttle[s] between identities' and names, from '*sati*-goddess' to 'Jasmine the reliable caregiver' and 'Jase the prowling adventurer. I thrilled to the tug of opposing forces', unless, presumably, these forces are so violent that they bring about disintegration and death (pp. 77, 176–7). As a figure for identity, the dead dog, like a number of other key figures and events in *Jasmine* (including, for example, the broken clay pitcher, the Partition Riots, bomb- and bullet-blasted bodies and the American farmer's body halved by carnivorous hogs), promotes a reading that Jasmine's affirmation of shuttling seems to deny. Although Mukherjee proclaims a liking for female characters in Jasmine's mould, the go-getters, or, as a manager in *The Coffin Tree* characterizes them, the 'iron butterfl[ies]' (p. 56), Jasmine's self-empowerment occurs at the expense of others.

At the end of the novel, Jasmine represents bicultural identity as a matter of choice, of wants fairly easily pursued. She is 'greedy with wants and reckless from hope', and, like 'a tornado, a rubble-maker, arising from nowhere and disappearing into a cloud', destroys her former identities in the process (p. 241). Jasmine-as-tornado also destroys others in a way that is directly criticized by one of her victims, Bud's ex-wife. 'I never got to travel', Karin says,

> Not like you. You travel around the world, swoop down in a small town and take the best man for yourself and don't even think of the pain you've left behind . . . You're leaving a path of destruction behind you.
>
> (pp. 204–5)

Various white American women experience Jasmine's destruction, but, as she notes of Karin, the changes, once so devastating, are eventually accepted. After all, in the USA, 'nothing lasts . . . Nothing is forever, nothing is so terrible, or so wonderful, that it won't disintegrate' (p. 181).

However, the terrible experiences of nonwhite women and men are a different matter. They prove particularly resistant to 'transformation, the fluidity of American character' since their racial difference is less easily domesticated and exoticized, and their poverty is less easily aestheticized (p. 138). Of this difference, Jasmine is often contemptuous, as when, for example, she describes Sikhs as terrorists and Chinese as naturally cruel in keeping with the yellow-peril stereotype. She also describes New York as 'an archipelago of ghettos seething with aliens' (p. 140). In particular, the Indian ghetto in Flushing leaves her feeling 'immured' by its 'artificially maintained Indianness', which seems, at least to Jasmine, unaffected by Americanness. Of Flushing, she proclaims: 'I'm dying in this limbo!' (pp. 145, 148–9). Significantly, this self-maintained limbo is not contextualized with reference to the way in which the USA contributes to the ghettoization of nonwhite groups.

Without this historical context, and, as number of Mukherjee's critics have noted, without history *per se*, Jasmine achieves her individuality in a manner that is consistent with the nationalized project of becoming American. But, then again, Jasmine is identified as 'special' (p. 72). In particular, her sexual allure becomes something of transcendent force in that it enables her to escape the psychological, physical and cultural limbo experienced by her immigrant peers. Crucial to Jasmine's iron butterfly persona are beauty and sexuality, as mainly defined by men. For this reason, David Leiwei Li claims, 'Jasmine's reincarnations through romance have not meant fundamental changes of her self but a recycling of her roles as caregiver, homemaker, and temptress in the process of patriarchal recuperation and nationalistic incorporation.'[43] She thus adheres to the acceptable stereotype of the immigrant, right down to those all-important 'give-away' shoes or 'Third World heels' that she quickly abandons for American running shoes (p. 132). Although more than likely also manufactured in the Third World, these shoes effectively function to differentiate Jasmine from ' "them," the knife-wielding undocumenteds hiding in basements webbing furniture' (p. 33).

Forced to join their numbers for financial and racial reasons, *The Coffin Tree*'s narrator similarly criticizes 'them.' Like Jasmine, she is given away by her shoes and clothes. For example, the female boss of an employment agency proclaims: 'Those shoes! You shouldn't be seen dead in them, much less go to an interview wearing them. They'd fire you before they hired you. . . . Here, take those off and wear mine.' These borrowed shoes only bring excruciating pain, not success at a job interview. She returns to her basement accommodation 'like a geisha in haste' (pp. 64–6). These American shoes do nothing to enhance her social mobility. If anything, they make her more Third World, as do the newly purchased giveaway outfits sister and brother wear for dinner at another of their father's political contacts. On arriving at Morrison's Park Avenue address, the narrator describes their 'bumbling stabs at presentability': 'Shan in his shiny suit that drooped at the shoulders, I in my lime green dress with shoes to match – a pair of bumpkins singing a song of our country' (pp. 46–7).

Their last meeting with Morrison was five years earlier, and it is made apparent to them now that he 'no longer wished to dabble in [Burmese] politics'. Instead, Morrison and his wife dabble with other countries in a supposedly more acceptable way through the consumption of foreign goods, including the Persian rugs that carpet their house and the fresh salmon flown in from Alaska that their Japanese butler was meant to serve at their dinner table. While Morrison is uncomfortable in the presence of the siblings, Mrs Morrison simply ignores them, her dismissive attitude being reinforced a day later in a telephone conversation. On inquiring about the money her father had sent to Morrison, the narrator is told or, more accurately, patronized by Mrs Morrison in 'the Voice of America' and the 'voice of . . . a nanny' that the couple have had 'no contact, financial or otherwise' with Burma. Presumably, poor, yet proud, refugees from Burma are not as liable to easy domestication or aestheticization as, say, a carpet, a fish and a servant (pp. 47–8). Indeed, the siblings' poverty resists aestheticization; it is instead contextualized via detailed references to poor housing, jobs and health.

Although not quite as much the iron butterfly as Jasmine, Law-Yone's narrator does, nevertheless, start to view her brother with contempt. She cringes at Shan's social interactions, also noting, when their lives take different turns how he 'never looked more like a refugee' (p. 72). While her new life has gradually improved, 'his new life – stripped of his dreams, his beliefs, his supports – was a blank.' As Shan's mental and physical health deteriorates, his sister becomes increasingly critical. She grudges, reproaches and mocks him for his lethargy and cowardice. His body is the main focus of her revulsion: 'I noted the discharge at the corners of his eyes, the untended hair, the greasy skin, the slackness of his body with its metallic smell – and felt disgust that all my powers of charity could not contain' (pp. 76, 79).

Both *Jasmine* and *The Coffin Tree* participate in immigrant bashing by characters that are themselves immigrants, suggesting that they, along with their American-born contemporaries, achieve self-empowerment at the expense of others. This similarity aside, the narrators respond to their immigrant bashing differently. In many respects, Law-Yone's narrator exhibits the legitimate, guilty response, even attempting suicide. She is subsequently institutionalized and rehabilitated, eventually remembering her brother apart from the immigrant stereotype of 'a creature degraded into an existence of cunning and shallow wants, like that of a crow, with one eye on the lookout for danger, the other on the prowl for shiny things' (p. 191). After reading Shan's book on the coffin tree legend about a spirit guide who will *'lead you/ To the home you choose'* in both life and death (p. 190), a book she heretofore considered 'a piece of chicanery, a fake map leading to a bogus treasure', the narrator realizes that her contempt and pity for her brother are misplaced: 'I had pitied Shan for being a cripple, but on his own he had found a crutch' in the legend 'while I, once able-bodied but now disabled, had nothing as yet to lean on' (p. 192). On the last page of the novel after also dreaming about the coffin tree, she finally gets her crutch, although it is not quite the 'dream to lighten the days': *'Living things prefer to go on living'* (pp. 192, 195).

In contrast, Jasmine does not experience shame or guilt, only relief, as she gives up her respectable life as caretaker to her disabled partner, Bud. How she comes to the decision to do this also seems shameless: 'I'm not leaving Bud . . . I have to see Du', albeit by way of her former lover 'Taylor the Rescuer' (pp. 240, 210). Du had previously left for Los Angeles to be with his only surviving relative. 'His eyes are glittery with a higher mission. Abandonment, guilt, betrayal: the boy in front of me would consider them banal dilemmas' (p. 221). Relatively speaking, the abandonment of his adopted parents is trivial:

he has lived through five or six languages, five or six countries, two or three centuries of history; he has seen his country, city, and family butchered, bargained with pirates and bureaucrats, eaten filth in order to stay alive.

(p. 214)

Considering these experiences, Du's Westward movement is understandable, but can the same be said of Jasmine's? She may repeatedly emphasize their similarities – 'We've been many selves. We've survived hideous times' (p. 124) – but this is to ignore their differences, most obviously, that Du is a wartime refugee and Jasmine is an undocumented immigrant who voluntarily travels to the USA for a reason directly opposed to survival, namely self-immolation. By homogenizing their experiences in this way, as well as having Du support her actions, Jasmine appropriates his higher mission in order to legitimate those actions. Here, it seems that whatever she does is acceptable. Given the legitimate and banal alternatives, as both involve some form of self-sacrifice, why should it not be? This question may seem frivolous, even 'Jasminesque', although it is posed here in order to highlight 'deeper and trickier contradictions', or, as Law-Yone's narrator observes, 'a stranger truth' (pp. 191–2). This truth involves acknowledging the way in which context problematizes absolute judgements with respect to real and fake, good and bad, right and wrong. This truth thus exceeds or, perhaps, falls between these binary oppositions much like Law-Yone's image of the coffin tree in the narrator's dream. As it turns out, this particular tree is identified as a juniper tree, although, this said, it is still accorded the revelatory power of the coffin tree. Its in-between status – as both coffin and a juniper tree in a 'dream which was more than a dream' – is reinforced by the fact that the tree falls down between 'two diverging streams' (pp. 194–5).

CONCLUSION

'Between worlds' is understood primarily in terms of the relationship between American-born writers, narrators and characters, and their immigrant counterparts, who experience, as *Jasmine* and *The Coffin Tree* in particular highlight, various traumas before and

after immigration. American-born Asians exacerbate their situation by stereotyping immigrants and by comparing them to
animals and, more often, by describing their physical appearance
as revolting. Immigrant narrators and characters respond to this
white and middle-class gaze in a number of ways. At times, they
appropriate it as do Mukherjee's and Law-Yone's narrators, who
regard other Asian immigrants with contempt, although, at other
times, as in *The Coffin Tree*, the white and middle-class gaze and
the racial self-hatred it generates are directly criticized.

'Between worlds' also applies to an understanding of ideology that
renders critique altogether more problematic. Many of the texts in
this chapter are by commercially successful writers, most obviously
Kingston, Tan and Mukherjee. Indeed, Mukherjee's immigrant
adventure novel is assumed to promote the assimilationist notion of
'America-the-good as white America' that *The Coffin Tree* and, more
generally, *Obasan* undermine.[44] As different as these literary texts are,
ideologically, thematically and formally, all seem to end happily, if not
with a wedding and proclamations of (Christian) love, then with a
death. In the case of Mukherjee's and Law-Yone's novels, rebirth
occurs more or less consistent with non-Western spiritual beliefs. In
The Joy Luck Club, this rebirth takes the form of the werewolf myth
and 'a mutant tag of DNA suddenly triggered, replicating itself insid-
iously into a *syndrome*, a cluster of telltale Chinese behaviors' (p. 267).

Such narrative closure suggests ideological closure, which, for
some Asian American critics, helps to explain why these writers have
achieved success in the literary marketplace. Closer analysis of these
texts, however, particularly their endings, highlights a discrepancy
between the words of the characters and their narrative contexts.
The characters may articulate desire for closure, as do certain
readers, but the narratives resist this desire. Like the coffin tree
legend, the narratives resemble 'a piece of chicanery, a fake map
leading to a bogus treasure' (p. 192). Other pieces of chicanery in *The
Coffin Tree* include a fake book and a fake tree. There is also a fake
book and a fake wedding in *Tripmaster Monkey*, and fake (wo)men in
M. Butterfly. These fake constructions do not make the experiences
described in these texts any less real – far from it since they, as Law-
Yone's narrator observes, help to ensure a future for their characters:
'some story to tell myself, some illusion to shape the future, some

dream to lighten the days' (p. 192). Whether these stories enable survival or not, they do nevertheless make possible other ways of being Asian American beyond absolute proclamations regarding real and fake, good and bad, right and wrong. They also make possible other ways of criticizing dominant ideologies that are responsive to the violence they perpetuate and to their complexities and contradictions.

SUMMARY OF KEY POINTS

- The 1965 Immigration Act and the Vietnam War meant that by the 1980s the Asian American population was predominantly immigrant.
- The model-minority stereotype circulated throughout American culture. Some Asian Americans achieved success, although others – for example, many post-1965 immigrants – struggled with poverty and violence. This struggle was exacerbated by immigrant bashing in a right-wing political climate.
- In the 1980s, the interracial and intergenerational romance proved commercially successful. Women's success with this traditional genre signalled to some critics their complicity with dominant American ideologies. For other critics, however, the possibility of transcending these ideologies through religious, sexual or familial love expressed the desire of the characters in a narrative context that problematized this desire.
- This desire for transcendence featured in immigrant narratives. Immigrant characters typically romanticized immigration and diaspora, as a movement from oppression to freedom, although their difficulties in the USA problematized this ideological understanding of immigration.

NOTES

1. Rubén G. Rumbaut, 'Vietnamese, Laotian, and Cambodian Americans', *Contemporary Asian America: A Multidisciplinary Reader*, ed. Min Zhou and James V. Gatewood (New York: New York University Press, 2000), pp. 193–5.

2. Elaine H. Kim, 'Beyond Railroads and Internment: Comments on the Past, Present, and Future of Asian American Studies', in *Privileging Positions: The Sites of Asian American Studies*, ed. Gary Y. Okihiro, Marilyn Alquizola, Dorothy Fujita Rony and K. Scott Wong (Pullman: Washington State University Press, 1995), pp. 12–13.

3. Viet Thanh Nguyen, *Race and Resistance: Literature and Politics in Asian America* (Oxford: Oxford University Press, 2002), p. 9.

4. Michael Omi and Howard Winant, *Racial Formation in the United States, from the 1960s to the 1990s* (New York: Routledge, 1994), pp. 143–4.

5. Steven Okazaki, quoted in Nguyen, *Race*, p. 167.

6. Sheng-mei Ma, *Immigrant Subjectivities in Asian American and Asian Diaspora Literatures* (New York: State University of New Press, 1998), p. 29.

7. Wendy Law-Yone, *The Coffin Tree* (London: Penguin, 1983), p. 45. Hereafter references to this edition are given in the text.

8. *Fortune* and *New Republic*, quoted in Ronald Takaki, *Strangers from a Different Shore: A History of Asian Americans* (Boston: Back Bay Books, 1998), p. 474.

9. Don T. Nakanishi, 'Surviving Democracy's "Mistake": Japanese Americans and the Enduring Legacy of Executive Order 9066', *Amerasia Journal* 19:1 (1993), 11, 13, 17.

10. Joy Kogawa, *Obasan* (New York: Anchor Books, [1981] 1994), p. 40. Hereafter references to this edition are given in the text.

11. Cheng Lok Chua, 'Witnessing the Japanese Canadian Experience in World War II: Processual Structure, Symbolism, and Irony in Joy Kogawa's *Obasan*', *Reading the Literatures of Asian America*, ed. Shirley Geok-lin Lim and Amy Ling (Philadelphia: Temple University Press, 1992), p. 104.

12. Linda Hutcheon, quoted in King-kok Cheung, *Articulate Silences: Hisaye Yamamoto, Maxine Hong Kingston, Joy Kogawa* (Ithaca, NY: Cornell University Press, 1993), p. 127.

13. Joy Kogawa and Ruth Y. Hsu, 'A Conversation with Joy Kogawa', *Amerasia Journal* 22:1 (Spring 1996), 205.

14. Cheung, *Articulate*, p. 128.

15. Scott McFarlane, 'Covering *Obasan* and the Narrative of Internment', Okihiro et al. (eds), *Privileging Positions*, pp. 407–8.

16. Ibid., p. 410. While the exclusion of stranded and deported Japanese Canadians from the redress settlement was the case in 1993 and, presumably, at the time of this essay's publication in 1995, some, but not all Japanese Canadians still in Japan who applied for the redress payment, received it. See for example, Tatsuo Kage 'Japanese Canadians Exiled to Japan' (21 September 2004), www.najc.ca/pdf/japancdnexiled.pdf [Accessed September 2007].

17. Kogawa and Hsu, 'Conversation', 211–12.

18. Deborah N. Misir, 'The Murder of Navroze Mody: Race, Violence, and the Search for Order', Zhou and Gatewood (eds), *Contemporary Asian America*, p. 504, pp. 506–7; Takaki, *Strangers*, pp. 481–4.

19. Ma, *Immigrant*, p. 25, p. 29.

20. Jersey citizen, quoted in Misir, 'Mody', p. 506.

21. Hwang, quoted in Ma, *Immigrant*, p. 27.

22. Ma, *Immigrant*, pp. 29–30.

23. Maxine Hong Kingston, *Tripmaster Monkey: His Fake Book* (New York: Vintage Books, 1989), pp. 3–5. Hereafter references to this edition are given in the text.

24. David Leiwei Li, *Imagining the Nation: Asian American Literature and Cultural Consent* (Stanford: Stanford University Press, 1998), p. 88.

25. David Henry Hwang, *M. Butterfly* (New York: Plume, [1988] 1989), p. 17. Hereafter references to this edition, including Hwang's Afterword, are given in the text.

26. Douglas Kerr 'David Henry Hwang and the Revenge of *Madame Butterfly*', *Asian Voices in English*, ed. Mimi Chan and Roy Harris (Hong Kong: Hong Kong University Press, 1991), p. 128.

27. Ibid., p. 130.

28. Andrew Shin, 'Projected Bodies in David Henry Hwang's *M. Butterfly* and *Golden Gate*', *MELUS* 27:1 (Spring 2002), 182, 187.

29. Sheng-mei Ma, 'Postcolonial Feminizing of America in Carlos Bulosan', *Ideas of Home: Literature of Asian Migration*, ed. Geoffrey Kain (East Lansing: Michigan State University Press, 1997), p. 129.

30. Gary Pak, quoted in Navtej Sarna, 'From the Far Corners: Review of Rajini Srikanth and Esther Y. Iwanaga's *Bold Words: A Century of Asian American Writing*', *TLS* (22 March 2002), 22.

31. Frank Chin, 'This is Not an Autobiography', *Genre* 18 (Summer 1985), 124.

32. Li, *Imagining*, p. 117.

33. Sau-ling Cynthia Wong, '"Sugar Sisterhood": Situating the Amy Tan Phenomenon', *The Ethnic Canon: Histories, Institutions, and Interventions*, ed. David Palumbo-Liu (Minneapolis: University of Minnesota Press, 1995), p. 191.

34. Amy Tan, *The Joy Luck Club* (London: Minerva, 1989), p. 17. Hereafter references to this edition are given in the text.

35. Li, *Imagining*, p. 112.

36. Wendy Ho, 'Swan-Feather Mothers and Coca-Cola Daughters: Teaching Amy Tan's *The Joy Luck Club*', *Teaching American Ethnic Literatures: Nineteen Essays*, ed. John R. Maitino and David R. Peck (Albuquerque: University of New Mexico Press, 1996), p. 331.

37. Li, *Imagining*, p. 115.

38. Wong, 'Sugar', p. 194.

39. Mukherjee, quoted in Anne Brewster, 'A Critique of Bharati Mukherjee's Neo-Nationalism', *SPAN* 34–5 (November 1992 and May 1993), 58.

40. Bharati Mukherjee, *Jasmine* (London: Virago, 1989), p. 118. Hereafter references to this edition are given in the text.

41. Bharati Mukherjee, 'Immigrant Writing: Give Us Your Maximalists!' *New York Times* (28 August 1988), 29; Runa Vignisson, 'Bharati Mukherjee: An Interview', in *SPAN* 34–5 (November 1992 and May 1993), 164–5.

42. Inderpal Grewal, 'The Postcolonial, Ethnic Studies, and the Diaspora: The Contexts of Ethnic Immigrant/Migrant Cultural Studies in the US', *Socialist Review* 24:4 (1994), 59.

43. Li, *Imagining*, p. 101.

44. Arnold Harrichand Itwaru, quoted in Grewal, 'Postcolonial', 59–60.

CHAPTER 5

Heterogeneity, Hybridity and Multiplicity, the 1990s

CONTEXTS AND INTERTEXTS

Writing at the beginning of the decade, in her highly influential essay 'Heterogeneity, Hybridity, Multiplicity: Marking Asian American Differences' (1991), Lisa Lowe reconfigured the debate so crucial to the development of Asian American literary studies between androcentric writers, specifically *The Big Aiiieeeee!* group comprising Jeffery Paul Chan, Frank Chin, Lawson Fusao Inada and Shawn Wong, and feminist writers like Maxine Hong Kingston, Amy Tan, Shirley Geok-lin Lim and Amy Ling. In her essay, Lowe is alert to the achievements of Asian American identity politics, particularly with regard to the way in which it enabled and continues to enable contestation and disruption of dominant American ideologies. The debate, however, has moved on. As Lowe says, 'we can afford to rethink the notion of ethnic identity in terms of cultural, class, and gender differences, rather than presuming similarities and making the erasure of particularity the basis of unity.' More than this, 'we can diversify our political practices to include a more heterogeneous group and to enable crucial alliances with other groups – ethnicity-based, class-based, gender-based, and sexuality-based – in the ongoing work of transforming hegemony.'[1]

What was it about the 1990s that made the acknowledgement of heterogeneity affordable as never before? According to Lowe, this decade was characterized by freedom, if contemporary Asian American experiences are understood historically and interracially. About this latter comparison, David Palumbo-Liu observes: 'it would be difficult to argue that Asian Americans . . . are "disadvantaged" in the same sense that blacks, Latinos/as, and indigenous peoples are still the objects of a virulent strain of American racism.'[2] The impact of Asian American identity politics, alongside other minority movements, and American economic interests in Asia go some way towards explaining why the point had been reached when marking Asian American differences had become a realistic option for advancement.

This developmental and homogenizing narrative, while it may well be relevant to some Asian Americans, assumes that class mobility makes possible the transcendence of differences and dominant hierarchies. This assumption is consistent with neoconservatism and, in the 1990s, neoliberalism, which, despite their apparent differences, ultimately share a similar agenda in terms of the determination to downplay the issue of race. With the emergence of racial minority states, including California, the site of the Rodney King beating and the Los Angeles urban uprising of 1992, the erasure of race and racism proves difficult, if not impossible. Perhaps it is better instead to manage a racially diverse USA by 'creating a normative, "productive", and well-contained pluralism', otherwise known as the 'multicultural phenomenon'?[3]

Beginning in the late 1980s, and continuing into the 1990s and 2000s, the debate about multiculturalism typically turns on a crucial question:

> Is multiculturalism a genuine attempt to move toward greater interethnic tolerance – toward a more equitable society in which different groups are awarded equal recognition – or is it a smokescreen that hides the continuing privilege of the dominant culture, and that defuses the ethnic tensions that threaten to divide the nation?[4]

Even more crucial than this either/or question is the fact that genuine multiculturalism is invariably implicated in the smokescreen version of multiculturalism that commodifies racial difference to the politico-economic advantage of dominant groups.

From this booming 'alterity industry' emerge 'celebrity minority' writers, often coming, so it seems, in threes.[5] For example: in theory, Bhabha, Said and Spivak, and in literature, Rushdie, Naipaul and Kureishi or Kingston, Mukherjee and Tan. As this final trio suggests, Asian American literature is part of this booming industry, of which the 1990s is typically identified as its most explosive period. It was explosive in terms of the number and the diversity of literary texts produced, as well as in terms of the emerging critical and theoretical paradigms within which these texts and earlier texts were read. As well as booming, Asian American literature in the 1990s engaged in 'bold explorations of gender and sexuality' in keeping with queer discourses.[6] These discourses understood queer Asian America not only in terms of sexuality (lesbian, gay, bisexual and transgendered Asian Americans) but also in terms of race and nation (biracial, diasporic and transnational Asian Americans). Moreover, these discourses were queer in their increased emphasis on poststructuralist and deconstructive theorizing. In short, 'queer', as David L. Eng and Alice Y. Hom propose in *Q & A: Queer in Asian America* (1998), refers to 'a political practice based on transgressions of the normal and normativity' as determined by white patriarchy.[7]

Much of the literature discussed in this chapter is queer in these various ways, although, this said, it is important to note that it does not simply represent the 1990s as liberated from a monocultural past. Possibilities are discussed, but so are difficulties, notably difficulties related to the issue of representation with respect to national and international violence. This violence impacts on the larger constituency of Asian Americans by rendering them abnormal. As Eng and Hom explain: 'this is a "queer" formation that traces its historical roots backward to shifting . . . legal definitions of the U.S. nation-state and the imagined formations of its citizenry' and humanity.[8]

Nationality and humanity or, more precisely, their disavowal with respect to Asians and Asian Americans, are most explicitly at issue during wartime, from the Spanish-American War (1898) to the atomic bombing of Japan (1945) and the Vietnam War (1959–75).

With the end of the Cold War in 1989, which was interpreted by right-wing American theorists and politicians as signalling the end of history (Francis Fukuyama) and a new world order (George H. W. Bush), it seems that in the dominant national psyche something else needed to take the place of communism 'in defining an essential ideological threat to the United States'. In the 1990s, the ideological threat was linked in some way to Asia: from East Asian capitalism or the 'Bamboo Network' to illegal Asian immigrants.[9]

When analyzing violence and warfare, as re-presented in Asian American and other multicultural literatures, the issue of referentiality proves crucial. Referentiality typically assumes a straightforward relationship between signifier and signified, as well as between sign and referent. Structuralism highlights the arbitrary nature of these relationships, with poststructuralism also unmasking their ideological and rhetorical workings. Although these theories radically problematize referentiality, it still persists, particularly in multicultural criticism and multicultural literature. Its persistence is discernible in smokescreen multicultural criticism, which presumes that multicultural literature is unproblematically, even naively, referential or mimetic. Its persistence is also discernible, and more complicatedly so, in multicultural literature, specifically, for example, in Cambodian and Vietnamese American autobiographies about the Vietnam War and its aftermath. Despite the difference between these 'refugee literatures', both are underpinned by an imperative to bear witness to violent experiences, including holocaust experiences.[10]

REFUGEE LITERATURES

In the context of holocaust, the ability to reference an historical event, argues Teri Shaffer Yamada in her analysis of Cambodian American autobiography, assumes 'more importance than it would in a non-Cambodian autobiography'. Historical accuracy is so important because autobiographical texts like Dith Pran's *Children of Cambodia's Killing Fields* (1997), Sophal Leng Stagg's *Hear Me Now* (1996) and Chanrithy Him's *When Broken Glass Floats* (2000) are used 'symbolically or ideologically, as depositional discourse' in the continuing human rights debate about the Pol Pot era (1975–9). In this era and later, Cambodians were victimized in both Cambodia and the USA. First, they were classified as enemies of the USA and the US-backed Pol Pot regime, and as such they were bombed and murdered. Second, they were classified as refugees and so were vulnerable to US social services. According to Yamada, Cambodian American autobiographies perform the 'movement from victim to plaintiff – an action signified by the rupture of an imposed silence.' This rupture allows for the emergence of truthfulness, a legally testifiable truthfulness in UN war crimes trials that is also important for self-rehabilitation.[11]

Self-rehabilitation via the autobiographical act is a complex process that involves talking about suffering experienced in both Cambodia and the USA in a way audible to the West. It also involves developing a 'hybrid identity' that balances Americanness and Cambodianness, political activism and personal expression, typically by way of reference to Cambodia before and during the Khmer Rouge regime.[12] For instance, Chanrithy Him demonstrates this hybrid identity through her political and literary writing. In a 2004 letter to US Congressman and Chair of the House International Relations Committee, Henry J. Hyde, Him expressed her concern about the lack of governmental support for the Resolution in support of Cambodian war crimes trials. In addition to insisting that it was his legal and moral responsibility not to hinder these trials, she writes,

> Like many survivors, I am a living symbol of suffering of innocent war victims. As a woman and a U.S. citizen, I spent painful years writing my autobiography, *When Broken Glass Floats* . . . [and] as a child survivor and a citizen of this world, I oblige myself . . . to make a difference.[13]

Although Him's letter went unanswered, it is still possible, despite this official blindsiding, for innocent war victims to be heard.

Japanese American poet Kimiko Hahn discusses this possibility in her 1997 poem, 'Blindsided'. This poem partly comprises quotations from a magazine interview with Cambodian refugees. 'Or perhaps a relative told their story to the doctor who told the interviewer.'[14] One refugee story is about how 'The Khmer Rouge took Chhean Im's brother and sister away. They killed/her father and another brother *before her eyes*' (p. 83). In addition to this interview, Hahn's speaker includes other non-fictional material to explain why so many women refugees subsequently experience 'vision / problems' even though 'there / is nothing physically wrong with their eyes' (p. 83). Apparently, *'conversion disorder'* and *'disassociation'* explain these instances of *'hysterical blindness'* (pp. 85, 87). However, Hahn's speaker challenges the interviewer's psychosomatic explanation: 'To view phenomena in more than polarities. Blind but not blind.' And, later, 'If a person cannot see, what do they *see?*' (pp. 86, 88). Hahn's speaker suggests that polarities conceal, as they claim to reveal, the complexity of 'the incidents of women turning . . . *mad'* (p. 83). However, these polarities do more than contribute to this madness, not least when gendered and racialized binary oppositions – 'virgins' versus 'damaged goods' and them versus us – generate and legitimate violence against others (pp. 85–6). For these reasons, then, it is madness to presume that Asian American women's wartime experiences can be articulated in polarities.

Hahn's speaker does not relinquish the possibility of these women being heard. Repeated five times at different points in the poem, 'Are you listening?' is asked of a mother and others. These listeners seem not to hear what the speaker is saying, until the poem's last three lines: ' "Are you, are you – " // When the interview is complete she turns toward the draft whistling in / beneath the door' (p. 88). Although the word listening remains unspoken and the question unfinished, the fact that 'Are you listening?' has been repeated so many times in the poem helps to ensure that Hahn's reader hears it here. In so doing, the reader offers a response to the woman in the penultimate line, enough for her to complete the interview. The reader has heard but not heard, just like the subaltern women in this poem are 'Blind but not blind' and 'speak but . . . will not speak' (pp. 86–7).

However complicated it is, the move from victim to plaintiff, from silence to speech, is also discernible in Vietnamese American autobiography, most notably Le Ly Hayslip's Vietnam-focused *When Heaven and Earth Changed Places* (1989) and US-focused *Child of War, Woman of Peace* (1993). Like her Cambodian

American counterparts, Hayslip has developed a politically active hybrid identity through campaigning for a medical charity. Oliver Stone's adaptation of Hayslip's autobiographies into the film *Heaven and Earth* (1994) adds to her representativeness regarding the Vietnam War and its aftermath. In short, she is regarded as the 'emblematic victim' of the Vietnamese experience.[15]

While Hayslip has been criticized for self-promotion and her autobiographies for misrepresentation, Viet Than Nguyen argues that her texts are more complex than this since they demonstrate in their historicism and idealism respectively both 'progressive' and 'regressive' ideological tendencies. This ideological conflict is represented in terms of a 'victimized body politic' whereby, as Nguyen highlights, 'the technologically enhanced, masculine body of the foreign and domestic aggressors violates the natural body of the woman as representative of the nation.'[16] The rehabilitation of a prewar and idealized Vietnameseness enables Hayslip, if not 'the Vietnamese voice' *per se* 'to withstand their catastrophic times and avoid the despair . . . because they are equipped with a rural background, rooted in their native soil, armed with a strong belief in their traditional values, or capable of dreaming harsh reality away.'[17]

LAN CAO, *MONKEY BRIDGE* (1997)

This ability or, more accurately, the inability to dream or imagine harsh reality away through a rehabilitating Vietnameseness is the focus of the matrilineal novel *Monkey Bridge* by Lan Cao (1961–). Unlike the Cambodian and Vietnamese American writers described thus far, Cao, more in the manner of Hahn in 'Blindsided', depicts rehabilitation as partial, if not impossible. In this sense, then, '*Monkey Bridge* doesn't forgive, it doesn't heal, and it doesn't nurture.' According to Michele Janette, the 'curative trajectory' is undermined by 'an unsettling gap' with respect to knowledge.[18] The high-rise bamboo constructions or monkey bridges that the Vietnamese villagers use to navigate the canal network analogically represent this gap. Similar to these bridges, this gap leaves Cao's narrators and readers with a feeling of precariousness – in terms of their knowledge about Vietnam's past in particular.

Yet, this precariousness is ideologically significant in the sense that is serves to unsettle dominant American discourses, most notably Orientalism. In, for example, the Hollywood film industry's representations of the Vietnam War, the Vietnamese are often Orientalized. For Cao, a film like *Heaven and Earth* domesticates the war, an opinion shared by *Monkey Bridge*'s main narrator, Mai Nguyen about an earlier film, *The Deer Hunter*.[19] As Mai sees it, the Hollywood film industry perpetuates 'one hallucinatory scene after another, against a disturbing background of incomprehensible grunts which supposedly constituted spoken Vietnamese, the roulettelike spin of a gun as arbitrary and senseless as Vietnam would dictate the life and death of American innocence.'[20] In contrast to these films, Cao's novel individualizes the Vietnamese, specifically Vietnamese refugees. *Monkey Bridge* also resists domesticating the war's violence as it continues to impact on the characters' lives in the USA against dominant American discourses that misrepresent both the war and the diaspora in terms of a movement from freedom to oppression.

While *Monkey Bridge* does seem to be successful with regard to its unsettling of American Orientalist and nationalist ideologies, the characters in *Monkey Bridge* and on monkey bridges where 'one wrong move' is liable to provoke disaster, would seem to invite a more unsettling reading of the gaps brought about by their experiences of the Vietnam War and its aftermath (pp. 25–7). Mai's mother, Thanh, is most unsettled by her past and present, as it is literalized in her disfigured face, body and mind. Her facial scarring happens during the war, while her depression, stroke and suicide come later. Mai describes Thanh as 'a war wound', and yet, she continues, 'mother hadn't seemed any more undone' than the other Little Saigon, Virginia residents (pp. 7, 255). Mai's narrative attempts to account for the historical specificity of Thanh's undoing within a more generalized experience of undoing as it applies to all those 'awkward reminder[s] of a war the whole country was trying to forget' (p. 15). Mai's narrative is enabled by the discovery of notepads and a suicide note that describe the 'untouchable part of my mother's nighttime life' in Vietnam (p. 46).

Thanh's nighttime life differs markedly from what Mai knows of their lives (mis)told to her thus far, particularly regarding two scars: that literal scarring of her mother's face, and, perhaps more crucially, the figurative scarring or 'ravenous expanse with no discernible seams and edges' brought about by her grandfather's disappearance (pp. 3, 10). While a kitchen fire seemingly explains Thanh's facial scarring, which, despite flare-ups, she has learnt to live with, the loss of Baba Quan is apparently another matter. When she was airlifted out of Saigon in April 1975, Thanh left without her father. According to Mai, her 'memory of that day continued to thrash its way through her flesh, and there were times when I thought she would never be consoled' (p. 5).

Following the philosophy of 'Simplify. Simplify. Everything will be alright', Mai assumes that Thanh's consolation will come via a simple telephone call to Baba Quan inviting him to leave the village of Ba Xuyen in the Mekong Delta, where he presumably still tends both the ancestral land and his ancestral spirits (p. 11). Once in the USA, he could assume responsibility for Thanh, and Mai could go away to college 'with the reassurance that she would not be – would not feel – abandoned' (p. 17). Following Mai's curative trajectory, Baba Quan's recovery is meant to aid Thanh's recovery, not least because his identity is as closely tied to Vietnam as his daughter's. Indeed, both carry 'the landscape of the delta in [their] flesh', along with articulating 'loyalty to . . . beginnings' via maintenance of traditional beliefs (pp. 115, 6).

However, Mai does not contact her grandfather since the nearest telephone connection to Vietnam would require crossing the US-Canadian border. This border crossing is impossible for a paranoid 'resident alien' to make given the USA's history of deporting unwanted Asians and Asian Americans, and Vietnam's 'history of defending, not crossing boundaries' (pp. 16, 29). And, anyway, Baba Quan hardly constitutes a cure because he is far removed from the idealized figure that Thanh constructs, unwittingly supported by Mai's adopted uncle, Colonel Michael MacMahon, of a land-loving farmer and twice-honoured hero. In Thanh's words: '*Baba Quan, the man I call Father, is a Vietcong from whom I am still trying to escape*' (p. 227).

More than Thanh's notepads, which focus on matrilineal themes – female chastity, birth, childhood and marriage, alongside an analysis of intergenerational and intercultural relationships – Thanh's suicide note details 'not the gorgeous fictional reimaginings of an improvised life – the life she wished she had – but the real one' (p. 255). This real life, which, owing to Baba Quan's history of '*sin, illegitimacy, and murder . . . sets in motion a* [karmic] *sequence of events*' (p. 229). These events not only include Baba Quan's prostituting his wife to Thanh's biological father, the rich landlord, Uncle Kwan, whom he eventually murders, but also Thanh's napalming while she is unsuccessfully attempting to bury her mother in her ancestral village consistent with Vietnamese tradition. At last, then, Mai knows the real story about her mother's scars, both the physical scar on her face and the psychological scar left by Thanh's father. Together with Thanh's sacrificial suicide, this knowledge apparently makes a '*new beginning*' possible for Mai: '*you will also have a different inheritance, an unburdened past, the seductive powers of an American future*', which she 'could walk right into' (pp. 253–4, 260).

In addition, to informing Mai's philosophy, this move towards health and truth is also a line of thinking promoted by her all-American best friend, Bobbie. And, Bobbie learnt it 'from her father's Alcoholics Anonymous pamphlets', with their 'storehouse of inspirational quotes, battle cries [of] . . . Think Positive' (p. 16). Even though 'Bobbie favored straight lines over detours,' Mai acknowledges that 'in her own way she too knew how to adapt' (p. 14). The differences of their childhood experiences notwithstanding, Bobbie's of an alcoholic father and Mai's of a depressive mother, both characters articulate a desire also shared by other characters in *Monkey Bridge* for '*a new frontier, clean, pristine, ready to be molded and shaped by any pair of skillful and pioneering hands*' (p. 56). As Mai observes of the Little Saigon community,

> It was the Vietnamese version of the American Dream; a new spin . . . to the old immigrant faith in the future. Not only could we become anything we wanted to be in America, we could change what we had once been in Vietnam.
>
> (pp. 40–1)

However, this 'rebirthing of the past' is more easily accomplished by 'a mere foreigner' – for example, Bharati Mukherjee's Jasmine – than by a Vietnamese since the latter's past is, as Mai notes, 'too long . . . to erase. Ours, after all, was an inescapable history that continued to be dissected and remodeled by a slew of commentators and experts' long after the Vietnam War ended (pp. 41–2). Cao's novel conveys this inescapable history through its retrospective narrative, from the 1970s back to the 1960s, if not '*two full generations before*' (p. 227). It articulates this history further via 'an eerie topography of misshapen memories and warped psychological space', which leaves its mark on the characters within the novel, as well as on the novel itself (p. 16). For example, Mai believes her parents' superstitions 'circulate inside my skin' (p. 17). She provides a more graphic example of this inescapable history in her opening sentence about 'the smell of blood, warm and wet' (p. 1), enough to make the novel a kind of wound and, ultimately, a kind of scar.

In her analysis of a scarred maternal body in the film of *The Joy Luck Club* (1993) (a scar resulting from, in this case, a kitchen accident, later being followed by the mother's sacrificial suicide for the daughter), Rey Chow argues that the scar functions as 'a narrative hinge' between histories, generations and, ultimately, 'them and us'. The scar 'allows us to return to the scene of the crime', specifically in *Monkey Bridge* the scene of a murder, a napalm attack and a failed burial; and, it 'links different generations of women together. If the daughter is scarred for life [by napalm], it is because her mother was scarred for life' by the shame of prostitution.[21] Mai, too, is scarred for life, although her scarring is not so much corporal as textual. This textual scarring befits her roles as narrator, 'first fighter' or woman warrior and 'scribe, writing down battlefield memories and dying declarations from those war-wounded who were too weak to write letters' in the Saigon military hospital where she worked as a volunteer in 1968 (pp. 118, 12).

Unlike her grandmother and mother, then, whose bodies are physically imperfect by traditional standards of chastity and beauty respectively, Mai's scar does not appear on her body, woman-warrior style. It instead appears on paper, specifically in the words and the images Mai chooses or, more accurately, that are chosen for her. Indeed, Mai's ever ready battlefield memory rushes against her head with 'violent percussive rage' that cannot be consciously controlled, even when she is awake. For instance, Thanh's hospitalization for a stroke and, presumably, her disfigured red face lead Mai 'back there again' (p. 1):

I knew I was not in Saigon. I was not a hospital volunteer. It was not 1968 but 1978. Yet I also knew . . . what I would see next. His face, not the face before the explosion, but the face after, motionless in a liquefied red that poured from a tangle of delicate veins.

(p. 2)

Although these faces are in different places – Thanh's in a US hospital, surrounded by green vegetation and a concrete car park that resembles the military hospital and militarized strategic hamlets in Vietnam – they are linked together in such a way so as to exceed Mai's conscious narrative control. More than it is with wounded faces and concrete lots, *Monkey Bridge* is overrun by images of whiteness, including 'anxious white' in the first chapter and 'funeral white' in the last chapter: 'everywhere a vast uninterrupted expanse of white as stark and endless as the white of a hospital hall' (pp. 1, 257).

Whether scars are corporeal or textual, they invariably function ambiguously in *Monkey Bridge* and elsewhere. Of the scar in multicultural texts, Chow asserts that 'it is a mark of the historical discrimination against peoples of color, a sign of the damage they have borne alongside their continual survival.'[22] Thanh says as much about the discriminating gaze she accords to Mai: '*She looks at her mother's face and sees scars, takes it for a sign for damage, not a badge of survival. Tender flesh the color of pearls makes her cringe*' (pp. 53–4). Here, Thanh recuperates the scar, although her aestheticization of it as a pearl-coloured badge does make it vulnerable to recuperation by dominant groups. Yet, as Chow observes, 'the scar is, as well, the mark of a representational ambivalence and inexhaustibility.' *Monkey Bridge* conveys this ambivalence in different yet related ways through images of ubiquitous whiteness, as old wounds heal to form pearly scars, the skin here taking 'on a new life'.[23] This new life is not equivalent to 'a brand-new slate' (p. 257) because in Chow's words 'the scar signifies . . . a series, a relation, a mark-made-on-the-other.'[24] Here, then, scars link generations and histories in inescapable ways, a point reinforced by Thanh's '*legacy*' to Mai about '*the worthwhile enterprise of learning to live with our scars*' (pp. 253, 53). Such an enterprise works against a curative trajectory towards absolute health and truth, although, like the past, these ideals prove inescapable. At the end of the novel, Mai is seen contemplating her new life at college, a place that the brochure describes as committed to ideals of openness, opportunity and excellence. It is a place of enlightenment, as is further suggested by the glossiness of the brochure and the emphasis on light – desk lamp, flashlight and the acceptance letter that 'whispered a starlight of reassurance'. 'I could walk right into it', this brand new future, Mai says, but in a way that also demonstrates she is learning to live with her scars as she notices, not the bloody wound that began the novel, but a night-time sky, only faintly marked (or scarred) by a 'sliver of what only two weeks ago had been a full moon [that] dangled like a sea horse from the sky' (p. 260).

SKY LEE, *DISAPPEARING MOON CAFÉ* (1990)

While Mai's narrative mainly spans a fifteen-year period from the late 1960s to the early 1980s, the historical span of *Disappearing Moon Café* by Sky Lee (1952–) is much longer. Lee's narrative shifts backwards and forwards between and within chapters and covers the period 1892 to 1987. The differences between Vietnamese American and Chinese Canadian histories notwithstanding, *Monkey Bridge* and *Disappearing Moon Café* are both stories 'full of holes'.[25] Two daughters, Mai and Kae Ying Woo respectively, attempt to fill these holes by waiting 'for enlightenment' from their mothers, Thanh and Bea(trice) Li Ying Wong, about secrets relating to troubled family histories (p. 20). While Thanh's history emerges in writing, Bea's history emerges in speech, as reported by her daughter: ' "You don't know, A Kae," whispers my mother, "but there has been much trouble in our family. It's best that what I tell you does not go beyond these four walls" ', the literal walls of the hospital where Kae recently gave birth, and the figurative walls of the 'boxed in . . . past – mine and my mother's, the four walls that we share!' (p. 23). As with Cao's novel and, perhaps more obviously, Kingston's *The Woman Warrior*, secrecy is pursued or requested by a mother. As is also the case in Lee's novel, these family histories are all open secrets, which Kae demonstrates in a highly self-conscious way in her role as the writer who is 'called upon to give meaning to three generations of life-and-death struggles' (p. 210).

In order to give meaning to almost a century of Wong familial struggles, Kae has to establish what happened first, not easy when even dates prove unreliable. The closest Kae comes to recording her complex family history into 'a suant, digestible unit' occurs in 'The Writer' (p. 19). This chapter represents the novel's postmodern form in a more intense way when, within a few pages, 'it experiments with a range of codes . . . from television interview, through séance and film, to domestic melodrama and Greek tragedy.'[26] This tragedy comes with a chorus of 'wailing women'.

> They all chant:
> Mui Lan lived a lie, so Fong Mei got sly.
> Suzie slipped away; Beatrice made to say,
> Kae to tell the story,
> all that's left of
> vainglory.
>
> (p. 188)

More precisely, Lee Mui Lan's lie refers to the 'baby deal' she strikes for her son, Wong Choy Fuk, who has both a wife, Fong Mei, and a mistress, Song Ang (p. 92). Neither woman is able to provide him with a legitimate heir because he is impotent, although this does not prevent two babies, Bea and Keeman, being born in 1926 to these women. Fong Mei goes on to have two more children, John and Suzie, again on the sly with her co-worker (and half-brother-in-law) at Disappearing Moon Café, the so-called orphan Wong Ting An. Alongside extra-marital affairs are inter-racial relationships between two generations of 'wild injun' women and 'chinamen' (p. 3). There are also incestuous relationships between Choy Fuk's non-biological children, Bea and Keeman, and between Ting An's biological children, Suzie and Morgan. Morgan also has a relationship with his half niece, Kae. Fong Mei responds violently to her daughters' incestuous relationships by holding both hostage, to pregnant Suzie's detriment in particular:

I'll see you dead first. You'll never marry him. You're going into . . . a prison for cheap sluts like you . . . And that thing in you is a deformed monster, so I'm giving it over to the government to raise.

(p. 203)

The last alternative proves unnecessary when the doctor fatally injures Suzie and Morgan's baby boy during delivery. Not long afterwards, Suzie commits suicide.

With this story told, Kae is called on to make meaningful this near century-long familial struggle. According to Richard Bromley, her act of 'feeding the dead' (pp. 185–90) represents 'a legacy of the repressed and the silenced', particularly 'migrants, native-born, and bi-racial people, with a focus on the doubly exiled women'.[27] This legacy necessitates revision of both Canadian history and identity. Kae's 'true sister', Hermia Chow, articulates this need for revisionism in terms of her own identity, as an 'overseas chinese from Switzerland' and 'the misplaced bastard daughter of a [Hong Kong] gangster and his moll' (pp. 38–9, 41). She asks:

Do you mean that individuals must gather their identity from all the generations that touch them – past and future, no matter how slightly? Do you mean that an individual is not an individual at all, but a series of individuals – some of whom come before her, some after her?

(p. 189)

Kae's 'other mother' and '(trans)parent', the Malayan-born, hindu-raised, tamil-speaking, overseas chinese Seto Chi further reinforces this need for revising traditional assumptions about identity and family (pp. 127, 129).

Together, then, these non-biological family members undermine the singularity, and by extension the presumed commonality, of Chinese Canadian identity as it is complicated by the Chinese diaspora. Kae imagines this diaspora in terms of China-centredness, whereby those from the mainland are purer in their Chineseness than Chinese from Hong Kong and Malaya. Of Chi, Kae insists,

Chi didn't come from China. . . . In a way, she wasn't even pure chinese . . . and she had learned her chineseness from my mother, which added tremendously to my confusion. All my life I saw double. All I ever wanted was authenticity; meanwhile, the people around me wore two-faced masks, and they played their lifelong roles to artistic perfection. No wonder no one writes family sagas any more!

(p. 128)

When considered alongside incestuous and transfamily relationships, this lack of authenticity serves to reinforce the disruption to 'the patriarchal idea and ideal of a continuous ethnic lineage' back to an originary identity, specifically an originary Chineseness.[28]

With regard to racial identities, white patriarchy is at its most regulatory during times of national crisis, as when, for example, Asian North Americans wore badges that 'shouted "China" (vs. jap) to the satisfaction of . . . [wartime] social exigencies' (p. 130). Not without some irony, Lee makes Chi the bearer of this badge, even though she was not pure Chinese. Although not a national crisis but more of a family crisis, the importance of racial purity is the focus of a conversation between Gwei Gang and his biological son, Ting An. Before this conversation, Ting An assumed he was an orphan, and that the family name Wong was given to him since 'Chinese bought and sold their identities' during the exclusion period, from 1923 to the 1940s (p. 232). Their biological relationship is revealed when Ting An informs Gwei Chang of his decision to marry 'a blonde demoness', not 'a real wife from China'. His father's definition of a wife angers Ting An because his own mother, Gwei Chang's rescuer and first wife, Kelora Chen, is, as he sarcastically puts it, 'a dirty half-breed, buried somewhere in the bush' (pp. 232–3).

In *Disappearing Moon Café*, racialized national ideals like pure Chineseness and pure Canadianness prove harmful and, ultimately, fatal. While Kae's attempt to claim her 'righteous inheritance to a pure bloodline' is problematized through transfamily and biracial family members, the fatal implications of purity are made most apparent through incest (p. 66). Bea and Suzie do not knowingly pursue incestuous relationships, unlike Kae, but, given the historical context, it is hardly surprising that Vancouver's Chinatown was 'ripe for incest' (p. 147). While Canadian anti-Chinese policies with regard to immigration, employment and miscegenation limited the Chinatown population both numerically and experientially, Chinese Canadians contributed to this diminishing population through their privileging of 'new immigrant blood' over native-born blood (p. 147). This blood–based hierarchy is particularly important for women. Not only does Gwei Chang proclaim Chinese immigrant women real wife material in contrast to dirty and demonic native-born women, but his real wife from China also endorses a similar hierarchy in relation to her immigrant daughter-in-law. Mui Lan assumes that Fong Mei would make an ideal 'receptacle' for a 'little boy who came from her son, who came from her husband, who also came lineally from that golden chain of male to male' (p. 31).

Disappearing Moon Café thus helps to historicize incest by high-lighting the ways in which the determination of patriarchies to ensure the purity of the bloodline leads ineluctably to a deviation from otherwise sacrosanct sexual mores. Incest becomes the best way of safeguarding purity, even if it is at the expense of women whose sexuality functions to demarcate 'the innermost sanctums of race, culture and nation, as well as the porous frontiers through which these are penetrated.'[29] If the frontiers of these sanctums or receptacles prove either too impenetrable or too penetrable, then death results for both pure and impure women. Suzie is one such impenetrable sanctum since she is impregnated by her half-brother, Morgan. Their baby boy is battered as much as his mother – at the hospital and in the family – and, a year after his birth and death, Suzie commits suicide. Alongside these two related deaths in *Disappearing Moon Café*, is the death, in 1924, of a Scottish nurse-maid, Janet Smith, whose sanctum, it would seem, is only too penetrable.

This working-class white woman is shot dead, and her co-worker, Wong Foon Sing, is suspected of her murder. While his surname would seem to link Foon Sing to the Wong family, he is, in fact, unrelated, as unrelated as Janet is to the Wong family. However, Hermia's transfamily identity, alongside her comment about serialized family relationships, does make possible a relation-ship between these unrelated characters. Apart from the Chinese houseboy, a rich playboy is suspected of Janet's murder. These differently raced and classed suspects ensure that the murder 'story had something for every kind of righteousness. For those who hated chinese and thought they were depraved and drug-infested. And for those who hated the rich and thought they were depraved and drug-infested' (p. 68). This depravity is also understood in sexual terms. Both suspects are described as boys, their emasculation signifying efforts to control their sexual desires, although, importantly, only Chinese immigrant men's desires are limited on an institutional level through Canadian anti-miscegenation laws.

However, laws prohibiting close working and marital relationships between white women and Chinese men for the purposes of protecting white femininity, and all it represents – family, freedom, happiness and Canadianness *per se* – actually generate the opposite scenario: 'white women got protected right out of a job' and, in Janet's case, out of a life (p. 68). Under white patriarchy, working-class women are vulnerable to men, whether rich and white, poor and Chinese or poor and white. White femininity effectively becomes the battleground between these men, enough to bring about the nursemaid's death, as well as Chinatown's persecution, 'not with clubs and stones this time but with the way they'd gotten them every time. It was dubbed the "Janet Smith" bill at the legislature' (p. 224).

Janet and Suzie, as well as the last male Wong heir, are linked by death, brought about in all three cases by ideals of racial purity within both the family and the nation. In other words, these three characters, particularly the women, are serially linked, forming part of Hermia's series of individuals that pertains as much to the Wongs as to Canada. Not a woman in her own right, Janet represents a national ideal and a segregationist bill. To this extent, she resembles other insubstantial female characters like Kerala, Mui Lan, Fong Mei and Suzie, who are similarly displaced in and by 'the male order' (p. 63). Significantly, 'the Janet Smith bill flopped and became Chinatown's first real success story', thanks to a new generation of media and legal savvy Chinatown statesmen (p. 227). This bill thus underpins both Chinese and white Canadian identities, notably male identities, and Janet's identity (as body and bill) serves to advocate and undermine legalized racial segregation.

Through its representation of incest and anti-miscegenation laws, *Disappearing Moon Café* differently represents the violent implications of racialized national ideals. In addition to being victims, women are also perpetuators of these ideals. As Kae observes, 'we turn on ourselves, squabbling desperately among ourselves about our common debasement . . . Willingly we fuel the white fire with which to scar other women' (p. 63). Kae has participated in this scarring, her perpetuation of female stereotypes arguably resembling those perpetuated by the Chinatown patriarchs. At the same time, however, 'The Writer', specifically in the subsection entitled 'Feeding the Dead', promotes a feminist understanding of the events in the novel beyond the personal. For the most part, this subsection has ghostly or subaltern women speak in an analytical and critical way about their actions as determined by patriarchal political economies. Here, it seems that Kae has fulfilled her self-appointed role of 'resolution to this story', albeit 'a neverending story' about a series of related and unrelated individuals who play and perform their identities (pp. 209–10). These performances do not make their identities any less real. As Kae makes clear in her response to Hermia's question about either living or writing 'A GREAT NOVEL': ' "I'd rather live one," I say' (p. 216).

MEI NG, *EATING CHINESE FOOD NAKED* (1998)

While trauma, in Kae's view, 'makes us want to rethink our lives or, to be more candid, rewrite it wherever possible' (p. 21), no such life-and-death struggle motivates the narrative in *Eating Chinese Food Naked* by Mei Ng (1966–). This New York based family saga may begin with Franklin Lee recounting the news to his wife, Bell, about 'all the people who got dead that day', but there is a certain banality about traumas monologically conveyed over the dinner table.[30] More significant, at least to Bell, is the fact that her youngest daughter, Ruby, has returned home to the family's laundry in Queens after four years away at college reading Women Studies and living 'like a regular American girl' (p. 25). Ruby's return is only temporary, and for financial reasons. It allows her to save enough money for her own apartment in an all-female building in Manhattan. Apart from approximately eight pages of first-person narration (in italics), this novel is omnisciently told and focuses on different characters in the Lee family, particularly on Ruby and her 'feeling of uneasiness, as if she had forgotten something, something important . . . The nagging feeling wouldn't leave her. She pushed it away, but it came back stronger each time' (pp. 14–15).

Ruby's uneasy feeling is to do with family and sexual relationships; as this feeling relates primarily to Bell: 'she realized that it was her mother she had forgotten; it was her mother she had left behind and had finally come back to get' (p. 16). This recovery also involves an articulation of Ruby's queer desires, which are made explicit in dreams: 'When Ruby was a kid . . . she was dreaming about marrying her mother and taking her away', and, as an adult, 'she dreamed she was having sex with her mother' (pp. 18, 168). She also masturbates while Bell is asleep in the bedroom that they share, as they used to do when Ruby was a child. Although Ruby is the main focus of generally eroticized desires – of both women and men, including her Jewish American boyfriend, Nick – Bell, too, discusses sex. Of her childhood sexual experiences, she tells Ruby 'about sleeping in the same bed with her brothers . . . and how they wouldn't listen when she told them to stop touching her' (p. 49).

The earlier experiences of incest, between Suzie and Morgan in *Disappearing Moon Café*, as well as between Bell and her brothers, suggest a negative understanding of incest. However, whether real, as in Kae's relationship with her half uncle or imagined, as in Ruby's relationship with her mother, the more recent experiences of incest seem less scandalous in comparison. These younger women articulate their sexualities in ways hardly imaginable as anything but pathological prior to the late 1960s and the sexual liberation movements.

In their explorations of sexual identity and racial identity, *Disappearing Moon Café* and *Eating Chinese Food Naked* represent an encounter between worlds typically assumed incongruent. In 'Maiden Voyage' (1997), Dana K. Takagi explores this sex–race encounter, principally by attending to the similarities and differences between being gay and Asian. Both groups affirm political identities against white patriarchal norms determined to render them invisible. In a bipolar racial formation, Asian American identity is invisible, and in Asian America, homosexuality is invisible. Takagi seeks to 'problematize the silences surrounding homosexuality in Asian America', with homosexuality also serving 'as an occasion to critique the tendency toward essentialist currents in ethnic-based narratives and disciplines.'[31] By the same token, argue David L. Eng and Alice Y. Hom, sex-based narratives and disciplines 'cannot be understood without a serious consideration of how social differences such as race constitute our cognitive perceptions of a queer world, how sexual and racial difference come into existence only in relation to one another.'[32]

For these three queer theorists, then, sexual and racial identities are mutually constitutive. The relationship between these identities is dynamic and open-ended. Can the same be said of Ng's novel, specifically with regard to Ruby and her relationships with Bell and Nick? Indeed, does *Eating Chinese Food Naked* promote a hierarchical understanding of identity – as either sex-based or race-based – or does it instead offer a more complicated, even dialogic, understanding of sexual and racial identity? For much of the novel, Ruby apparently decentralizes race, specifically Chineseness, in favour of sex and sexuality. 'She hated the entire [multicultural] borough of Queens and particularly the laundry and the people who lived behind it', presumably like 'a regular American girl' preoccupied with partying, cooking, dating and 'fucking' (pp. 24–5).

More specifically, sexual politics within both the private and the public spheres are highlighted. Both spheres encourage women's servitude in a dictatorial way, although Ruby's secretarial work is preferable to Bell's factory work. Ruby and her sister Lily also describe their father as dictatorial. His childrearing skills are dominated by fear, although Bell also 'threatened them with China – China and the bogeyman, so they became one and the same' (p. 41). In addition to hitting Ruby's brother, Van, Franklin plays his daughters off against each other and against their mother. However, it is Franklin's relationship with Bell that receives the most criticism, as well as the most explanation:

> Sometimes he knew he was too harsh with her. Washing other
> people's dirt every day wore him down, and the only way he
> knew of boosting himself up again was to make his wife feel

small, so he found fault with the way she salted the fish, the
way she did her hair, the way she said good morning.

(p. 32)

In short, Franklin's '*women's work*' apparently explains his persecution of his family (p. 30).

Given that patriarchy powerfully dictates the Lee family's
behaviour, leaving them all trapped in victor and victim roles – the
tyrannical husband, the subaltern wife and, in Ruby's case, the
'treacherous' daughter (p. 58) – it is hardly surprising that Ruby's
primary concern is with sexual politics. Moreover, her educational
training in Women's Studies, alongside her reading of Jane Austen's
novels, would presumably enable her to theorize about gender and
sexual stereotypes and their transcendence in a variety of ways.
Ruby imagines transcendence in terms of killing her father, escap-
ing to Florida with her mother and sexual liaisons with strange
white men in the city. Theorizations aside, Ruby embarks on her
maiden voyage by returning to the betrayed and forgotten mother,
specifically to her mother's room in the basement where she has an
awakening about her sexual and racial identity.

After moving out of her mother's bedroom, Ruby moves into this
other feminized space in the basement where her feelings for Nick
are made apparent, at least more so than at anytime previously,
when she reluctantly has sex with him: 'All that touching and
moving and breathing was almost painful, like being woken from a
deep sleep.' Thus awakened, Ruby moves into the female-only city
apartment block only a couple of pages later. This move is supported by Bell, who seems similarly awakened after listening to the
couple having sex in the basement: 'You're a big girl now. No good
to live with your ma anymore' (pp. 212–13). Like her daughter, Bell
becomes more independent, which, in turn, improves her relationship with Franklin. Reciprocity marks their marriage, as it used to
do, even in the smallest of gestures to do with their consumption of
food. These gestures had previously gone unnoticed by their
American-born daughter.

After the basement scene, however, Ruby learns to read these
gestures or, more precisely, lack of gestures in Nick. He eats
Chinese food naked and worse:

he was eating all the good meaty bits and leaving the bony
parts for her . . . She had been taught to give the good bits to
the other person and that the other person would give her the
good bits, and in this way, they would take care of each other.

(p. 234)

The consumption of Chinese food thus makes possible an understanding of heterosexual relationships.

More than this, both the basement and eating Chinese food
naked scenes promote an understanding of the way in which
sexual and racial identities come into existence in relation to one
another. Ruby is increasingly preoccupied with Nick's whiteness,
most obviously when she describes him as 'contaminated' by
whiteness (p. 224). After the basement scene, 'he seemed too tall
or maybe too pale . . . How soft and white he was when he was
sleeping. Like a worm . . . her sweet white worm' (p. 231). When
he eats Chinese food naked, however, sweetness and whiteness
become incompatible. As he greedily consumes white Chinese
food and Chinese food that turns white, Ruby notices that
dumplings, noodles and rice do not 'fit with . . . the sight of his
soft penis' (p. 233). The couple also argue in this scene, not so
much because of Ruby's sexual identity, but more because of her
racial identity or, more accurately, his racist identity: 'I was thinking, Who is that ugly Chinese woman standing in my room? But
now here you are and you're beautiful. I don't even notice your
Chineseness. You're just Ruby who I love' (p. 236).

Given this emphasis on the ugly qualities of Chineseness, it is
hardly surprising that Ruby struggles with her racial identity. As a
child, for example, she endured 'Ching Chong, Ching Chong'
taunts, accompanied by slant-eyed gestures. Even her teacher proclaimed her homework 'some kind of crazy Chinese crossword
puzzle', overwriting it with 'a big red X' (pp. 237–8). Moreover,
'when she got older, people would get mad at her for trying to act
black or white or Puerto Rican' (p. 65). Among white friends, she is
Chinese: 'Yes, you are my friend . . . and, yes, I am your friend, but
I am your Chinese friend', even though, among Chinese friends, she
felt that 'they were Chinese in a way she didn't know how to be'
(p. 119). As Ruby understands it, then, her Chineseness is either

hypervisible to non-Chinese or invisible to Chinese, most poignantly in her relationship with Nick.

Like her peers and teacher at school, Nick makes Ruby inferior. His whiteness, alongside his colour-blind yet racist comment – 'I don't even notice your Chineseness. You're just Ruby' – make her so upset that 'her face . . . twisted shut'. The narrative continues:

> Her angry face, her ugly Chinese face. Not you too, Nick, she said to him in her head, not when I trusted you with my face, trusted you not to slap it and twist it out of shape. / She dressed quietly.
>
> (p. 238)

In this context, Chineseness is only available to Ruby in twisted or limited terms, and it is so violently imposed that she is left quiet. She is subjugated, as Bell once was in her marriage to tyrannical Franklin.

Given that Ruby is doubly subordinated on the basis of her gender and her race, it is hardly surprising that she wishes 'she had been born into another family', presumably a non-Chinese family (p. 246). No sooner is this wish articulated than the narrative suggests other possibilities for Ruby's identity through the figure of the Chinese immigrant mother. Once dominated by both her husband and daughter, Bell is ultimately represented in terms of freedom. Ruby imagines her mother running free in her birthday gift of running shoes. Also significant is the fact that Bell's voice authoritatively and imperatively 'rings out' in the final paragraph of the novel when she returns her daughter's call, albeit via an answer machine message about a long-desired fish dish: 'First, pick a sea bass with clear eyes, not cloudy . . . Watch out for small bones' (p. 252). This message also conveys another, deeper message about the possibility of a future for this mother–daughter relationship, and a future – crucially, only an hypothetical future – for Ruby and Nick:

> If only she were fifty years old and tired of affairs. If only he weren't so white and didn't sweat up her pillowcases. If only he were a woman. Or, if he were more of a man. Or if he could just learn to cook a good pot of rice.
>
> (p. 160)

Or, is she tricking herself, particularly as she anticipates leaving him again for a woman?

CHANG-RAE LEE, *NATIVE SPEAKER* (1995)

While *Eating Chinese Food Naked* and *Disappearing Moon Café* differently queer Asian North American sexual identity in relation to racial identity, Chang-rae Lee's novels from the 1990s, specifically his spy story *Native Speaker* and his war story *A Gesture Life* (1999), explicitly queer racial identity. In his final novel to date, *Aloft* (2004), Lee queers or de-essentializes Asian Americanness as it pertains to his narrator who is an aging Italian American father of mixed-race children from his marriage to a Korean American woman. More than do the later suburban novels, *Native Speaker* represents mixed characters in mixed relationships in mixed settings, specifically multicultural Queens, New York. *Native Speaker*'s narrator is a Korean American man, who, like his equally 'amiable' counterparts in the other novels, is compelled to analyze his complicity with patriarchal political economies.[33]

Although it also has fatal consequences in *Native Speaker*, the complicity at issue in *A Gesture Life* occurs in circumstances that are altogether more violent and involve war crimes: 'the days over fifty years ago, when Koreans were made servants and slaves in their own country by the Imperial Japanese Army. How our mothers and sisters were made the concubines of the very soldiers who enslaved us' through the Comfort Woman system (p. 142). For the most part, however, *Native Speaker* is not concerned with this wartime history, but with postwar historical events. At least three contemporary events are represented in the novel: first, the 1992 uprising in Los Angeles; second, the 1993 *Golden Venture* incident in New York when a ship carrying illegal Chinese immigrants ran aground; and, third, 'Giuliani time'. Rudolph Giuliani's election to mayor of New York in 1994 signalled a change in the city's politics, towards revanchism or nativism and racism.[34] One of the most forceful expressions of racial reaction in *Native Speaker* occurs when an inadequately policed crowd of mostly white working-class men proclaim that 'Spanish niggers' and 'greasy gooks' have stolen their jobs, future and country. This crowd demand 'AMERICA FOR AMERICANS', to which end they want the deportation of Latino and Asian immigrants (p. 308).

In this violent context, Lee's narrator Henry Park operates as a professional spy. It is one of his many roles in 'a string of serial identity' (p. 30). He is not a spy in the glamorous sense – political, patriotic and heroic. His motivations are 'entirely personal' and 'determined by some calculus of power and money' (pp. 6, 15). Park and his colleagues at Glimmer and Co. 'deal in people. Each of us engaged our own kind, more or less. Foreign workers, immigrants, first-generationals, neo-Americans', about whom they write 'unauthorized biographies' for multinational corporations, foreign governments and powerful individuals (p. 16). In spying on his own kind, Park adheres to the 'ugly immigrant's truth' of exploiting those who are already economically and racially exploited for his personal advancement in keeping with dominant American ideologies (p. 297).

More than a spy, then, Park is a 'traitor', his treachery emerging not only in his role of servant, arguably 'whitey's boy', but also in his role as dictator (pp. 5, 181). As the novel's narrator, he effectively dictates interpretations of the other characters. Not only is the immigrant politician John Kwang in Park's sights but so, too, are his dead immigrant father, dead biracial son, Mitt, and estranged white wife, Leila. More than he does his wife and son, Park stereotypes these two Korean immigrant men, both of whom, he believes, are liable to easy understanding because of their respective allegiances to familiar immigrant stories of achievement (pp. 45–6, 130). Importantly, Park does problematize the authority of his narrative by insisting that 'truth, finally, is who can tell it' and by highlighting his preference for simulacrum and invention (p. 6). Self-reflexivity on this count suggests that his narrative is not simply the expression of a race traitor.

The issue of race treachery is further complicated in relation to Park's victim, Kwang, who, as 'sweet-ass veal' to the wolves at Glimmer and Co., would seem to represent the antithesis of a race traitor (p. 39). According to Rachel C. Lee, Kwang represents an idealized Asian American and his 'bid to be elected mayor of New York presumes and burnishes the ideal self-image of the US nation-state as a kind of heteroglossic utopia.'[35] Not an exploiter, then, like Park and his colleagues, Kwang is champion and friend of the exploited, from unregistered voters to undocumented workers and 'every boat person in between' (p. 283). Kwang's constituency resembles a multicultural family, and his campaign attempts to diversify Asian American political practices in the manner described by Lisa Lowe through the formation of intraracial and interracial relationships.

For example, Kwang's powerful, if problematic, speech to a multiracial Brooklyn audience focuses on the Korean–black relationship. He encourages this audience to imagine this relationship apart from the sensationalist views held by the media and the current mayor of interracial relationships as characterized by boycotts, shoot-outs and riots in keeping with yellow-peril and black-peril stereotypes. Kwang concludes his speech by emphasizing the similarities between Korean and African Americans regarding historical traumas of enslavement and racial self-hatred. In his words, 'Know that what we have in common, the sadness and pain and injustice, will always be stronger than our differences' (p. 142). Kwang's response to the injustice perpetuated by the white patriarchal political economy is a 'giant money club, our huge *ggeh* for all . . . with people other than just our own' giving and receiving financial support (p. 261).

This alternative economic system potentially threatens white economic advantage, making Kwang's downfall unsurprising. Fundamental to his fall is Park's report for Glimmer and Co. In its original format, this report simply listed Kwang's colleagues, as well as confirming that *ggeh* was a non-profit making organization. However, the report reproduced by the Immigration and Naturalization Service lists undocumented immigrants and unregistered lending activities. Kwang's fall from idealized to criminalized Asian American – 'Smuggler Kwang' (p. 308) – is something of an inevitability, a necessity even. As Kwang is Park's 'necessary invention', Park is Kwang's 'necessary phantom' (pp. 130, 290), and their relationship is played out, as Min Hyoung Song notes, in the manner of a Greek tragedy. This tragedy is determined by powerful forces, which include 'the machinations of powerful repressive state apparatuses', most obviously Glimmer and Co.'s client, the INS.[36]

In this repressive context, Kwang had to go, his untimely demise remarkably similar to Mitt's. Not only are both characters described as children but they also suffer racial abuse by sporting crowds. Their respective ends, in scandal and in death, arguably represent, as Lee puts it in an interview, 'the end of "a way of thinking about the future", the idea that may be the time was not quite right for such a "subversive, historic, unprecedented" blending of ethnicities.'[37] More precisely, Mitt is called 'mutt, mongrel, half-breed, banana, twinkie' by some white boys, who, after they proclaim eternal friendship, crush him to death in a *stupid dog pile* (pp. 96–9). Kwang is called 'every ugly Asian name' by a multiracial mob who chant as if they lived 'always at a football match'. This mob grab at Kwang. As he crouches down to avoid the mob, Park compares him to 'a broken child, shielding from me his wide immigrant face' (pp. 315–18). Significantly, Park, too, despite the oppositional role he has assumed throughout the novel in relation to Kwang – as wolf to veal – effectively becomes a child in his wife's English language class.

In becoming children and in leaving public life, Kwang by returning to Korea and Park by going back to school, the novel queries the progress of Asian Americans. The potentially transformative alliances that both characters sought via their respective multicultural non-biological families do little to change the 'old syntax' of at least thirty years before (p. 183). This syntax is as relevant now as it was when Park's immigrant father was also confined to the domestic sphere, not so much by choice but by historical conditions within a bipolar racial formation. Whether wolf or veal, victimizer or victimized, Lee's characters in leaving American public life seem to come across as failures. And yet, as Rachel C. Lee argues:

what is really at stake in the novel . . . [is not] a failed literary representation of Korean Americans as much as a failure of American political rhetoric, evident in those living breathing working people in New York who – in the logic of American citizenship – cannot be represented in the public sphere.[38]

If there is an ugly immigrant truth in *Native Speaker*, then, it has less to do with exploitation within and between racial minority groups and more to do with the category 'American'. The notion that for many Americans, particularly those committed to revanchism, an American is white or European in origin makes Asian Americans queer in the sense of abnormal. At the same time, however, Lee's novel queers the category of American, most directly via the 'gentlest, queerest voice' of a Scottish American who makes her living out of being an English-language speaker (p. 324). Making their livings in a similar way are the unauthorized biographer Park, the politician Kwang and the novelist Lee. Yet, queerly, ESL (English as a Second Language) teacher Leila alone is accorded nativity, if only according to nativist and racist white Americans. In this way, then, *Native Speaker* queers or, as Liam Corley argues, 'contests the interpellation of racially marked immigrant subjects as always already excluded from the category of "American" by making the more controversial claim that terrorizing and exploiting immigrants is quintessentially American.' In short, Park's ugly immigrant truth is American truth, and 'his memoir of complicity' is American history.[39] Finally, illegal immigrants from Puritan to Chinaman and every boat person in between are 'the quintessential Americans'.[40]

With the historical and ideological underpinnings of Americanness unmasked, thinking about a multicultural future becomes a possibility again, even if in a city-sponsored ESL classroom for schools that do not have adequate English language facilities of their own. In addition to suggesting that the city and state, not Kwang, are out of sync with the changing multicultural landscape, these supplementary classes suggest how language and education, as much as party politics, participate in the state's 'disciplinary tactics that both subjugate and produce the modern subject'.[41] This subject or 'a good citizen' can just as easily play up to this role as mess it up, which, in 'a city of words', suggests that 'horsing with the language' has subversive, historic, unprecedented possibilities, after all (pp. 324, 319).

CONCLUSION

A heterogeneous, hybrid and multiplicitous Asian America necessarily includes those who have apparently made it, like, for example, Chang-rae Lee's John Kwang, and those who struggle with traumatic pasts as they continue into the present and are exacerbated by intraracial and interracial differences. The traumas represented in the literary texts selected here include wartime violence, specifically in Vietnam, Cambodia and Korea. Apart from the Comfort Woman system in *A Gesture Life* other traumas relating to sexuality include incest in *Disappearing Moon Café* and *Eating Chinese Food Naked*. As different as these traumas are, they all resist easy telling and easy healing, the texts in which they are the focus typically articulating this difficulty thematically and formally through fragmented texts full of holes.

The holes or gaps function in at least two ways. First, they work against the assumption that Americanization is a smooth process. The gaps in *Monkey Bridge* and *Disappearing Moon Café* in particular help to highlight the asymmetrical relations within North American culture, both past and present. Hence the need in *Native Speaker* for a minority politician such as Kwang to represent non-white interests in a city where immigrants, along with those commonly perceived as immigrants, are particularly vulnerable. This vulnerability was exacerbated by anti-immigration legislation in the 1980s and 1990s, for example, California's Proposition 187 in 1994, which, although not overtly racialized, adversely affected specific racial groups. As regards the impact of this and other laws, Angelo N. Ancheta highlights how they were most powerfully felt by 'Asian Americans and Latinos because of the large numbers of immigrants within their communities and because of the linkage between nativism and race.'[42]

Second, the holes or gaps enable resistance to the appropriative strategies of dominant ideologies, even when they appear at their most benevolent. For example, multiculturalism may permit others to speak, although, in its uncritical form, it ultimately functions as a smokescreen with which others are rendered complicit in the manner of Chang-rae Lee's Henry Park. By analyzing this complicity and, moreover, by problematizing the idealism that assumes it can be transcended once and for all the literary texts in this chapter articulate ways of being Asian American that involve learning to live with complicity. As it is represented by Lan Cao's novel via the analogy of the scar, such an act does not imply that the old wound has healed completely, nor does it imply that the damage and the survival have been completely forgotten. Indeed, the scar gestures towards the old wound and the new skin simultaneously. In so doing, it offers a way of critically engaging absolutes, whether in terms of the complete cure, the final truth or the authentic way of being Asian American, apart from white patriarchy.

SUMMARY OF KEY POINTS

- The 1990s were marked by new possibilities for some Asian Americans, relative to Asian American history and other racial minority groups.
- The model-minority stereotype circulated throughout American culture, although, with the rise of East Asian capitalism, yellow-peril fears began to resurface in the popular media. According to the right-wing press and politicians, illegal immigrants also imperilled the USA. Although the illegal immigrant was not raced, this identity was nonetheless racialized (as Asian and Latino/a) consistent with colour-blind political theory.
- In the 1990s, the multicultural phenomenon boomed, as represented by celebrity minority writers.
- Asian American literature and criticism also boomed. The 1990s was identified as a particularly productive decade in terms of the number and diversity of Asian American texts produced.
- A demographically and ideologically diverse Asian America was reinforced via Southeast Asian refugee and Asian Canadian literatures. For many critics, the 1990s were associated with queer writing, with Asian American texts queering both the category of Asian American and American in complicated ways.

NOTES

1. Lisa Lowe, 'Heterogeneity, Hybridity, Multiplicity: Marking Asian American Differences', *Diaspora* 1:1 (Spring 1991), 39–40.
2. David Palumbo-Liu, *Asian/American: Historical Crossings of a Racial Frontier* (Stanford: Stanford University Press, 1999), p. 4.

3. David Palumbo-Liu (ed.), 'Introduction', *The Ethnic Canon: Histories, Institutions, and Interventions* (Minneapolis: University of Minnesota Press, 1995), p. 14, p. 6.
4. Graham Huggan, *The Postcolonial Exotic: Marketing the Margins* (London: Routledge, 2001), p. xiii.
5. Ibid., p. vii, p. xii, p. 4.
6. Sau-ling Cynthia Wong and Jeffrey J. Santa Ana, 'Review Essay: Gender and Sexuality in Asian American Literature', *Signs* 25:1 (1999), 197, 203–14.
7. David L. Eng and Alice Y. Hom (eds), 'Introduction', *Q & A: Queer in Asian America* (Philadelphia: Temple University Press, 1998), p. 1.
8. Ibid., p. 6.
9. Palumbo-Liu, *Asian/American*, p. 207, p. 361.
10. Renny Christopher, '*Blue Dragon, White Tiger*: The Bicultural Stance of Vietnamese American Literature', *Reading the Literatures of Asian America*, ed. Shirley Geok-lin Lim and Amy Ling (Philadelphia: Temple University Press, 1992), p. 259.
11. Teri Shaffer Yamada, 'Cambodian American Autobiography: Testimonial Discourse', *Form and Transformation in Asian American Literature*, ed. Zhou Xiaojing and Samina Najmi (Seattle: University of Washington Press, 2005), pp. 152–4.
12. Ibid., pp. 153–5.
13. Chanrithy Him, 'Letter, May 5, 2004', http://www.yale.edu/cgp/HenryHyde1.DOC [Accessed January 2007].
14. Kimiko Hahn, 'Blindsided', *Making More Waves: New Writing by Asian American Women*, ed. Elaine H. Kim, Lilia V. Villanueva and Asian Women United of California (Boston: Beacon Press, 1997), p. 84. Hereafter references to this poem are given in the text.
15. Thomas A. DuBois, quoted in Viet Thanh Nguyen, *Race and Resistance: Literature and Politics in Asian America* (Oxford: Oxford University Press, 2002), p. 112.
16. Nguyen, *Race*, p. 123, p. 108, p. 113.
17. Qui-Phiet Tran, 'From Isolation to Integration: Vietnamese Americans in Tran Dieu Hang's Fiction', Lim and Ling (eds), *Reading the Literatures*, p. 283, p. 281.

18. Michele Janette, 'Guerrilla Irony in Lan Cao's *Monkey Bridge*', *Contemporary Literature* 42:1 (Spring 2001), 51, 54.

19. Cao, quoted in Janette, 'Guerrilla', 65: ' "Heaven and Earth" . . . fails to transform America's apparently irresistible impulse to view Vietnam as anything other than a domestic theater.'

20. Lan Cao, *Monkey Bridge* (New York: Penguin, 1997), pp. 100–1. Hereafter references to this edition are given in the text.

21. Rey Chow, *Ethics After Idealism: Theory-Culture-Ethnicity-Reading* (Bloomington: Indiana University Press, 1998), p. 99, p. 106.

22. Ibid., p. 112.

23. Ibid., p. 112.

24. Ibid., p. 107.

25. Sky Lee, *Disappearing Moon Café* (Vancouver: The Seal Press, 1990), p. 160. Hereafter references to this edition are given in the text.

26. Roger Bromley, *Narratives for a New Belonging: Diasporic Cultural Fictions* (Edinburgh: Edinburgh University Press, 2000), p. 113.

27. Ibid., p. 110.

28. Chow, *Ethics*, p. 107.

29. Ania Loomba, *Colonialism/Postcolonialism* (London: Routledge, 1998), p. 159.

30. Mei Ng, *Eating Chinese Food Naked* (London: Penguin, 1998), p. 11. Hereafter references to this edition are given in the text.

31. Dana Y. Takagi, 'Maiden Voyage: Excursion into Sexuality and Identity Politics in Asian America', Elaine Kim et al. (eds), *Making More Waves*, p. 145, p. 148.

32. Eng and Hom, 'Introduction', p. 12.

33. Chang-rae Lee, *Native Speaker* (London: Granta Books, 1995), p. 6. Hereafter references to this edition are given in the text.

34. Liam Corley, ' "Just another Ethnic Pol": Literary Citizenship in Chang-rae Lee's *Native Speaker*', *Studies in the Literary Imagination* 37:1 (Spring 2004), 61–3, 66–7.

35. Rachel C. Lee, 'Reading Contests and Contesting Reading: Chang-rae Lee's *Native Speaker* and Ethnic New York', *MELUS* 29:3/4 (Fall/Winter 2004), 341, 349.

36. Min Hyoung Song, 'A Diasporic Future? *Native Speaker* and Historical Trauma', *LIT* 12 (2001), 94.
37. Lee, quoted in Pam Belluck, 'Being of Two Cultures and Belonging to Neither; After an Acclaimed Novel, a Korean-American Writer Searches for his Roots', *New York Times Book Review* (10 July 1995), 1.
38. Lee, 'Reading', 349.
39. Corley, 'Ethnic', 75.
40. Lee, 'Reading', 351.
41. Ibid., 346.
42. Angelo N. Ancheta, *Race, Rights, and the Asian American Experience* (New Brunswick, NJ: Rutgers University Press, 1998), p. 14.

Conclusion

Chang-rae Lee's novel *Native Speaker* (1995) as much as it represents historical events specific to the 1990s – for example, the 1992 Los Angeles uprising and the 1993 *Golden Venture* incident – anticipates a continuing socio-political climate hostile to Asian Americans and other racial minorities. Indeed, the future that the white working-class men demand back from Asian and Latino immigrants in the mob scene that occurs towards the end of the novel seems more of a possibility now than it did in the mid-1990s. On 26 October 2001, the USA Patriot Act was passed, partly in response to the terrorist attacks on Washington DC and New York City on 11 September 2001. This act adversely affected the civil liberties of immigrants from the Middle East, as well as South and Southeast Asia, some of whom were deported because their loyalty to the USA was in doubt. According to Rajini Srikanth in *The World Next Door* (2004), this act could also 'spell the end of civil liberties as we know them for all U.S. residents – immigrants and citizens alike – if its provisions are allowed to solidify and extend indefinitely.'[1]

While the Patriot Act would seem to suggest that the contradiction between democratic political rhetoric and undemocratic political reality was suddenly rendered irresolvable by 9/11, this would be to ignore the way in which this contradiction is built into the American democratic system. So much depends on this contradiction, most obviously white hegemony. On the matter of the dominant racial hierarchy, Yan Phou Lee observed in 1889, as did other Asian American writers for over a century after him,

> The founders of the American Republic asserted the princi-
> ple that all men are created equal . . . How far this Republic
> has departed from its high ideal and reversed its traditionary
> policy may be seen in . . . the actions of this generation of
> Americans in their treatment of other races.

Lee goes on to suggest that discriminatory actions put into question this generation's Americanness, along with bypassing the fact that Asians, specifically the Chinese, are fit for naturalization because of their appreciation of the Republic and its founding ideals. This ideological contribution to the USA is reinforced materially, principally by 'the application of Chinese "cheap labor" to the building of railroads, the reclamation of swamp-lands, to mining, fruit-culture, and manufacturing.'[2] Later nation-building applications include the defence industry, particularly in the Second World War, after which the exclusion laws established between the 1880s and the 1930s were finally rescinded. And, yet, Asian Americans, right up until today, continue to be excluded, if not from the nation-state, then from mainstream American culture.

Exclusionism has historically rendered Asian Americans invisible. National discourses like American history and American literature, if they mentioned them at all, typically focused on negative stereotypes such as the yellow peril. The so-called positive stereotype of the model minority makes Asian Americanness visible, even hypervisible, at the detriment of poor Asian Americans and African Americans in particular. This history of misrepresentation was most directly challenged by Asian American cultural nationalism in the late 1960s and 1970s. In highlighting the discrepancy between anti-Asian stereotypes and Asian Americans in a supposedly democratic racial formation, cultural nationalist and other critics also evidenced a dependency on the very condition they criticized.

This dependency raises important questions for the future, particularly with regard to the paradoxes inherent in the formulation of Asian Americanness as a category. On the matter of Asian

America, for example, Viet Thanh Nguyen draws attention to the fact that it depends on 'the endurance of the conditions that mark Asian Americans as being racially different.' He continues: as critics attempt to resolve these conditions by creating 'a space for Asian Americans in the American nation', they 'must then ask themselves to what end that space – Asian America – is created'. If racial inequality were resolved, then there would seem to be little need for Asian Americanness since the resolution would entail equal recognition of the demographic and ideological diversity of all Americans.[3]

The possibility of racial democracy and by extension a post-nationalist and post-assimilationist future – beyond Asian America – obliges Asian American writers to ask questions about what it means both to be and to write as an Asian American. What forms will Asian American critique take in the twenty-first century and how will Asian American literature contribute to this critique? At present, Asian American critics propose at least two apparently oppositional strategies when critically engaging dominant American ideologies. The first approach is outward-looking in the sense that it urges Asian American studies to turn toward the Americas, the Pacific Rim and Asia. It necessitates that Asian American studies redefine not only the 'America' but also the ' "Asia" in Asian American, or to reach out to strange black and brown peoples' consistent with transnationalist critique.[4] The second approach is inward-looking in the sense that it urges Asian American studies to turn toward language. It necessitates that Asian American studies analyze the category of Asian American as rhetorically and ideologically constructed, consistent with poststructuralist critique. What links these apparently oppositional discourses is the suggestion that Asian American studies become more self-reflexive with regard to its geo-political and theoretical boundaries or essentialisms.

In addition to the challenge posed by dependency on racial inequalities that it simultaneously seeks to resolve, Asian American studies is challenged by its dependency on identity. Asian American critics like, for example, Lisa Lowe and, later, Anne Anlin Cheng in *The Melancholy of Race* (2001) and Viet Thanh Nguyen in *Race and Resistance* (2002), are alert to the achievements of Asian American identity politics, particularly with regard to the way in which it enabled and continues to enable contestation and disruption of dominant American ideologies. At the same time, however, they cannot ignore the way in which Asian American identity is 'the very ground upon which both progress and discrimination are made'.[5] For the most part, intraracial discrimination is a key concern of Asian American critics who exceed the cultural nationalist ideal of English-speaking Chinese and Japanese American heterosexual men. As well as being criticized by feminist and queer theorists, this ideal is also challenged by transnationalist discourses. These discourses urge denationalization and, more generally, the de-essentializing of Asian American studies as a basis of self-critique via analyses of its US-centrism and by extension American colonialism, imperialism and capitalism.

For example, Sucheta Mazumdar observes in her critical writing that a US-centric Asian American studies 'has proved incapable of disentangling how colonialism has warped its own world view' when it repeats the isolationist and exceptionalist logic of US foreign policy.[6] In his critical writing, specifically about Hawaii, Nguyen implies that the decentralization of this US-centric world view risks 'reiterating American nationalism and the related historical amnesia that concerns imperialism and its effects' by claiming the local culture, which is, for some native Hawaiians, an Asian settler culture, as its own.[7] Whether or not decentralization is pursued, it, in both cases, risks reiterating American imperialism. This is also the case in locations without a history of annexation, say, certain tourist destinations in Asia. As destinations for Americans and other Westerners, these countries are effectively transformed into playgrounds for foreign and local elites to the detriment of poorer locals who are kept away from private beaches and golf courses.

Even if trips to a pacific island paradise, a mysterious faraway land in Asia and, more mundanely, ethnic enclaves in the USA, are not literally realized, these exotic destinations can still be reached by Americans (and other Westerners) through reading travel literature, specifically Asian American tour-guiding texts.[8] Such a classification is relevant to a number of Asian American literary texts discussed in this volume, from early texts like Yan Phou Lee's *When I Was a Boy in China*, Winnifred Eaton's *Miss Spring Morning* and, perhaps, Edith Eaton's 'Its Wavering Image' to later texts, particularly by commercially successful writers such as Maxine Hong Kingston, Amy Tan, Salman Rushdie and Arundhati Roy. According to their more critical commentators, these celebrity writers owe their success to their ability to provide Western readers with exoticized descriptions of Asia and Asian diasporic cultures that ultimately cohere with the dominant racial hierarchy.

In 'Prizing Otherness', from *The Postcolonial Exotic* (2001), Graham Huggan discusses the relationship between some Asian diasporic writers and one of the world's top literary prizes. The British Booker Prize is ambivalently regarded on account of its patron's colonial past on the Guyanan sugar plantations and, for some, its neocolonial present. Postcolonial writers, including Asian diasporic writers, are frequently awarded prizes and short listed, their English-language novels effectively ' "writing back" to a literary Empire'. At the same time, however, the prize-giving process is 'bound to an Anglocentric discourse of benevolent paternalism' consistent with neocolonialism.[9] Prize-winning and short-listed writers include Rushdie, who won in 1981 with *Midnight's Children*. He also won the 1993 Booker of Bookers, and he has appeared several times on the shortlist. His *The Ground Beneath Her Feet* (1999) did not make a more recent shortlist, even though the British media proclaimed it a likely finalist for the Booker Prize with Vikram Seth's *An Equal Music* (1999). Anita Desai, Kazuo Ishiguro, Rohinton Mistry, Timothy Mo and V. S. Naipaul have all won, as well as repeatedly making it on to the shortlist. Other Booker Prize winners include Michael Ondaatje for *The English Patient* (1992) and Arundhati Roy for *The God of Small Things* (1997).

Of these Asian diasporic writers, Kazuo Ishiguro stands out. According to *Time* magazine critic and travel writer Indian American Pico Iyer, Ishiguro is 'a paradigm of the polycultural order', arguably because he, unlike fellow British Asians such as Rushdie and Mo, represents 'a baffling and enigmatic case of a writer who neither writes about his own ethnicity nor about ethnic themes'.[10] In his essay, 'China Man Autoeroticism and the Remains of Asian America' (1998), Tomo Hattori proposes that Ishiguro's prize-winning novel *The Remains of the Day* (1989) contributes towards the de-essentializing of Asian American literature by resisting regulation by both 'the author-concept' and 'the boundaries of ethnic or national identity'.[11] The novel features neither Japanese nor British Asian characters, let alone Asian American characters, unlike, for example, Rushdie's *Fury* (2001). Instead, Ishiguro's central protagonist is an English butler in the service of an English aristocrat before the Second World War.

According to Hattori, *The Remains of the Day*'s ethnicity derives not so much from its author as from the questions it raises about cross-cultural relationships under imperialism. In particular, Ishiguro's butler, in his loyalty to service even if it entails complicity with Nazi ideology, 'illuminates . . . a putatively subversive nostalgia for the faded but glorious day of loyal subjects and model minorities.' On this count, then, Ishiguro's novel, argues Hattori, allows an understanding of

> the role that U.S. ethnic groups play within the world economic system and the way in which their often willing cooptation into the pluralist model of U.S. multiculturalism turns them into apologists for the further penetrations of the world by American capital, culture, and political ideology.

Thus understood, *The Remains of the Day* also allows an interpretation of Asian American literature that includes 'Asian literatures that bear traces of American culture', Asian literature that is available to the American reader, and 'American literature, not necessarily by or about Asians, but which [has] felt the influence of Asian philosophy, religion, science, popular culture or consumer trends.'[12]

Outside Britain, the denationalizing of Asian American literature could include not only Asian Canadian literature but also Asian-influenced Canadian literature. In *Asian/American* (1999), for example, David Palumbo-Liu discusses William Gibson's cyberspace novel, *Neuromancer* (1984), which opens in Chiba (Japan), before moving to the Sprawl (USA). Palumbo-Liu details how this white Canadian writer's representation of Japan emerges from an American anti-Chinese cartoon, a Vancouver bar for Japanese tourists and Gibson's airport drops for Japanese ESL students.

Perhaps this is pushing the boundaries of Asian American literature too far, especially as it is difficult to discern whether *Neuromancer* Americanizes Asia, Asianizes America or 'recompartmentalizes' Asia and America.[13]

Two characters beyond the boundaries of Gibson's novel help to clarify the Americanization of Asia and the Asianization or, more specifically, the Indianization of America. In fact, both characters extend their remarks to everyone and everything. According to Salman Rushdie's Professor Malik Solanka in *Fury*:

> Everyone was an American now, or at least Americanized: Indians, Iranians, Uzbeks, Japanese, Lilliputions, all. America was the world's playing field, its rule book, umpire and ball. Even anti-Americanism was Americanism in disguise, conceding, as it did, that America was the only game in town and the matter of America the only business at hand.[14]

Conversely, 'Mr Everything Comes From India' in the popular British television comedy series *Goodness Gracious Me* (1998–2001) proclaims that English, European and American figures, from William Shakespeare and Leonardo Da Vinci to Superman, as well as the majority of English words, come from India. Of the British royal family, he proclaims: 'Indian! Have arranged marriages. Live in the same house and all work for the family business. Indian!' In one episode, 'Mr Everything Comes From India' is seen moving books from the English and Chinese literature sections into the Indian literature section.[15] As different as these characters are, both satirize and ultimately critique an understanding of the world that obliterates differences in the manner of Gibson's *Neuromancer* to the point that everyone and everything conforms to their universalizing perspectives.

Aside from these British and Canadian turns toward Asia, Asian America and the USA, recent Asian American writers have also turned their attention towards Asia. Contemporary texts by Asian Americans who employ settings that are mostly in Asia include, for example, Jessica Hagedorn's Philippine-based novel and play *Dogeaters* (1990 and 2003), Meena Alexander's Indian-based novel *Nampally Road* (1991), Selvadurai Shyam's Sri Lankan-based novel *Funny Boy* (1994), and Amitav Ghosh's novel *The Glass Palace* (2001), which is set in Burma, Malaysia and India. Amy Tan's 2005 novel, *Saving Fish From Drowning* is also set in Burma, albeit at a different time to Ghosh's. Of a similar celebrity status to Tan, is Bharati Mukherjee, who also turns toward Asia and the wider world in both *The Middleman and Other Stories* (1988) and *The Holder of the World* (1993).

Mukherjee's short story collection opens with 'The Middleman', which is narrated by a Jewish Iraqi American from Baghdad, Bombay and Queens who is wary of becoming black in his current location 'deep in Mayan county, Aztecs, Toltecs, mestizos, even some bashful whites with German accents. All that and a lot of Texans.' Other stories in *The Middleman* feature, for example, a white Vietnam veteran in 'Loose Ends', a Trinidadian Indian woman in 'Jasmine' and a Sri Lankan teacher in 'Buried Lives'. Set in seventeenth-century New England, Old England and India, *The Holder of the World* reimagines Nathaniel Hawthorne's Hester Prynne in *The Scarlet Letter* via her earlier incarnations as Hannah Easton, the Salem Bibi and White Pearl. By providing one of America's most canonical literary texts with a history that firmly ties it to Europe and Asia, Mukherjee 'slalom[s] between *us* and *them* . . . deconstruct[s] the barriers of time and geography'.[16]

Perhaps Mukherjee can afford to slalom between 'us' and 'them' because her national identity is relatively secure on account of her professional middle-class position. In 'On Being an American Writer', Mukherjee's essay in the US-government-sponsored publication *Writers on America* (December 2002), she conveys this security, and her confidence in it, by reconstructing, rather than deconstructing, the binary opposition between us and them. Here, in the USA, she proclaims, 'there is no history, there are no barriers, no taboos, no fatwa can be launched, and no secret police will knock on your door.' And, anyway, if they do knock on your door, 'you at least have means of redress', apart from, that is, if you fit the racial profile for a terrorist.[17] More so than this one, however, Mukherjee's version of the immigrant experience into a freedom not available in countries only too tied to history is most visible in American national discourses after 9/11.

While national discourses seek to render invisible working-class immigrant experiences, Asian American critics also risk rendering this class invisible if they view transnationalism or denationalization too positively. In her essay 'Denationalization Reconsidered' (1995), Sau-ling Cynthia Wong proposes that an overly positive view of denationalization lacks historical specificity because it assumes a 'developmentalist narrative' with respect to Asian American studies 'based on a "forgetting" of the inherently coalitional spirit of the pan-Asian American movement'. For Wong, this narrative depends on 'an overdrawn and dehistoricized dichotomy' between 'the narrow-minded, essentialist' 1960s and 1970s and the 'deconstructivist and internationalist' 1980s and 1990s. Clearly, this dichotomy is not peculiar to Asian American studies; it marks the Western academy generally as it has shifted from blatant monoculturalism towards multiculturalism(s). In its overdrawn form, however, this dichotomy obscures the way in which early Asian American criticism 'was already witness to much critical interest beyond the domestic American scene'. Such witnessing was demonstrated by criticism of the Vietnam War, specifically by activist poets, for example, Janice Mirikitani. Asian American activists also utilized the theories of Malcolm X, Mao Zedong and other revolutionary figures when protesting against exclusion from US institutions. For Wong, then, these relationships between revolutionary peoples challenge the assumption that Asian American criticism in the 1960s and 1970s was narrow-minded or US-centric.[18]

On the matter of essentialism, Wong again insists that the argument is overdrawn. Early Asian American criticism was 'more anti-essentialist than it has been given credit', if mainly because of its demographic and ideological diversity. And, anyway, as Wong observes, essentialism is hardly a period specific concern when the concept of diaspora, so popular in current arguments for transnationalism, has 'an essentialist core' in its assumption of a collective identity, as in the Chinese diaspora or the Indian diaspora. Wong also implies that overly positive denationalizing discourses are narrow-minded for essentializing earlier Asian American criticism. They are also narrow-minded in the sense that they privilege a middle-class transnational identity that is able to exploit technologies such as air travel and the Internet in a manner that marginalizes the way in which other Asian Americans and Asian immigrants continue to be oppressed in the USA.[19]

Overall, then, Wong claims that 'the concept of *Asian Americans* is one that doesn't travel well, and for good reason: explicitly coalitional . . . it grew out of a specific history of resistance and advocacy within the United States.'[20] Moreover, racial discrimination and violence from the mid-1990s onwards, as exemplified, for instance, in the rise in anti-Arab and anti-Muslim hate crimes following 9/11, further reinforce Wong's reason for a domestic focus in Asian American studies. Transnational critics are not oblivious to this reasoning, with Rajini Srikanth, for one, acknowledging that a diasporic and global focus does risk being misread by non-Asian Americans as evidence of Asian American disloyalty to the USA. The assumption of disloyalty is consistent with a history of anti-Asian discrimination and violence, for the most part justified by the stereotype of the perpetual foreigner, who is, for this reason, excludable (between 1882 and 1952), internable (between 1941 and 1946) and generally disposable. At the same time, however, Srikanth insists that transnationalist critique enables insight into the complex relationships between the USA and Asia, as it impacts on the lives of those in and beyond Asian America.

Fundamental to this transnational relationship is the act of reading, not just merely reading but rather a ' "proper" risky' act whereby what is read – whether a literary text or a discursively produced world – depends for its significance on how it is read.[21] This proper risky act of reading is opposed to the sort of reading practices performed by 'Mr Everything Comes From India' and his counterpart 'Mr Everything is America', although, this said, both characters do satirize these universalisms and ways of reading that adhere to the logic of the same. In so doing, they also gesture towards a different understanding of transnational relationships that does not merely involve appropriation. Such an understanding involves '*partial* reading . . . in both senses of the word – as the biases with which we read, and as the ways in which those biases contribute to gaps in our understanding.'[22]

Certain biases recur in the reading of Asian American literary texts, some of which are also common in readings of multicultural literature. While critics respond to these biases in different ways, it is best to acknowledge the impossibility of fully overcoming bias. As much as biases limit understanding, they do at the same time generate the very categories and debates so crucial to Asian American critique – past, present and future. One particular bias stands out: the binary opposition between 'them' and 'us', typically, but not exclusively, between white Americans and Asian Americans. This relationship is both a thematic and formal concern in Asian American literary texts, as well as emerging in certain readings of the literature.

As they are read in this book, Asian American literary texts – from the first case study of Chinese American Yan Phou Lee's *When I Was a Boy in China* (1887) to the last, Korean American Chang-rae Lee's *Native Speaker* (1995) – include as part of their content a theorization of the relationship between them and us. As different as these texts are from each other, they are nevertheless written in cultural historical contexts in which the self-legitimizing inhabitants of the nation–state claim that the USA is solely theirs. For these Americans, America is white and American means white. Between these two texts are other Asian American literary texts also claiming Americanness for their Asian American protagonists (and writers), a claim consolidated in the cultural nationalist period through the representation of Asian American culture and history. Importantly, this claim did not necessarily entail the erasure of Asian American specificity consistent with the traditional understanding of assimilation as a unilateral process.

For example, Maxine Hong Kingston conveys this specificity in her literary texts, despite the claims of other cultural nationalists such as Frank Chin, Jeffery Paul Chan and Ben Tong. Although the latter read her semi-autobiographical novels, specifically *The Woman Warrior* and *China Men*, as claiming Americanness at the expense of Chinese Americanness, other critics highlight how these texts exceed this traditional genre and its underlying ideological assumptions. From Benjamin Franklin (1706–90) onwards, autobiographical writing has contributed to the formulation of an idealized Americanness: individual, heroic and progressive. In Kingston's case, however, this genre is denationalized formally by Asian talk-story. She combines Asian and American literary traditions to produce specifically Asian American forms. It is a strategy used by other Asian American writers, including, Toshio Mori (*shibai*), Hisaye Yamamoto (*haiku*), John Okada ('Momotaro'), Frank Chin (Kwan Kung), Amy Tan (talk-story), Jessica Hagedorn (*tsismis*) and Ruthanne Lum McCunn (wooden fish song).[23]

While Asian American literary texts complicate the binary opposition between them and us, certain critics within and beyond Asian American studies reproduce it by adhering to 'the autobiographical imperative', 'information retrieval' and 'coercive mimeticism'.[24] These different yet related ways of reading emphasize constraint not universally applied to white American literature. When critics simply read Asian American literature as authentic authorial expression, true cultural historical information and a reliable reflection of the world, they bypass its creativity, literariness, playfulness and, ultimately, critical potential.

In 'Required Reading and Other Dangerous Subjects' from *The Opposite of Fate* (2003), Amy Tan tries to recuperate that which has been bypassed when certain critics 'dictat[e] what literature must do and mean and say'.[25] Tan identifies as racist the way in which 'minority writers tend to be perceived as different from their white colleagues. Our responsibilities are supposedly more specific' (p. 314). Moreover, mainstream recognition and respect is accorded to those writers who most seem to adhere to minority-specific responsibilities relating primarily to the concept of representation. Good minority texts must be representative of the writer and the writer's group, which, in Tan's case, is 'not just Chinese-Americans but sometimes all Asian culture'. Good minority texts must also be realistic, so realistic, in fact, that they 'may not be read as literary fiction, or as American fiction, or as entertainment; they will be read more likely as sociology, politics, ideology, cultural lesson plans in narrative form' (pp. 305, 308–9).

However, this them-and-us approach is more than a mainstream issue, having, as Tan notes, 'crept into the fold' of the margin (p. 309). The authority of experience is presumed in both instances, albeit for apparently different reasons and in relation to different minority texts. It is a form of censorship. 'And woe to you', Tan maintains, 'if the Asian-American reviewer champions both ethnic correctness and marginalism, and believes your fiction should *not* depict violence, sexual abuse, mixed marriages, superstitions,

Chinese as Christians, or mothers who speak in broken English'
(p. 311). Such championing may be for the good reason of avoiding
negative stereotyping, but it simultaneously risks authorizing the
authority of experience: 'If you're an Asian-American, you must
write about modern, progressive characters, no harking back to the
bad old days.' Similarly,

If you're gay, you must write about AIDS and explicit safe
sex . . . If you're African-American, you must write about
oppression and racism. And who are *you* to question these mandates if you're not a member of the particular minority at issue?

(p. 309)

If you are a member of the particular minority at issue, and if you
do question these mandates, you risk being 'treated as a traitor, pub-
licly branded and condemned' as 'a running-dog whore sucking on
the tit of the imperialist white pigs' (pp. 316, 320).

Both imperialists and marginalists seek dominance of multicultural literature and multicultural criticism, with each side demand-
ing authenticity as defined by them for didactic, cathartic and, in
Tan's estimation, propaganda purposes. For her, literature provides
'freedom and danger, satisfaction and discomfort, truth and contradiction' (p. 322). This potential for contradiction has meant that
Tan's literary texts have been both applauded and condemned, typically in terms of their perceived relationship to racist stereotyping.
For example, Frank Chin categorizes Tan's novels as fake in the tradition of Kingston, while other Asian American critics proclaim her
ideological balancing act in a novel like *The Joy Luck Club* so slick
that she can bring together apparently oppositional discourses:
'neoconservative rhetoric' and dominant American ideologies on
the one hand, and 'poststructural and multicultural celebrations of
diasporic subjectivity' on the other.[26]

But, Asian American and other multicultural literatures do not
only affirm traditional aesthetic categories – didacticism, catharsis
and mimesis. As Tan puts it in an interview:

All I'm saying is that there's work to be done . . . so that people
don't use them entirely for lessons outside of literature, outside

the pleasure of reading, outside of the whole nature of story. What people read these books for seems to be so much about role models, cultural explanation, historical point of view and that's not bad in and of itself. But *by* itself . . . It does something to literature . . . not just multicultural literature . . . turning our literature into very limited rhetoric.[27]

Ultimately, this is all this book is saying. Yes, Asian American literature can be used as cultural history, particularly as so many of the texts focus on historical experiences of exclusionism from both the nation-state and mainstream American culture. Yes, Asian American literature can help to explain what being an Asian American must be like, apart from racist stereotypes of a threatening yellow peril and a controllable model minority. It can also help to render this identity heterogeneous through the depiction of demographic and ideological diversity. It can affect readers emotionally, as well as critically, through a range of genres and forms such as memoir, autobiography, Bildungsroman, interracial and intergenerational romance, satire and comedy. In addition to being about 'them', Asian American literature is about 'us' and, finally, about itself in the sense that it is about the nature of story and the linguistic and the ideological processes involved in reading and representation. This last function ensures that Asian American literature is not turned into the very limited rhetoric, whereby literary texts are made to mean and reference reliably.

To end this book with a possible future, albeit a 'back to the future' scenario: African American Anne Deavere Smith's solo performance of *Twilight: Los Angeles, 1992*, which premiered in 1993. In addition to addressing the general point differently raised by Tomo Hattori and Amy Tan regarding the de-essentializing of Asian American literature, this play re-presents historical experiences in a way that foregrounds the issue of representation. *Twilight* is based on some of Smith's interviews with people variously involved in the Los Angeles uprising of 1992 following the acquittal of the white policemen who attacked African American Rodney King. While the beating and the trial were understood according to the black-white racial dichotomy, the uprising forced a renegotiation of this traditional opposition to include Korean Americans and Latinos. Although the American press depicted the uprising as the nation's first multiracial riot, race scholars emphasized the importance of 'stripping these incidents of the aura of the extraordinary'.[28] This aura of the extraordinary has consistently been applied to so-called mistakes in the racial formation of the United States, despite the fact that acts of racial violence against individuals, small groups, ethnic groups and entire races are not anomalous but integral to this formation. Thus euphemized, such anomalies can quite easily become banal, even resembling an ordinary spectator sport.

In her essay on the Los Angeles uprising, Korean American Elaine H. Kim recalls how 'European Americans discuss[ed] the conflicts as if they were watching a dogfight or a boxing match'. Presumably, the material and psychological damage incurred by other Americans during these sports meant that they were the losers.[29] Even when racial minorities win, when they have, for example, a winning hand by playing the 'race card', their 'liability [is] transmuted to asset and reformed yet again as liability' according to a vernacular that underplays 'race and racial matters in America'. Anne Anlin Cheng continues:

What does it mean that the deep wound of race in this country has come to be euphemized as a card? . . . One would 'play' a card only because one is already *outside* the larger game, for to play a card is to exercise the value of one's disadvantage, the liability that is asset. The paradox doubles: the one who plays with a full deck not only need not play at all but indeed has no such 'card' to play. Only those playing with *less* than a full deck need apply.[30]

With the game so well rigged against people whose racially marked bodies tie them to violence and discrimination, it seems that, in Rodney King's words, 'We're all stuck here for awhile.' But, 'can we all get along?'[31] This question finds a response in Smith's play, *Twilight*. Slaloming between us and them when she mimics on stage some of her interviewees, Smith crosses class, gender and racial boundaries. Such mimicry offers the possibility of cross-cultural understanding, particularly when Smith is pacifist gang member

Twilight Bey, who asserts: 'I can't forever dwell in darkness, / I can't forever dwell in the idea, / just identifying with people like me, and understanding me and / mine.'[32] Compared to other acts of slaloming, by, for example, Bharati Mukherjee in *Writers on America*, Smith's *Twilight* promotes the insight that for cross-cultural understanding to be more than merely appropriative it has to acknowledge its partiality and limitations. Such an acknowledgement does not entail a movement from darkness to lightness, only into the twilight – although, at least here, there is still the possibility of a future for debate on Asian American literature as it generates insights with respect to identity, history and ideology beyond the boundaries of this book.

NOTES

1. Rajini Srikanth, *The World Next Door: South Asian American Literature and the Idea of America* (Philadelphia: Temple University Press, 2004), p. 203.
2. Yan Phou Lee, 'The Chinese Must Stay', *North Atlantic Review* 148:389 (April 1889), 476, 479.
3. Viet Thanh Nguyen, *Race and Resistance: Literature and Politics in Asian America* (Oxford: Oxford University Press, 2002), pp. 170–1.
4. Sucheta Mazumdar, quoted in Srikanth, *World*, p. 155.
5. Anne Anlin Cheng, *The Melancholy of Race: Psychoanalysis, Assimilation, and Hidden Grief* (Oxford: Oxford University Press, 2001), p. 24.
6. Mazumdar, quoted in Srikanth, *World*, p. 155.
7. Nguyen, *Race*, p. 157.
8. See, for example, Sau-ling Cynthia Wong, 'Autobiography as Guided Chinatown Tour? Maxine Hong Kingston's *The Woman Warrior* and the Chinese-American Autobiographical Controversy', *Multicultural Autobiography: American Lives*, ed. James Robert Payne (Knoxville: University of Tennessee Press, 1992), pp. 262–4.
9. Graham Huggan, *The Postcolonial Exotic: Marketing the Margins* (London: Routledge, 2001), pp. 106–11, p. 119.

10. Pico Iyer and anonymous panellist, quoted in Tomo Hattori, 'China Man Autoeroticism and the Remains of Asian America', *Novel* 31:2 (Spring 1998), 218.

11. Hattori, 'China Man', 220.

12. Ibid., 227–8, 220.

13. David Palumbo-Liu, *Asian/American: Historical Crossings of a Racial Frontier* (Stanford: Stanford University Press, 1999), pp. 380–2.

14. Salman Rushdic, *Fury* (London: Vintage, 2001), p. 87.

15. http://www.bbc.co.uk/comedy/guide/articles/g/goodness-gracious_66601650.shtml [Accessed January 2007].

16. Bharati Mukherjee, *The Middleman and Other Stories* (London: Virago, 1988), pp. 3–4, p. 7; Bharati Mukherjee, *The Holder of the World* (London: Virago, 1993), p. 13, p. 11.

17. Bharati Mukherjee, 'On Being an American Writer', *Writers on America*, ed. George Clack, Paul Malamud, Mark Jacobs and Michael Bandler, http://usinfo.state.gov/products/pubs/writers/mukherjee.htm [Accessed February 2007].

18. Sau-ling Cynthia Wong, 'Denationalization Reconsidered: Asian American Cultural Criticism at a Theoretical Crossroads', *Amerasia Journal* 21:1 & 2 (1995), 12–13, 3.

19. Ibid., 17.

20. Ibid., 17.

21. Gayatri Chakravorty Spivak, quoted in Srikanth, *World*, p. 13.

22. Srikanth, *World*, p. 16.

23. Helena Grice, *Negotiating Identities: An Introduction to Asian American Women's Writing* (Manchester: Manchester University Press, 2002), pp. 87–9.

24. Hattori, 'China Man', p. 220; Gayatri Chakravorty Spivak, *The Post-colonial Critic: Interviews, Strategies, Dialogues*, ed. Sarah Harasym (New York: Routledge, 1990), p. 9; Rey Chow, *The Protestant Ethnic and the Spirit of Capitalism* (New York: Columbia University Press, 2002), p. 95.

25. Amy Tan, *The Opposite of Fate* (London: Flamingo, 2003), p. 308. Hereafter references to this edition are given in the text.

26. David Leiwei Li, *Imagining the Nation: Asian American Literature and Cultural Consent* (Stanford: Stanford University Press, 1998), p. 117.

27. David Stanton, 'Breakfast with Amy Tan', *Paintbrush* 22 (Autumn, 1995), 7–8.
28. Robert Gooding-Williams (ed.), 'Introduction: On Being Stuck', *Reading Rodney King / Reading Urban Uprising* (New York: Routledge, 1993), p. 2.
29. Kim, 'Home is where the *Han* is', in Gooding-Williams, *Rodney*, p. 217, p. 215.
30. Cheng, *Melancholy*, p. 103.
31. Rodney King and T-shirt slogan, quoted in Gooding-Williams, 'Introduction', p. 3.
32. Anne Deavere Smith, *Twilight: Los Angeles, 1992* (New York: Dramatists Play Service, Inc., 2003), p. 171.

Student Resources

GLOSSARY

Identities and Places

Amerasian A term coined in the Second World War period and refers to children of Asian mothers and American fathers left fatherless in Asia. It is more commonly used to refer to the biracial children of US serviceman stationed in Southeast Asia during the Vietnam War.

Asian America Both the real and the imagined spaces Asian Americans occupy in the USA – for example, San Francisco Chinatown and other urban ethnic spaces; the Sierra Nevadas and other rural spaces; the annexed Philippines and Hawaii; and, in the national imagination, an extra-US space that renders Asian Americans perpetually foreign.

Asian American An identity, a census category and a socio-political consciousness. It is a unifying and homogenizing racial category that was developed during the cultural nationalist period in the late 1960s. It refers to a person of Asian descent, both American- and foreign-born, living in the USA, including Hawaii, or, more generally, North America.

Asian-American Used by some cultural nationalist critics to emphasize the Americanness of Asian Americans against the perpetual foreigner stereotype. The hyphen is meant to link Asian and American, thus inhibiting cultural and psychological alienation. However, other critics argue that it has the opposite effect in that hyphenation reinforces the so-called real Americanness of racially unmarked groups, specifically white Americans.

Asian Pacific American A more recent development on Asian American, although it is more explicit in its inclusion of Asian Pacific Islanders, for example, Fijian, Guamanian, Hawaiian, Samoan and Tongan Americans, and of Asian Canadians.

East Asian American People of Asian descent from China, Japan, North and South Korea, Taiwan and Tibet.

Eurasian (or Hapa) The biracial children of Asian and European parents living in the USA.

South Asian American People of Asian descent from Bangladesh, Bhutan, India, Maldives, Nepal, Pakistani and Sri Lanka. South Asian Americans have also been labelled Asian Indians, Indian Subcontinentals, and Indo-Americans.

Southeast Asian American People of Asian descent from Burma (now Myanmar), Cambodia (now Kampuchea), Indonesia, Laos, Malaysia, Philippines, Singapore, Thailand and Vietnam.

West Asian American Arab Americans, both Muslim and non-Muslim. West Asia is also the Middle East. Although not usually included in definitions of Asian American, some critics include Arab Americans and Muslim Americans in their discussions, especially after the 9/11 terrorist attacks and the backlash against people deemed to fit the racial profile of the terrorist on the basis of their skin colour and religion.

Ideas and Ideologies

Asian American Studies Began in the late 1960s following student campaigns for ethnic studies at some US colleges and universities. Like other area studies, it is an interdisciplinary field involved in the analysis of culture, history, politics, sociology and literature. Historically, the **Asian American literature** studied, which, in part, generates its definition, tends to be Anglophonic US-centric prose, poetry and drama by East Asian American writers.

Assimilation Typically understood as a process whereby all immigrants integrate into American culture (the melting pot). In the 1960s, cultural nationalist critics understood assimilation in terms of Anglo-conformity; they argued that it constituted racial self-denial and promoted racial self-hatred. More recently, Asian American critics complicate assimilationism by arguing that Asianness is intrinsic to the material and ideological production of Americanness.

Bildungsroman A novel of formation, traditionally that of a Euro-American hero from childhood naivety towards adult insight and knowledge. The Bildungsroman also offers a model for understanding the modern nation, as progressing from violence towards civility. Some Asian Americans critics argue that the Bildungsroman serves an assimilationist function by reconciling individuals both inside and outside novels of formation with the dominant social order. However, other critics propose that this reconciliation remains incomplete, particularly in Bildungsromans by women and racial minorities.

Cultural Nationalism and Yellow Power The socio-political movements that emerged in the late 1960s when Asian Americans defined themselves principally by representing past traumas and the heroic struggle against them. Whether in the form of labour strikes, legal cases, interethnic and interracial alliances or Asian American literary and cultural critique (see Chronology), this struggle underpinned the cultural nationalist project of self-redefinition *vis-à-vis* nativist, racist and Orientalist stereotypes.

Yellow Power is the most forceful articulation of cultural national-ism and is mainly directed towards whites and race traitors, especially assimilationist (because feminist and Christian) Asian American women. Yellow Power does not advocate separatism in, for example, the manner of Black Power.

Essentialism Reductionist typification that necessarily occurs when theorizing complex phenomena. For example, it operates when people are organized into groups on the basis of a set of shared defining physical and psychological features, and can easily degenerate into harmful stereotyping. Essentialist categories include 'the Oriental', 'the Asian American', 'Asianness' and 'Americanness', the singularity of these categories potentially over-riding the complexity of the identity and the group to which they apparently refer.

Ethnicity A concept related to race. These two terms have been regarded as antonyms in a logic that opposes the biological and physiological (race) to the cultural and historical (ethnicity), and as synonyms on the basis that both are ideological categories. Typically, Asian American is understood as a racial category, while Chinese American, Vietnamese American and so on are identified as ethnic categories. Ethnicity theorists are criticized by critical race theorists for conflating experiences of immigration and assimilation without enough attention to cultural historical differences between whites and nonwhites. For critical race theorists, ethnicity theory is Eurocentric, as well as ahistorical and politically conservative.

Model Minority A term coined in the USA in mid-1960s to refer to Asian Americans who had successfully assimilated into American culture through strong commitment to work, education and family. The model minority is a stereotype that helps to main-tain the dominant racial hierarchy by misrepresenting the success of some Asian Americans as representative of the racial group, which in turn obscures continuing economic and political inequal-ities in and beyond Asian America. Model-minority figures include Charlie Chan, Lotus Blossom and, more recently, Science Nerd.

Nativism An ideology that is typically articulated by white Americans who oppose another group of Americans on the basis of their perceived foreignness.

Oriental (and Mongolian) An old-fashioned and derogatory term, which was replaced with Asian American in the late 1960s. This shift from Oriental to Asian American is similar to the shift from Negro to African American.

Orientalism An ideology first discussed in detail by Edward W. Said in *Orientalism: Western Conceptions of the Orient* (1978). Said's Orient is the Middle East, as it is systematically Orientalized by Anglo-French writers who, with little or no reference to modern conditions in these countries, render it either exotic, feminine, childlike and, therefore, controllable, or irrational, undeveloped, barbaric and, thus, threatening. Similar to its European counterpart, American Orientalism approaches Asians as biologically and culturally inferior or Other, to the point that they are rendered perpetually foreign.

Race A cultural category used to differentiate people into groups, most obviously black, white and Asian. Although race is assumed to be dependent on visible physical differences such as skin colour, hair texture, and nose and eye shape, critical race theorists argue that people learn to see these differences. As such, then, racial categorization involves cultural historical processes that are not in themselves stable.

Racism An ideology that seeks to stabilize by naturalizing and essentializing racial categories for reasons of power and inequality. Racism can be articulated by prejudiced individuals within dominant and subordinate racial groups, although, particularly from the 1960s onwards, it is understood in terms of institutional racism. Institutional racism sustains white advantage through the economic and political exploitation of nonwhite racial groups. This dominant racial hierarchy is integral to American cultural history, underpinning the formation of American citizenship in terms of freedom, civility and development against such figures as 'the enslaved African', 'the wild Indian' and 'the heathen Chinese'.

Transnationalism and denationalization Ways of theorizing the nation within a global context. With respect to Asian American studies, transnational critics, often, but not exclusively, affiliated with postcolonial and diaspora studies, criticize its US-centric perspective.

Yellow Peril A term popularized in the USA in the mid-nineteenth century at a time of increased Asian migration. Like its apparently opposite stereotype of the model minority, the yellow-peril stereotype represents Asian Americans as perpetually foreign, albeit in much more threatening terms. Yellow-peril figures include Dr Fu Manchu, Dragon Lady and, more recently, Asian Millionaire Businessman.

SELECTED ELECTRONIC RESOURCES

Cultural History Websites

http://www.asian-nation.org provides an overview of Asian American historical, political, demographic and cultural issues. This site briefly defines key terms, including stereotypes, and includes articles on, for example, the Vietnam War. It also features current 'Asian-Nation News Blog'.

http://www.digitalhistory.uh.edu/asian_voices/asian_voices.cfm is part of an academic site that includes a comprehensive Asian American timeline, 1587–1998, and a detailed discussion of Asian American history. This site also lists online Asian American history resources.

http://www.goldsea.com or *Goldsea Asian American Daily* is a topical site and covers issues specific to Asian America (e.g. business, crime, entertainment, fashion and sport) and Asia (e.g. geopolitics).

http://www.modelminority.com is a topical site that provides articles, along with commentaries, stories and other documents on Asian American culture, government and experiences.

http://www.pbs.org/ancestorsintheamericas/ is the companion
website for the PBS series *Ancestors in the Americas* by Loni Ding.
It features an Asian American timeline covering the period
1600–1945, with images, quotations and explanation. It also provides classroom guides, with discussion questions, as well as links
to Asian American history and media websites.

Encyclopaedic sites containing facts and figures on Asian
American cultural history, along with references and links to other
Asian American resources: http://americanhistory.about.com/
od/asianamerhistory/AsianAmerican_History.htm http://en.
wikipedia.org/wiki/Asian_American and http://www.infoplease.
com/spot/asianhistory1.html

Literary Websites

http://falcon.jmu.edu/~ramseyil/asialit.htm is a pedagogical site
for schoolteachers and is sometimes overly didactic. Its annotated
bibliography includes articles and books on teaching multicultural
literature to children and teenagers. The rest of the bibliography
lists fictional and non-fictional Asian American texts, many of
which come with a recommended age range.

http://voices.cla.umn.edu/VG/index.html or *VG: Voices from the
Gaps, Women Artists and Writers of Color* is a transnational academic site that includes information on some Asian American women
writers and artists. It contains biographical, critical and historical
material, as well as interviews. One of VG's links is to *Voice of
the Shuttle* at http://vos.ucsb.edu/ where other links to Asian
American literature and Asian American studies can be found.

http://web.ade.org/bulletin/ is an academic site for the Association
of Departments of English or *ADE Bulletin*. Its spring 1985 edition
includes essays on Asian American literature by Amy Ling
(http://web.ade.org/ade/bulletin/N080/080029.htm), Elaine
Kim http://web.ade.org/ade/bulletin/N080/080034.htm) and
Linda Cheng Sledge (http://web.ade.org/ade/bulletin/N080/
080042.htm).

http://www.alexanderstreet2.com/aadrlive/ or *Asian American Drama* brings together 252 plays by forty-two Asian American playwrights, along with related biographical, production and theatrical material. This site expands on the playwrights listed in *Asian American Playwrights: A Bio-Bibliographical Critical Sourcebook* edited by Miles Xian Liu. It is available through either one-time purchase of perpetual rights or annual subscription.

http://www.english.uiuc.edu/maps/ is a companion site for the *Anthology of Modern American Poetry* edited by Cary Nelson. This site includes some Asian American poets, as well as entries for 'Angel Island Poetry' and 'Japanese American Concentration Camp Haiku'. It provides close readings of individual poems and related biographical, critical and historical material. Other online Asian American poetry resources are also listed.

http://www.georgetown.edu/tamlit/ is an academic site sponsored by Georgetown University and D. C. Heath. Its 'Syllabus Library for Teaching American Literatures' includes Amy Ling's essay, 'Teaching Asian American Literature', from the *Heath Anthology Newsletter* (http://www.georgetown.edu/tamlit/essay/asian_am.html). The first half of this essay succinctly addresses terminology, after which Ling clarifies the meaning and function of Asian American literature. The second half of Ling's essay refers to the ten Asian American authors included in the *Heath Anthology*. Other online essays, as well as syllabi and discussion questions, on Asian American literature can also be found on 'tamlit'.

http://wwwlibrary.csustan.edu/pcrawford/asianlit/ is an academic site that provides a selective bibliography of Asian American literature. Twenty-six anthologies are listed, followed by selected literatures that are divided historically (pre- and post-1950) and ethnically.

http://www.poets.org is a poetry site that includes information on some Asian American poets along with essays and interviews.

http://www.sjsu.edu/faculty/awilliams/AsianAmResources.html is an academic site that lists sources for researching Asian American literature. Among these sources are important journals and publishers, as well as other Asian American studies programmes.

The following are further sites for Asian American studies, including Asian American literary studies:

http://eslibrary.berkeley.edu/aasc.htm
http://www.aasc.ucla.edu/
http://www.aasp.cornell.edu/
http://www.aasp.uiuc.edu/
http://www.asamst.ucsb.edu/
http://www.iaas.umb.edu/
http://polyglot.lss.wisc.edu/aasp/
http://www.sfsu.edu/~aas/
http://www.utexas.edu/cola/centers/aas/

GUIDE TO FURTHER READING

Aguilar-San Juan, Karin (ed.), *The State of Asian America: Activism and Resistance* (Boston: South End Press, 1994).

Alexander, Meena, *Fault Lines: A Memoir* (New York: The Feminist Press, 1993).

Ancheta, Angelo N., *Race, Rights, and the Asian American Experience* (New Brunswick, NJ: Rutgers University Press, 1998).

Ang, Ien, *On Not Speaking Chinese: Living Between Asia and the West* (London: Routledge, 2001).

Bahri, Deepika and Mary Vasudeva (eds), *Between the Lines: South Asians on Postcolonial Identity and Culture* (Philadelphia: Temple University Press, 1996).

Berson, Misha (ed.), *Between Worlds: Contemporary Asian-American Plays* (New York: Theatre Communications, 1990).

Bow, Leslie, *Betrayal and Other Acts of Subversion: Feminism, Sexual Politics, Asian American Women's Literature* (Princeton: Princeton University Press, 2001).

Brada-Williams, Noelle and Karen Chow (eds), *Crossing Oceans: Reconfiguring American Literary Studies in the Pacific Rim* (Hong Kong: Hong Kong University Press, 2004).

Brewster, Anne, 'A Critique of Bharati Mukherjee's Neo-Nationalism', *SPAN* 34–5 (November 1992 and May 1993), 50–9.

Bromley, Roger, *Narratives for a New Belonging: Diasporic Cultural Fictions* (Edinburgh: Edinburgh University Press, 2000).

Bruchac, Joseph (ed.), *Breaking Silence: An Anthology of Contemporary Asian American Poets* (Greenfield Center: Greenfield Review, 1983).

Bulosan, Carlos, *America Is in the Heart: A Personal History* (Seattle: University of Washington Press, [1946] 1973).

Cao, Lan, *Monkey Bridge* (New York: Penguin, 1997).

Cao, Lan and Himilce Novas, *Everything You Need to Know About Asian-American History* (New York: Plume, 1996).

Chan, Jeffery Paul, Frank Chin, Lawsan Fusao Inada and Shawn Hsu Wong (eds), *Aiiieeeee! An Anthology of Asian-American Writers* (Washington, DC: Howard University Press, 1974).

Chan, Mimi and Roy Harris (eds), *Asian Voices in English* (Hong Kong: Hong Kong University Press, 1991).

Chan, Sucheng, *Asian Americans: An Interpretative History* (New York: Twayne Publishers, 1991).

Chandrasekhar, S. (ed.), *From India to America: A Brief History of Immigration, Problems of Discrimination; Admission and Assimilation* (La Jolla, CA: A Population Review Book, 1992).

Chang, Juliana (ed.), *Quiet Fire: Asian American Poetry, 1892–1970* (New York: Asian American Writers' Workshop, 1996).

Cheng, Anne Anlin, *The Melancholy of Race: Psychoanalysis, Assimilation, and Hidden Grief* (Oxford: Oxford University Press, 2001).

Cheung, King-kok, 'The Woman Warrior versus The Chinaman Pacific: Must a Chinese American Critic Choose between Feminism and Heroism?' in *Conflicts in Feminism*, ed. Marianne Hirsch and Evelyn Fox Keller (New York: Routledge, 1990), pp. 234–51.

Cheung, King-kok, *Articulate Silences: Hisaye Yamamoto, Maxine Hong Kingston, Joy Kogawa* (Ithaca: Cornell University Press, 1993).

Cheung, King-kok (ed.), *An Interethnic Companion to Asian American Literature* (Cambridge: Cambridge University Press, 1997).

Cheung, King-kok and Stan Yogi (eds), *Asian American Literature: An Annotated Bibliography* (New York: MLA, 1988).

Chin, Frank, 'Confessions of the Chinatown Cowboy', *Bulletin of Concerned Asian Scholars* 4:3 (1972), 58–70.

Chin, Frank, *The Chickencoop China and The Year of the Dragon* (Seattle: University of Washington Press, 1981).

Chin, Frank, 'This is Not an Autobiography', *Genre* 18 (Summer 1985), 109–30.

Chin, Frank, *The Chinaman Pacific and Frisco R.R. Co.* (Minneapolis: Coffee House Press, 1988).

Chin, Frank and Jeffrey Paul Chan, 'Racist Love', *Seeing Through Shuck*, ed. Richard Kostelanetz (New York: Ballantine Books, 1972), pp. 65–79.

Chin, Frank, Jeffery Paul Chan, Lawson Fusao Inada and Shawn Wong (eds), *The Big Aiiieeeee! An Anthology of Chinese American and Japanese American Literature* (New York: Meridian, 1991).

Chow, Rey, *Ethics After Idealism: Theory–Culture–Ethnicity–Reading* (Bloomington: Indiana University Press, 1998).

Chow, Rey, *The Protestant Ethnic and the Spirit of Capitalism* (New York: Columbia University Press, 2002).

Chu, Louis, *Eat a Bowl of Tea* (New York: Lyle Stuart Books, [1961] 2002).

Chu, Patricia, *Assimilating Asians: Gendered Strategies of Authorship in Asian America* (Durham, NC: Duke University Press, 2000).

Chuh, Kandice, *Imagine Otherwise: On Asian Americanist Critique* (Durham, NC: Duke University Press, 2003).

Chuh, Kandice and Karen Shimakawa (eds), *Orientations: Mapping Studies in the Asian Diaspora* (Durham, NC: Duke University Press, 2001).

Cole, Jean Lee, 'The Winnifred Eaton Digital Archive', http://etext.lib.virginia.edu/eaton/ [Accessed January 2007].

Corley, Liam, ' "Just another ethnic pol": Literary Citizenship in Chang-rae Lee's *Native Speaker*', *Studies in the Literary Imagination* 37:1 (Spring 2004), 61–82.

Dabydeen, Cyril (ed.), *Another Way to Dance: Contemporary Asian Poetry from Canada and the United States* (Toronto: TSAR, 1996).

Davis, Rocío G., *Transcultural Reinventions: Asian American and Asian Canadian Short-story Cycles* (Toronto: TSAR, 2001).

Davis, Rocío G. and Sami Ludwig (eds), *Asian American Literature in an International Context: Readings on Fiction, Poetry, and Performance* (Munster: Lit Verlag, 2002).

Diana, Vanessa Holford, 'Biracial/Bicultural Identity in the Writings of Sui Sin Far', *MELUS* 26:2 (Summer 2001), 159–86.

Duncan, Patti, *Tell this Silence: Asian American Women Writers and the Politics of Speech* (Iowa City: University of Iowa Press, 2004).

Eng, David L., *Racial Castration: Managing Masculinity in Asian America* (Durham, NC: Duke University Press, 2001).

Eng, David L. and Alice Y. Hom (eds), *Q & A: Queer in Asian America* (Philadelphia: Temple University Press, 1998).

Eng, Franklin, Judy Yung, Stephen Fugita and Elaine Kim (eds), *New Visions in Asian American Studies: Diversity, Community, Power* (Pullman: Washington State University Press, 1994).

Espiritu, Yen Le, *Asian American Panethnicity: Bridging Institutions and Identities* (Philadelphia: Temple University Press, 1992).

Grewal, Inderpal, 'The Postcolonial, Ethnic Studies, and the Diaspora: The Contexts of Ethnic Immigrant/Migrant Cultural Studies in the US', *Socialist Review* 24:4 (1994), 45–74.

Grice, Helena, 'Asian American Fiction', in *Beginning Ethnic American Literatures*, ed. Helena Grice, Candida Hepworth, Maria Lauret and Martin Padget (Manchester: Manchester University Press, 2001), pp. 133–88.

Grice, Helena, *Negotiating Identities: An Introduction to Asian American Women's Writing* (Manchester: Manchester University Press, 2002).

Gyhmn, Esther Mikyung, *Images of Asian American Women by Asian American Women Writers* (New York: Peter Lang, 1995).

Hagedorn, Jessica (ed.), *Charlie Chan is Dead: An Anthology of Contemporary Asian American Fiction* (New York: Penguin, 1993).

Hattori, Tomo, 'China Man Autoeroticism and the Remains of Asian America', *Novel* 31:2 (Spring 1998), 215–36.

Hattori, Tomo, 'Model Minority Discourses and Asian American Jouis-Sense', *Differences* 11:2 (1999), 228–47.

Higashida, Cheryl, 'Re-Signed Subjects: Women, Work, and World in the Fiction of Carlos Bulosan and Hisaye Yamamoto', *Studies in the Literary Imagination* 37:1 (Spring 2004), 35–60.

Hirabayashi, Lane Ryo (ed.), *Teaching Asian America: Diversity and the Problem of Community* (Lanham: Rowman, 1998).

Ho, Wendy, 'Swan-Feather Mothers and Coca-Cola Daughters: Teaching Amy Tan's *The Joy Luck Club*', in *Teaching American Ethnic Literatures: Nineteen Essays*, ed. John R. Maitino and David R. Peck (Albuquerque: University of New Mexico Press, 1996), pp. 327–45.

Hom, Marlon K. (ed., intro. and trans.), *Songs of Gold Mountain: Cantonese Rhymes from San Francisco Chinatown* (Berkeley: University of California Press, 1987).

Hong, Maria (ed.), *Growing Up Asian American: An Anthology* (New York: Morrow, 1993).

Hongo, Garrett (ed.), *The Open Boat: Poems from Asian America* (New York: Anchor-Doubleday, 1993).

Hongo, Garrett, *Under Western Eyes: Personal Essays from Asian America* (New York: Anchor-Doubleday, 1995).

Hsiao, Ruth Yu, 'A Practical Guide to Teaching Asian-American Literature', *Radical Teacher* 41 (1992), 20–3.

Hsu, Kai-yu and Helen Palubinskas (eds), *Asian-American Authors* (Boston: Houghton Mifflin, 1972).

Huang, Guiyou (ed.), *Asian American Poets: A Bio-Bibliographical Critical Sourcebook* (Westport, CT: Greenwood Press, 2002).

Huang, Guiyou, *The Columbia Guide to Asian American Literature Since 1945* (New York: Columbia University Press, 2006).

Huggan, Graham, *The Postcolonial Exotic: Marketing the Margins* (London: Routledge, 2001).

Hune, Shirley and Hyung-chan Kim, Stephen S. Fugita and Amy Ling (eds), *Asian Americans: Comparative and Global Perspectives* (Pullman: Washington State University Press, 1991).

Hwang, David Henry, *M. Butterfly* (New York: Plume, [1988] 1989).

Hyoung Song, Min, 'A Diasporic Future? *Native Speaker* and Historical Trauma', *LIT* 12 (2001), 79–98.

Janette, Michele, 'Guerrilla Irony in Lan Cao's *Monkey Bridge*', *Contemporary Literature* 42:1 (Spring 2001), 50–77.

Jen, Gish, *Who's Irish?* (New York: Vintage, 1999).

Kafka, Phillipa, *(Un)Doing the Missionary Position: Gender Asymmetry in Contemporary Asian American Women's Writing* (Westport, CT: Greenwood Press, 1997).

Kain, Geoffrey (ed.), *Ideas of Home: Literature of Asian Migration* (East Lansing: Michigan State University Press, 1997).

Kang, Laura Hyan Yi, *Compositional Subjects: Enfiguring Asian/American Women* (Durham, NC: Duke University Press, 2002).

Kim, Elaine H., *Asian American Literature: An Introduction to the Writings and their Social Context* (Philadelphia: Temple University Press, 1982).

Kim, Elaine H., 'Defining Asian American Realities through Literature', *Cultural Critique* 6 (Spring 1987), 87–111.

Kim, Elaine H., ' "Such Opposite Creatures": Men and Women in Asian American Literature', *Michigan Quarterly Review* 29 (1990), 68–93.

Kim, Elaine H., 'Home is where the *Han* is', in *Reading Rodney King / Reading Urban Uprising*, ed. Robert Gooding-Williams (New York: Routledge, 1993), pp. 215–35.

Kim, Elaine H., Lilia V. Villaneuva and Asian American Women United of California (eds), *Making More Waves: New Writing by Asian American Women* (Boston: Beacon Press, 1997).

Kingston, Maxine Hong, *The Woman Warrior: Memoirs of a Girlhood Among Ghosts* (London: Picador, 1976).

Kingston, Maxine Hong, *China Men* (London: Picador, 1980).

Kingston, Maxine Hong, 'Cultural Mis-readings by American Reviewers', in *Asian and Western Writers in Dialogue*, ed. Guy Armirthanayagam (London: Macmillan, 1982), pp. 55–65.

Kingston, Maxine Hong, *Tripmaster Monkey: His Fake Book* (New York: Vintage Books, 1989).

Knippling, Alpana Sharma (ed.), *New Immigrant Literatures in the United States: A Sourcebook to Our Multicultural Literary Heritage* (Westport, CT: Greenwood Press, 1996).

Kogawa, Joy, *Obasan* (New York: Anchor Books, [1981] 1994).

Kogawa, Joy and Ruth Y. Hsu, 'A Conversation with Joy Kogawa', *Amerasia Journal* 22:1 (Spring 1996), 199–216.

Koshy, Susan, 'The Fiction of Asian American Literature', *The Yale Journal of Criticism* 9:2 (1996), 315–46.

Kudaka, Geraldine (ed.), *On a Bed of Rice: An Asian American Erotic Feast* (New York: Anchor, 1995).

Lai, Him Mark, Genny Lim and Judy Yung (eds), *Island: Poetry and History of Chinese Immigrants on Angel Island, 1910–1940* (Seattle: University of Washington Press, 1991).

Lawrence, Charles R., 'Beyond Redress: Reclaiming the Meaning of Affirmative Action', *Amerasia Journal* 19:1 (1993), 1–6.

Lawrence, Keith and Floyd Cheng (eds), *Recovered Legacies: Authority and Identity in Early Asian American Literature* (Philadelphia: Temple University Press, 2005).

Law-Yone, Wendy, *The Coffin Tree* (London: Penguin, 1983).

Lee, Chang-rae, *Native Speaker* (London: Granta Books, 1995).

Lee, Chang-rae, *A Gesture Life* (London: Granta Books, 1999).

Lee, Josephine (ed.), *Performing Asian America: Race and Ethnicity on the Contemporary Stage* (Philadelphia: Temple University Press, 1997).

Lee, Josephine, Imogene L. Lim and Yuko Matsukawa (eds), *Re/Collecting Early Asian America: Essays in Cultural History* (Philadelphia: Temple University Press, 2002).

Lee, Rachel C., *The Americas of Asian American Literature: Gendered Fictions of Nation and Transnation* (Princeton: Princeton University Press, 1999).

Lee, Rachel C., 'Reading Contests and Contesting Reading: Chang-rae Lee's *Native Speaker* and Ethnic New York', *MELUS* 29:3/4 (Fall/Winter 2004), 341–52.

Lee, Sky, *Disappearing Moon Café* (Vancouver: The Seal Press, 1990).

Lee, Yan Phou, *When I Was a Boy in China* (Philadelphia, PA: Xlibris, [1887] 2003).

Lee, Yan Phou, 'The Chinese Must Stay', *North Atlantic Review* 148:389 (April 1889), 476–83.

Leong, Russell (ed.), *Asian American Sexualities: Dimensions of Gay and Lesbian Experience* (New York: Routledge, 1996).

Li, David Leiwei, 'The Naming of a Chinese American "I": Cross-Cultural Sign/ifications in *The Woman Warrior*', *Criticism* 30:4 (Fall 1988), 497–515.

Li, David Leiwei, *Imagining the Nation: Asian American Literature and Cultural Consent* (Stanford: Stanford University Press, 1998).

Lim, Shirley Geok-lin, 'Japanese American Women's Life Stories: Maternality in Monica Sone's *Nisei Daughter* and Joy Kogawa's *Obasan*', *Feminist Studies* 16:2 (Summer 1990), 289–312.

Lim, Shirley Geok-lin and Amy Ling (eds), *Reading the Literatures of Asian America* (Philadelphia: Temple University Press, 1992).

Lim, Shirley Geok-lin and Mayumi Tsutakawa (eds), *The Forbidden Stitch: An Asian American Women's Anthology* (Corvallis, OR: Calyx, 1989).

Ling, Amy, *Between Worlds: Women Writers of Chinese Ancestry* (New York: Pergamon Press, 1990).

Ling, Amy and Annette White-Parks (eds), *Mrs Spring Fragrance and Other Writings* (Urbana: University of Illinois Press, 1995).

Ling, Jinqi, *Narrating Nationalisms: Ideology and Form in Asian American Literature* (Oxford: Oxford University Press, 1998).

Loomba, Ania, *Colonialism/Postcolonialism* (London: Routledge, 1998).

Lowe, Lisa, 'Heterogeneity, Hybridity, Multiplicity: Marking Asian American Differences', *Diaspora* 1:1 (Spring 1991), 24–44.

Lowe, Lisa, *Critical Terrains: French and British Orientalisms* (Ithaca, NY: Cornell University Press, 1991).

Lowe, Lisa, *Immigrant Acts: On Asian American Cultural Politics* (Durham, NC: Duke University Press, 1996).

Ma, Sheng-mei, *Immigrant Subjectivities in Asian American and Asian Diaspora Literature* (New York: SUNY Press, 1998).

Ma, Sheng-mei, *The Deathly Embrace: Orientalism and Asian American Identity* (Minneapolis: University of Minnesota Press, 2000).

Mazumdar, Sucheta, 'Through Western Eyes: Discovering Chinese Women in America', in *A New Significance: Re-envisioning the History of the American West*, ed. Clyde A. Milner II (Oxford: Oxford University Press, 1996), pp. 158–68.

Miller, Stuart Creighton, *The Unwelcome Immigrant: The American Image of the Chinese, 1785–1882* (Berkeley: University of California Press, 1969).

Min, Pyong Gap (ed.), *Asian Americans: Contemporary Trends and Issues* (Thousand Oaks, CA: Sage Publications, 1995).

Minh-ha, Trinh T., *Woman, Native, Other: Writing Postcoloniality and Feminism* (Bloomington: Indiana University Press, 1989).

Mirikitani, Janice, *We, the Dangerous: New and Selected Poems* (London: Virago, 1995).

Mirikitani, Janice, Luis Syquia Jr., Buriel Clay II, Janet Campbell Hale, Alejandro Murgia and Roberto Vargas (eds), *A Time to Greez! Incantations from the Third World* (San Francisco: Glide-Third World, 1975).

Mori, Toshio, *Yokohama, California* (Seattle: University of Washington Press, [1949] 1985).

Morris, Rosalind, '*M. Butterfly*: Transvestism and Cultural Cross-Dressing in the Critique of Empire', in *Gender and Culture in Literature and Film East and West: Issues of Perception and Interpretation*, ed. Nitaya Masavisut, George Simson and Larry E. Smith (Honolulu: University of Hawaii Press, 1994), pp. 40–59.

Mukherjee, Bharati, 'Immigrant Writing: Give Us Your Maximalists!', *New York Times* (28 August 1988), 1, 28–9.

Mukherjee, Bharati, *The Middleman and Other Stories* (London: Virago, 1988).

Mukherjee, Bharati, *Jasmine* (London: Virago, 1989).

Mukherjee, Bharati, *The Holder of the World* (London: Virago, 1993).

Mukherjee, Bharati, 'On Being an American Writer', *Writers on America*, ed. George Clack, Paul Malamud, Mark Jacobs and Michael Bandler at http://usinfo.state.gov/products/pubs/writers/mukherjee.htm.

Nakanishi, Don T., 'Surviving Democracy's "Mistake": Japanese Americans and the Enduring Legacy of Executive Order 9066', *Amerasia Journal* 19:1 (1993), 7–35.

Nelson, Emmanuel S., *Reworlding: The Literature of the Indian Diaspora* (Westport, CT: Greenwood Press, 1992).

Nelson, Emmanuel S. (ed.), *Asian American Novelists: A Bio-Bibliographical Critical Sourcebook* (Westport, CT: Greenwood Press, 2000).

Nelson, Graham (ed.), *Asian American Drama: Nine Plays from the Multiethnic Landscape* (New York: Applause, 1997).

Ng, Frank (ed.), *The Asian American Encyclopedia*, 6 vols (New York: Cavendish, 1995).

Ng, Mei, *Eating Chinese Food Naked* (London: Penguin, 1998).

Ng, Wendy L., Gary Y. Okihiro and James S. Moy (eds), *Reviewing Asian America: Locating Diversity* (Pullman: Washington State University Press, 1995).

Nguyen, Viet Thanh, *Race and Resistance: Literature and Politics in Asian America* (Oxford: Oxford University Press, 2002).

Nomura, Gail M., Russell Endo, Stephen H. Sumida and Russell C. Leong (eds), *Frontiers of Asian American Studies* (Pullman: Washington State University Press, 1989).

Okada, John, *No–No Boy* (Seattle: University of Washington Press, [1957] 1979).

Okihiro, Gary Y., *Margins and Mainstreams: Asians in American History and Culture* (Seattle: University of Washington Press, 1994).

Okihiro, Gary Y., Marilyn Alquizola, Dorothy Fujita Rony and K. Scott Wong (eds), *Reflections on Shattered Windows: Promises and Prospects for Asian American Studies* (Pullman: Washington State University Press, 1988).

Okihiro, Gary Y., Marilyn Alquizola, Dorothy Fujita Rony and K. Scott Wong (eds), *Privileging Positions: Sites of Asian American Studies* (Pullman: Washington State University Press, 1995).

Omi, Michael and Howard Winant, *Racial Formation in the United States, from the 1960s to the 1990s* (New York: Routledge, 1994).

Palumbo-Liu, David, *The Ethnic Canon: Histories, Institutions, and Interventions* (Minneapolis: University of Minnesota Press, 1995).

Palumbo-Liu, David, *Asian/American: Historical Crossings of a Racial Frontier* (Stanford: Stanford University Press, 1999).

Payne, James Robert (ed.), *Multicultural Autobiography: American Lives* (Knoxville: University of Tennessee Press, 1992).

Revilla, Linda, Shirley Hune and Gail M. Nomura (eds), *Bearing Dreams, Shaping Visions: Asian Pacific American Perspectives* (Pullman: Washington State University Press, 1993).

Said, Edward W., *Orientalism: Western Conceptions of the Orient* (London: Penguin, 1995).

Shankar, Lavina Dhingra and Rajini Srikanth (eds), *A Part, Yet Apart: South Asians in Asian America* (Philadelphia: Temple University Press, 1998).

Shea, Pat, 'Winnifred Eaton and the Politics of Miscegenation in Popular Fiction', *MELUS* 22:2 (Summer 1997), 19–32.

Shimikawa, Karen, *National Abjection: The Asian American Body Onstage* (Durham, NC: Duke University Press, 2002).

Shin, Andrew, 'Projected Bodies in David Henry Hwang's *M. Butterfly* and *Golden Gate*', *MELUS* 27:1 (Spring 2002), 177–97.

Shohat, Ella, 'Notes on the "Post-Colonial"', in *The Pre-Occupation of Postcolonial Studies*, ed. Fawzia Afzal-Khan and Kalpana Seshadri-Crooks (Durham, NC: Duke University Press, 2000), pp. 126–39.

Shukla, Sandhya, *India Abroad: Diasporic Culture of Postwar America and England* (Princeton: Princeton University Press, 2003).

Solberg, S. E., 'Sui Sin Far/Edith Eaton: First Chinese-American Fictionist', *MELUS* 8:1 (Spring 1981), 27–39.

Sone, Monica, *Nisei Daughter* (Seattle: University of Washington Press, [1953] 1979).

Spivak, Gayatri Chakravorty, *The Post-colonial Critic: Interviews, Strategies, Dialogues*, ed. Sarah Harasym (New York: Routledge, 1990).

Srikanth, Rajini, *The World Next Door: South Asian American Literature and the Idea of America* (Philadelphia: Temple University Press, 2004).

Stanton, David, 'Breakfast with Amy Tan', *Paintbrush* 22 (Autumn 1995), 5–19.

Tachiki, Amy, Eddie Wong, Franklin Odo and Buck Wong (eds), *Roots: An Asian American Reader* (Los Angeles: UCLA Asian American Studies Center, 1971).

Takaki, Ronald, *Strangers from a Different Shore: A History of Asian Americans* (Boston: Back Bay Books, 1998).

Tan, Amy, *The Joy Luck Club* (London: Minerva, 1989).

Tan, Amy, *The Opposite of Fate* (London: Flamingo, 2003).

Ty, Eleanor, *The Politics of the Visible in Asian North American Narratives* (Toronto: Toronto University Press, 2004).

Ty, Eleanor and Donald C. Goellnicht (eds), *Asian North American Identities: Beyond the Hyphen* (Bloomington: Indiana University Press, 2004).

Uno, Roberta (ed.), *Unbroken Thread: An Anthology of Plays by Asian American Women* (Amherst: University of Massachusetts Press, 1993).

Vignisson, Runa, 'Bharati Mukherjee: An Interview', *SPAN* 34–5 (November 1992 and May 1993), 153–68.

Wand, David Hsin-Fu (ed.), *Asian-American Heritage: An Anthology of Prose and Poetry* (New York: Washington Square, 1974).

Watanabe, Sylvia and Carol Bruchac (eds), *Into the Fire: Asian American Prose* (Greenfield Center: Greenfield Review, 1996).

Weglyn, Michi, *Years of Infamy: The Untold Story of America's Concentration Camps* (New York: Morrow, 1976).

Wong, Jade Snow, *Fifth Chinese Daughter* (Seattle: University of Washington Press, [1950] 1989).

Wong, Sau-ling Cynthia, 'Autobiography as Guided Chinatown Tour? Maxine Hong Kingston's *The Woman Warrior* and the Chinese-American Autobiographical Controversy', in *Multicultural Autobiography: American Lives*, ed. James Robert

Payne (Knoxville: University of Tennessee Press, 1992), pp. 248–79.

Wong, Sau-ling Cynthia, *Reading Asian American Literature: From Necessity to Extravagance* (Princeton: Princeton University Press, 1993).

Wong, Sau-ling Cynthia, 'Denationalization Reconsidered: Asian American Cultural Criticism at a Theoretical Crossroads', *Amerasia Journal* 21:1 & 2 (1995), 1–27.

Wong, Sau-ling Cynthia and Jeffrey J. Santa Ana, 'Review Essay: Gender and Sexuality in Asian American Literature', *Signs* 25:1 (1999), 171–226.

Wong, Sau-ling Cynthia and Stephen Sumida (eds), *A Resource Guide to Asian American Literature* (New York: MLA, 2001).

Wong, Shawn (ed.), *Asian American Literature: A Brief Introduction and Anthology* (New York: HarperCollins, 1996).

White-Parks, Annette, 'A Reversal of American Concepts of "Other-ness" in the Fiction of Sui Sin Far', *MELUS* 20:1 (Spring 1995), 17–34.

Wu, Frank H., *Yellow: Race in America Beyond Black and White* (New York: Basic Books, 2002).

Wu, William F., *The Yellow Peril: Chinese Americans in American Fiction, 1850–1940* (Hamden, CT: Archon Books, 1982).

Xiaojing, Zhou and Samina Najmi (eds), *Form and Transformation in Asian American Literature* (Seattle: University of Washington Press, 2005).

Yamamoto, Hisaye, *Seventeen Syllables and Other Stories* (New Brunswick, NJ: Rutgers University Press, 1998).

Yamamoto, Traise, *Masking Selves, Making Subjects: Japanese American Women, Identity, and the Body* (Berkeley: University of California Press, 1999).

Yep, Laurence (ed.), *American Dragons: Twenty-Five Asian American Voices* (New York: Harper, 1993).

Zhou, Min and James V. Gatewood (eds), *Contemporary Asian America: A Multidisciplinary Reader* (New York: New York University Press, 2000).

Index

African American, 1–2, 8, 10, 30,
    33, 45–6, 55, 82–3, 90, 96,
    110, 144, 169, 178, 189,
    190–1, 198, 199
Alexander, Meena
    Fault Lines, 1–6, 16, 17
    The Shock of Arrival, 16
American citizenship, 10, 29,
    45–6, 53, 58–9, 68, 69, 70n,
    81, 88, 145, 170, 199
Ancheta, Angelo N., 7, 29, 172
Androcentrism, 13–14, 32, 54,
    57–8, 76, 85–6, 100, 102, 108,
    143
Ang, Ien, 5–6
Anti-communist Confession
    Program, 91–2, 125
Anti-miscegenation laws, 13, 32,
    43, 49n, 60, 76, 79, 158–60
Asian American movement, 12,
    72, 75, 103n, 185
Asian American stereotypes *see*
    model minority and yellow
    peril

Asian American studies, 4, 6,
    16–17, 19, 21–2, 72, 75, 85,
    143, 179–80, 185–6, 197
Asian-identified traditions, 13, 51,
    62, 69, 73, 77, 80–2, 86, 88–9,
    102, 126–7, 129, 136, 138,
    149, 152–3, 187–8
Assimilationism, 33–4, 37, 44, 46,
    47, 61, 64–5, 74, 76, 100, 123,
    138, 172, 179, 187, 197
Autobiography, 2, 6, 9–10, 11,
    13–14, 18–19, 34, 47, 48n,
    76–7, 86, 146–7, 187–8

Bildungsroman, 6, 7, 18, 19,
    113–14, 190, 197
Bulosan, Carlos, *America Is in the
    Heart*, 11, 54, 55–60, 64, 65,
    67–8

Cambodian Pol Pot regime,
    146–8
Cao, Lan, *Monkey Bridge*, 15, 22,
    149–55, 172–3

Chan, Jeffery Paul, 13–14, 18, 72, 76, 79, 143, 187
Chan, Sucheng, 9
Charlie Chan, 11, 14, 74, 84, 198; *see also* model minority
Chin, Frank
  Aiiieeeee! and other criticism, 13–15, 18–19, 72, 76–8, 83, 86–8, 89, 92, 95, 100–1, 107–8, 116–17, 120, 122, 127–8, 143, 187, 188, 189
  The Chickencoop Chinaman, 80–3, 84–5, 86, 92, 99
  The Chinaman Pacific and Frisco R. R. Co., 80, 85, 101
  The Year of the Dragon, 22, 83–4
Cheng, Anne Anlin, 179–80, 191
Cheung King-kok, 85, 93, 111–12
Chow, Rey, 153, 154
Christianity, 13, 18, 33, 34, 35, 45, 48n, 59, 77, 108, 113, 129, 138, 189, 198
Chu, Louis, *Eat a Bowl of Tea*, 78–9, 80–1
Chu, Patricia, 57–8, 81
Cold War, 11, 146
Colonial complex, 59–60, 63, 95, 121
Colonialism
  American, 11, 29, 58, 60, 180
  British, 129–31, 181
  see also neocolonialism and postcolonialism
Corley, Liam, 171

Cultural nationalism, 6, 8, 11, 12–15, 37, 54, 65, 72–4, 76, 83, 86, 102, 108, 110, 128, 144, 178, 180, 187, 195, 196, 197–8

Denationalization *see* transnationalism
Dr Fu Manchu, 9, 11, 14, 200; *see also* yellow peril

Eaton, Edith (or Sui Sin Far), *Mrs Spring Fragrance and Other Writings*, 7, 10, 28, 30–2, 33–4, 37–8, 39–42, 43–4, 45, 46, 47, 121, 181
Eaton, Winnifred (or Onoto Watanna)
  'An Unexpected Grandchild', 39
  Miss Numè of Japan, 37, 43
  Miss Spring Morning, 26–8, 38–9, 42, 45, 180
  The Old Jinrikisha, 38–9
Eng, David L. and Alice Y. Hom, 16–17, 145, 163
Essentialism, 2, 3, 27–8, 32, 60, 109, 123–4, 126–7, 163, 179–80, 185, 190, 198
Ethnic studies, 15–16, 75, 102, 197
Exclusion
  from American culture, 7, 63, 86–7, 90, 93, 101, 178, 185, 190
  from Canada, 110–11, 114–15, 141n, 158
  from USA, 8, 14, 28–9, 36, 50, 53, 67, 76, 91, 95, 178, 190

Feminisms, 14–15, 31, 32, 44, 76,
   85–6, 88, 89, 92, 100–1, 102,
   108, 123, 143, 161, 180, 198
First World War, 55

Golden Venture, 167, 177
Goodness Gracious Me, 183, 186
Grewal, Inderpal, 132

Hagedorn, Jessica, 14
Hahn, Kimiko, 15, 22, 147–8
Harte, Bret, 9, 33
Hate crime, 108, 115–16, 186
Hattori, Tomo, 22, 181–2, 190
Hayslip, Le Ly, 15, 148–9
Him, Chanrithy, 15, 146–7
Ho, Wendy, 125
Hsiao, Ruth Y., 78
Hsu, Ruth, 115
Huggan, Graham, 181
Hwang, David Henry
   FOB, 116
   M. Butterfly, 17, 116, 118–21,
      127–8, 138

Immigrant bashing, 15, 108–9,
   115–17, 122, 136, 139; see also
   racial self-hatred
Internment
   Japanese American, 3, 12, 15,
      52–5, 61–5, 91, 109–10, 113
   Japanese Canadian, 110–15, 141n
Ishiguro, Kazuo, 181–2

Janette, Michele, 149

Kerr, Douglas, 120
Kim, Daniel Y., 84

Kim, Elaine H., 34, 97, 101,
   191
Kingston, Maxine Hong
   China Men, 73, 86, 92–101,
      108, 187
   'Cultural Mis-Readings by
      American Reviewers' and
      other criticism, 14, 74, 76,
      87–8, 128, 143
   The Woman Warrior, 18, 73,
      86–92, 93, 100, 101, 117, 125,
      126–7, 155, 187
   Tripmaster Monkey, 116–18,
      122, 138
Kogawa, Joy, Obasan, 18, 73,
   110–15, 118, 138
Koshy, Susan, 3–4

Law-Yone, Wendy, The Coffin
   Tree, 15, 128–37, 138–9
Li, David Leiwei, 87, 91, 100, 118,
   123, 134
Lim, Shirley Geok-lin, 63
Ling, Jinqi, 54, 92–3, 97
Lee, Chang-rae, Native Speaker,
   167–71, 172, 177, 187
Lee, Rachel C., 57–8, 168–9, 170
Lee, Sky, Disappearing Moon Café,
   17, 155–61, 167
Lee, Yan Phou
   When I Was a Boy in China,
      9–10, 28, 34–7, 45, 180, 187
   'Why the Chinese Must Stay',
      36–7, 46, 178
Los Angeles uprising, 144, 167,
   177, 190–2
Lowe, Lisa, 15, 19, 143–4, 169,
   179

Ma, Sheng-mei, 60, 116
Madame Butterfly, 14, 39, 42,
    118–20
Mazumdar, Sucheta, 180
Mirikitani, Janice, 14, 22, 72, 73,
    74–5, 96, 97–8, 99, 185
Model minority, 8, 11, 74, 91–2,
    102, 108–9, 139, 173, 178, 182,
    190, 198; see also Charlie Chan
Mori, Toshio, Yokohama,
    California, 12, 13, 18, 51–2,
    54–5, 57, 68, 188
Mukherjee, Bharati
    Jasmine, 128–37, 138, 152
    'On Being an American Writer'
        and other criticism, 128, 130,
        184, 192
    The Holder of the World, 184
    The Middleman and Other
        Stories, 184
Multiculturalism, 17, 21–2, 144–5,
    146, 169, 172, 173, 182,
    186–7, 188–90

Nakanishi, Don T., 109–10
Naturalization laws, 10, 29, 45–6,
    68, 69
Neocolonialism, 16, 132, 181
Ng, Mei, Eating Chinese Food
    Naked, 17, 161–7
Nguyen, Viet Thanh, 7–8, 19–20,
    21–2, 54, 149, 179–80

Okada, John, No-No Boy, 12, 13,
    50–1, 54, 61, 62–3, 64, 65–6,
    68, 72, 73, 188
Omi, Michael and Howard
    Winant, 7–8, 23n

Orientalism, 8, 27–8, 29, 35–6,
    37, 38, 41–2, 45, 46, 47, 77,
    83–4, 86–8, 98, 116, 119–21,
    122, 126, 129, 132, 150,
    199

Palumbo-Liu, David, 144,
    182–3
Paper son, 81
Pen war, 14–15, 76, 85, 101, 102
Postcolonial studies, 15–16, 200
Postcolonialism, 131, 181
Poststructuralism, 17, 145, 146,
    179

Queer
    desire and identity, 83, 119–21,
        162, 166–7
    theory, 16–17, 145, 162–3, 167,
        171, 173, 180

Racial self-hatred, 13, 76–7, 84,
    95, 116–17, 121, 128, 138,
    169, 197; see also immigrant
    bashing
Romance genre, 10, 19, 37, 44, 45,
    47, 118, 121–2, 139, 190
Rushdie, Salman, 181, 183

Second World War, 12, 50–5, 62,
    66–7, 68–9, 70n, 76–7, 96,
    109–11, 125, 145, 167, 178
Sexuality, 9, 14, 17, 30, 31–2, 42,
    43, 45, 58–60, 62, 67–8, 69,
    78–9, 80–1, 94–5, 119–21,
    134, 145, 159–60, 162–5,
    172
Smith, Anne Deavere, 190–2

Sone, Monica, *Nisei Daughter*, 12, 54, 61–3, 64–5, 68
Songs of Gold Mountain, 10–11, 29–32, 33, 38, 42, 45–6, 59–60
Spanish-American War, 145
Srikanth, Rajini, 5, 15–16, 177, 186

Takagi, Dana K., 162–3
Tan, Amy
  The Joy Luck Club, 18, 121–7, 153, 188, 189
  The Opposite of Fate, 188–90
Terrorisms, 5, 134, 171, 177, 184, 196
Transnationalism, 17, 22, 145, 179–86, 200

Vietnam War, 14, 72, 96–9, 107, 119, 120, 137, 139, 145, 146, 148–51, 152–4, 172, 175n, 185

Whitman, Walt, 17
Wong, Jade Snow, *Fifth Chinese Daughter*, 11, 76–8, 80–1, 86
Wong, Sau-ling Cynthia, 16, 122, 185–6
Wu, William F., 29

Yamamoto, Hisaye, *Seventeen Syllables and Other Stories*, 12, 13, 51–2, 54, 61, 62–4, 66–7, 68, 73, 188
Yellow peril, 8, 9–10, 26, 29–30, 32–3, 40, 45, 46, 50, 67, 69, 74, 109, 134, 169, 173, 178, 190, 200; *see also* Dr Fu Manchu